Praise for *The School of Sophisticated Drinking*

"It's seldom we get chance to see the European viewpoint on the history of booze, and I can't think of a more delightful way of discovering how the industry looks from the other side of the Atlantic than by reading *The School of Sophisticated Drinking*. It's a very entertaining book that deserves a leather armchair, a fine cigar, and a double measure of cognac."

GAZ REGAN, author of *The Joy of Mixology*

"*The School of Sophisticated Drinking* is an entertaining and insightful resource into the elaborate history of the spirits we all work with today. Kerstin Ehmer and Beate Hindermann have penned a detailed and insightful look into the development and sometimes comical past of the world of cocktail recipes and their stories."

FRANKIE SOLARIK, co-owner, Barchef Toronto and author of *The Bar Chef: A Modern Approach To Cocktails*

"*The School of Sophisticated Drinking* is just as much of a must-read book for the seriously cocktail-minded as it is for the professional bartender. Erudite, hedonistic and charming in the extreme, I can give this publication no greater compliment than to say it is The Victoria Bar in book form."

PHILIP DUFF, award-winning spirits educator and Director of Education for Tales of the Cocktail

"For years, American bartenders looked to the Germans for inspiration. My only wish is that this wonderful tome of knowledge had been available ten years ago!"

JEFFREY MORGENTHALER, author of *The Bar Book: Elements of Cocktail Technique*

T0124637

The School of Sophisticated Drinking

THE SCHOOL OF
SOPHISTICATED
DRINKING

AN INTOXICATING HISTORY *of* SEVEN SPIRITS

KERSTIN EHMER *&* BEATE HINDERMANN

FOREWORD BY **KEVIN BRAUCH**

WITH ILLUSTRATIONS BY **ANGELA DWYER**

GREYSTONE BOOKS

Vancouver/Berkeley

The School of Sophisticated Drinking
© Greystone Books Ltd., 2015

Originally published in German as
Victoria Bar, DIE SCHULE DER TRUNKENHEIT
© Metrolit Verlag BmbH & Co. KG, Berlin 2013

Translation copyright © Jamie McIntosh, 2015

Translated from the original German, *Die Schule der Trunkenheit:
Eine kurze Geschichte des gepflegten Genießens* by Kerstin Ehmer
and Beate Hindermann © 2013 Metrolit
Foreword copyright © Kevin Brauch, 2015

15 16 17 18 19   5 4 3 2 1

Greystone Books Ltd.
www.greystonebooks.com

Cataloging data available from Library and Archives Canada
ISBN 978-1-77164-119-7 (pbk.)
ISBN 978-1-77164-120-3 (epub)

Editing by Lana Okerlund
Cover design by Peter Cocking
Text design by Nayeli Jimenez
Illustrations by Angela Dwyer
Printed and bound in Canada by Friesens
Distributed in the U.S. by Publishers Group West

We gratefully acknowledge the financial support of the Canada
Council for the Arts, the British Columbia Arts Council, the Province
of British Columbia through the Book Publishing Tax Credit, and
the Government of Canada through the Canada Book Fund for
our publishing activities.

Greystone Books is committed to reducing the consumption
of old-growth forests in the books it publishes.
This book is one step towards that goal.

TABLE OF CONTENTS

Preface: Why We Drink & Why This Book　*vii*

Foreword by Kevin Brauch　*xv*

First Semester: BRANDY　*1*

Second Semester: VODKA　*35*

Third Semester: WHISKY　*61*

Fourth Semester: RUM　*91*

Fifth Semester: GIN　*125*

Sixth Semester: TEQUILA　*155*

Seventh Semester: CHAMPAGNE　*177*

Cocktail Recipes　*217*

Notes　*233*

Selected Bibliography　*241*

PREFACE

Why We Drink & Why This Book

ASKED WHETHER HE believed in God, Frank Sinatra once answered, "I'm for anything that gets you through the night, be it prayer, tranquilizers, or a bottle of Jack Daniel's."[1]

If we see the night as the refuge of the sinister, the seat of the invisible and unknown, the time when we are exposed to fears and reservations without distractions, then it quickly becomes apparent why alcohol, despite all its inherent dangers, still hasn't bowed out of our culture. With the onset of dusk the seductive call for drinks becomes louder. For centuries there has been a battle between the do's and don'ts, between purging and purgatory. It remains a draw. Euphoria and intoxication demand their price. Headaches the day after, swollen livers or actual addictions threaten, and still we are unable to keep our hands off alcohol.

It soothes our doubts and releases us from the merciless passage of time. In the happy, ecstatic realms of intoxication neither clocks nor worries play a role. As euphoric versions of ourselves we land unconditionally in the here and now. Past and future are blanked out. Thoughts flow freely.

Ancient Greece knew the symposium, a ritualized form of wining and dining, binding excessive wine drinking with witty reflection on specific topics. Herodotus told us that the ancient Persians usually spoke about important matters in a state of intoxication and reassessed them the next day when sober. Vice versa, decisions made when sober were retested in a drunken state. This initial, pretty sensible-sounding use of alcohol increasingly fell into disuse in subsequent millennia.

Places of cultivated drinking are on the precipice of excess. But a venerable gastronomic provision that the Americans introduced to Europe at the World's Fair in 1889 pointed to a way out of this dilemma. At the foot of the newly erected Eiffel Tower they presented in the American bar both a completely new handling of mixed alcohols and a new gastronomical concept that moved away from the rigid seating plans of restaurants and enabled the free choice of variable conversation partners. Up until that time, the ladies were expected to amuse themselves after dinner while the men withdrew to the library for a cherished cigar. Now, with the American bar, there was even room for women and communication between the sexes. It probably wasn't the last time that alcohol was the fuel of social progress, although it can't be denied that it has also often acted as brake fluid.

The bar is actually nothing more than the workplace of the barkeeper, but in this new concept of the taproom the bar was, on the one hand, a boundary separating the guest from the bar staff and the spirits, and, on the other, the hub and eponymous trademark of this gastronomical novelty. The barkeeper, now in focus, advanced to master of ceremonies. A barkeeper is, if required, comforter, friend, and accomplice, yet also someone of authority who has to tell some guests that enough is enough for one evening.

SEPTEMBER 25, 2001. Berlin. Taxis, taxis, a never-ending stream of taxis deposited elegantly dressed clients on the rain-glistening pavement outside 102 Potsdamer Strasse. Onlookers gawped. Discreet makeup, real jewelry, and suits and ties were not usually part of the scenery here.

Pickpockets sought out their prey, as did the ladies of the oldest profession, who despite the harsh weather conditions were still showing plenty of skin between their boots and Day-Glo hot pants. The tea in glasses in the Turkish cafés grew cold and the horseracing on the monitors of the nearby betting shops went unnoticed. The sign of the fast-food kiosk next door, a tap-dancing sausage, laughed deliriously and unswervingly at the newcomers to the local nightlife.

Everybody warned us. Potsdamer Strasse was not the place for an aspiring upmarket bar. But it was here of all places that we found the rooms we had sought for so long: more generously proportioned than most bars, with high walls offering space for our art collection. We stripped the rooms down to the core, designed wallpaper and hired artists to make murals, and had furniture and panels made by craftsmen. Wood and leather made an entrance. And our wonderful guests? Not letting the sinister surroundings bother them, they ignored the prophets of doom and followed their trusted barkeepers.

It was an address with tradition. Less than a century ago, Berlin, the Moloch, the voracious beast, had caused the disappearance of numerous poor souls behind the gleaming teeth of its delights.

At the beginning of the twentieth century, Potsdamer Strasse was a pulsating arc connecting the old imperial Berlin behind the Brandenburg Gate to the newly built areas of the aspiring West. They began at Potsdamer Platz, site of the luxurious Hotel Aldon with the first proper cocktail bar in Berlin;

next door was the bizarre stronghold of Berlin entertainment, the gigantic building of the Haus Vaterland with room for up to three thousand guests. It accommodated nine themed restaurants, including a Japanese tearoom, a Turkish café, and a Wild West bar with a black cowboy as barkeeper who came to Berlin as the son of an African chieftain, fell in love, and stayed. But that is another story. The main attraction was the *Rheinterrassen* (the Rhine terraces). The huge hall was bordered by a semicircular backdrop depicting a Rhine landscape complete with the ruins of a castle perched on the cliffs of Loreley. On the hour the backdrop became darker and a storm brewed with simulated thunder and lightning and "real" raindrops, followed by illuminations of the sun's return. Tables nearest the backdrop had to be protected from the splattering rainfall by glass panels.

In Potsdamer side streets, popular bars frequented by homosexuals had become established in the 1920s. At night, men minced around in high heels and evening dresses, feather boas fluttering from muscular shoulders. Marlene Dietrich found the inspiration for later film costumes at the Eldorado. The pink *chapeau claque* (opera hat) that she wore in *The Blue Angel* originally belonged to the cloakroom attendant at this red-velvet bar who, naturally, was a man dressed up as a woman in a man's clothes. In turn, tuxedos and bow ties were the preferred attire of the many women dressed as *garçons* who frequented this, in many ways, confusing bar.

About half a mile down Potsdamer Strasse was another Berlin institution: the Sportpalast, which could seat up to ten thousand people for major events. The ice rink made ice hockey popular in Germany, and the poet and playwright Bertolt Brecht watched the boxer Max Schmeling knock out his opponent.

Once a year the city held *Sechstagerennen* (six-day racing), the poor in the cheap seats below the roof and the rich gathered in grandstand boxes at the side of the racetrack. Those who wished to be seen chose one of the standing places inside the track. For six days, twenty-four hours a day, people ate and above all drank while the bike riders completed their circuits in all the hurly-burly.

The Sportpalast was also used as a major political arena. The workers' leader Ernst Thälmann spoke there at the Communist congress; Adolf Hitler found there the monumental framework for his bellowed diatribes; and Joseph Goebbels, his minister of propaganda, encouraged "total war" there.

Hitler's seizure of power marked the end of the pulsating nightlife in the New West, and bombs did the rest. In 1945 Potsdamer Platz and its pleasure domes lay in ruins. Years of occupation by the Allies, which limited nightlife to the officers' mess, were followed in 1962 by the event that would finally put Potsdamer Strasse to sleep for decades. Overnight Potsdamer Strasse was divided abruptly by a twelve-foot-high wall of concrete and barbed wire. With the erection of the Berlin Wall, West Berlin was an island surrounded by the grey seas of East German socialism.

The Sportpalast was provisionally reconstructed, and gigs by the Beach Boys, Jimi Hendrix, and Deep Purple ensured that the enclosed citizens felt that they belonged to the Western world, but large numbers of people seeking entertainment were missing. The building was not economically viable and was finally demolished in 1973.

Student riots shook the isolated city; those who could, abandoned *le bateau ivre* (the drunken boat). Squatters rescued some run-down buildings from complete ruin, opening bars in Potsdamer Strasse. The soundtrack of the street was now punk.

At Haus Nr. 96, a few musicians managed to turn an abandoned movie theater into a concert venue, the Quartier Latin, attracting acts like John Cale and The Cramps to play there, but that all came to an end in 1989.

Suddenly, as quickly as it had appeared, the Berlin Wall fell. Nightlife began moving in the opposite direction towards the eastern part of the city. House and techno clubs sprouted in the cellars and halls of the decaying industrial architecture of the former socialist half of the city. Musically, Berlin was becoming Germany's Detroit.

Potsdamer Platz sprang up from nothing on a site that in the meantime had become a green field. Grand Hyatt and Ritz Carlton opened branches. The Berlin Film Festival moved to newly opened movie theaters there.

When the Victoria Bar opened in 2001, the glamour had not moved particularly far down the south side of the street. Only the arrival of a number of aspiring Berlin galleries signaled the slow awakening of the area. Empty sites were filled with owner-occupied apartments, and families began to move in. A fresh wind blew through the street. The transformations boded well.

Regardless of all that was happening outside its doors, the Victoria Bar served its renowned, precisely measured cocktail creations to new and old guests—actors, artists and their collectors, the brass section of the Berlin Philharmonic, the artistes from the neighboring Wintergarten Varieté (Wintergarten Variety Theatre) who sometimes conjured up coins from the ears of astonished attorneys at the bar. Sometimes a politician would saunter in, not to mention the large group from various branches of the medical profession with an affinity to alcohol. During the Berlinale (Berlin International Film Festival), the bar is flooded by movie buffs from all over the world, and from time to time we cater for top-ranked premiere parties.

SHORTLY AFTER OPENING, we—that is, the manager of the Victoria Bar, Stefan Weber; his associate Kerstin Ehmer;

barkeeper Gonçalo de Sousa Monteiro, who in the meantime has set up his own business with the Buck and Breck; and, the soul of the business, barkeeper Beate Hindermann—began tracing the history of alcohol. On closer inspection of the development of our most common spirits, expanded by the eventful five-hundred-year history of champagne, we were astonished by the tight link of political and economic processes to the shaping of individual spirits. Every shift in power, every war, every technical innovation left an impression on the appearance and taste of alcohol brands up to their present state. New markets were found, old ones collapsed, exotic ingredients were discovered in far-flung corners of the world, vineyards and factories burst into flames only to rise up again, and tax on alcohol made some wars possible while also financing schools and railways. Politicians, generals, writers, musicians, and actors found inspiration and downfall.

The results of our research were poured into the School of Sophisticated Drinking. On a cold and foggy November day in 2003, flanked by a set menu of five cocktails, we held the first lecture in the now-legendary series in the Victoria Bar.

AS DURING THE liquid part of the lecture some of the knowledge imparted was blurry by the next morning, there was a need for a work that would make the collected knowledge accessible at home. So we settled down and edited and expanded the lecture material into its present form.

Every time the long bar is full of new students, each drinking the same drink and toasting a long-gone historical figure, it is still an impressive picture. Five cocktails, even for a well-trained student, is quite a serious challenge—the subject matter is too. During the final assessment, some people begin to flounder. Often a neighbor will help out, even if the teaching staff do not really approve. A chapter of *The School of Sophisticated*

Drinking links people and, through their exertions to acquire knowledge, turns strangers into friends.

We highly recommend an appropriate drink to accompany the reading matter. One or, at the very most, two. Then stop, sleep, and on with the next chapter tomorrow.

Cheers, prost, skol, salud, na sdarówje, and à votre santé!

KERSTIN EHMER AND BEATE HINDERMANN

FOREWORD

WHY DO WE drink? Well, we drink for joy! To see the stars, celebrate life, and laugh. We also drink to grieve, forget, and forgive. To find a smile or maybe a friend, and sometimes to get through the day (or toast the end of one). We drink to birth and to death, for love, and yes, even just to burn off some steam or bitch and complain. We have so many reasons and excuses to have a drink—and if we don't, just wait five minutes, we can probably come up with one.

Drinking is cultural, political, and religious; it's also different for each and every one of us, even if we often do it together and in the exact same way. Some drinking traditions are handed down to us, taught by family and friends or bestowed upon us by coworkers. The most sacred ones are generally those we feel we created personally, however we chose to go about it. Those are the ones worth learning, the ones worth reading about.

I found some of my own traditions in Germany. Like many foreigners, I began my very first trip in Munich, a city made famous by Oktoberfest. People come for the beer, they stay for the parties, and I can't believe they make it home in one piece.

And yet they return again, year after year after year. It's not the best example of cultured German drinking, but it is a significant one. Berlin is not Munich; they may be brotherly cities, but they were separated at birth and have grown up to be polar opposites. I last traveled to Berlin several years ago while making a science documentary, and when we weren't working, we played the way the Berliners do. Berlin is Germany's cool kid. You go out during the day in Munich. You go out all night in Berlin!

There's so much to love about Berlin, and if you do your research right, you should find yourself on the Potsdamer Strasse where the vibe is as hip as any you've felt anywhere. And if you're lucky enough, you'll pull up a stool at the bar or collapse into a comfortable leather sofa in the modern trappings of the Victoria Bar, home to Die Schule der Trunkenheit, which translates as The School of Drunkenness—or as we in the industry would rather think of it, The School of Sophisticated Drinking.

Most people didn't like school. I often pretended to be sick to miss a test or skip the class of a particular teacher who was mean to me, or I'd procure a note to leave early, avoiding a bully who was causing me grief. But "school" is not really what The School of Sophisticated Drinking is all about. Imagine a school that you like, a school where you can drink... that's my kind of place. That's what Kerstin Ehmer and Beate Hindermann dreamed up for their legendary lecture series on alcohol's storied origins, first hosted at the Victoria Bar and now published as a book.

In these pages, you'll absorb a delicious curriculum of libational learning. As each semester opens, your realm of study moves on to a different tipple. You start off easy in the first semester, with brandy, and by the seventh semester, you're popping the cork off a bottle of champagne. Along the way you'll immerse yourself in the scholarly study of our favorite beverages; reading about historical boozehounds ranging from Hemingway to the Queen Mum, you'll realize that this school has some important alumni.

We all could spend a semester or two at The School of Sophisticated Drinking. I like to think I graduated with Honors and may even return someday to complete my Masters: an excuse to drink, if there ever was one.

Cheers und prosit!

KEVIN BRAUCH, celebrity bartender, host of *The Thirsty Traveler*, and floor reporter on *Iron Chef America*

BRANDY

Willy Brandt and the High Art of Diplomatic Drinking

OCTOBER 12, 1965. Early evening. A black Mercedes approached Checkpoint Charlie. In the back seat was the mayor of West Berlin, Willy Brandt, and his wife, Rut. The car passed the control point unhindered and glided through the dark streets beyond the wall.

They hadn't visited the eastern section of the city for years, and silently they let the cityscape pass by. The air smelled of burned brown coal, and the street lighting was dim. In the facades of the soot-blackened buildings they could still see the bullet holes from the final battle for the capital of the German Reich. The huge edifice of the Russian embassy, in Unter den Linden, the only illuminated building, loomed surreally, looking like a stranded ocean liner. The first visit to the archenemy.

The Allies had been informed; the German government, too. West Berlin had disappeared behind the wall five years earlier, and in its shadows the war still seemed unfinished. But the Russian ambassador, Pyotr Abrassimov, had invited the Brandts, and they had accepted. Brandt was hoping to improve the situation for his part of the divided city, which was suffering from isolation.

Brandt was familiar with the drinking habits of the Russians and had fortified himself with a tin of sardines in oil beforehand. In the lavish dining hall decked with red silk wall hangings, the tables groaned under the weight of caviar, eggs, minced meats, trout, and stuffed veal roulades. The charming and convivial cellist, Mstislav Rostropovich, had been invited to loosen the tense atmosphere, and he did his best. By the time Brandt requested switching from vodka to cognac, the mayor and ambassador were on first-name terms. The ladies withdrew to be entertained by a film about Russian traditions and landscapes, and the gentlemen began to find a way to talk over glasses of cognac. The politics of cautiously getting to know each other had begun.

Twenty-four years and many empty bottles later, the wall was gone. In the form of Willy Brandt, time had found the hard-drinking character it needed to establish trust between the former enemies in the East and the new, democratic Germany. Some reservations, some bad memories were literally drunk under the table. Brandt loved his alcohol, preferably alcohol that had been distilled from wine—hence his nickname "Weinbrand Willy" (Brandy Willy). "Can he drink!" Henry Kissinger was said to have exclaimed, somewhat concerned, on meeting him years later as chancellor of the Federal Republic. He also loved his women. But it was precisely these obvious weaknesses, vulnerabilities, and contradictions that endowed him with credibility and made him one of the most popular politicians of subsequent decades. After his resignation in 1974 he was asked about his plans in an interview, and he replied that now, at last, he could drink his brandy in peace. A former TV repairman shared the plausible story that Brandt used to give away bottles of Rüdesheim brandy to delivery and tradesmen at Christmas so that others could share his pleasure, along the lines of "it's done me so much good…"

Brandy and the Economic Miracle

IN THE LAND of the "Economic Miracle" a bottle of brandy on the kidney-shaped coffee table was a symbol of affluence. First and foremost, drinks, like meals, had to be nourishing. EGGNOGS went through a renaissance. It was almost an outrage, after all the privations, to waste a whole egg on a drink. In 1957 the RÜDESHEIM COFFEE arrived, a specialty combining Asbach Uralt brandy and a strong coffee. With the addition of sugar and cream sweetened with vanilla sugar and a sprinkling of chocolate chips, it was certainly not a pleasure low on calories. The health-promoting properties of brandy were also touted; a warm brandy and an aspirin served as an effective home remedy for a cold.

In 1943 under the Nazi regime, brandy vanished from shelves. Allied air raids in the Rhine-Main region had also hit the brandy distilleries. The distillery of Hugo Asbach in Rüdesheim was destroyed by American bombers. What strict legislation couldn't achieve in America had unintentionally become reality: after war and Nazi terror, Germany had become the driest country in Europe. The Germans, unwittingly, had become a nation of teetotalers.

In these times of emergency a drink became popular in the Rhine Valley; its name, knolli-brandy, was the only connection to the original spirit. Farmers distilled the appalling but effective hooch from sugar beet; Maria Halkin, mother to a Victoria Bar barkeeper, who lived through the times, claimed the drink made people blind. With the associated impaired vision, men failed to find their way home, and if somehow they did succeed, their wives failed to recognize them in this state.

3

An improvement in the situation occurred only with monetary reforms, the introduction of the deutsche mark, and economic aid from the Marshall Plan. The spirit industry began to reorganize. Some distilleries succeeded in rescuing stocks and machinery that had been hidden at the end of the war. At the beginning of the 1950s, brandy production restarted. Even in East Germany they no longer drank only vodka.

Where the "Spirit of Wine" Is Bottled

THE GERMAN TRADITION of wine distilleries began early in the nineteenth century in Uerdingen on the Rhine. It was here that the first distillery was founded by Heinrich Melcher and his sons. He imported his wine from France, and together with his supplier he started another business: Dujardin, the first German cognac. Other entrepreneurs followed in their footsteps. The private distillery of Jacobi Frankfurt was founded in 1880, followed in the next decade by Asbach in Rüdesheim, Mariacron in Oppenheim, and Scharlachberg in Bingen.

Gains made in these early boom years and the good relationship with winegrowers both sides of the Rhine suffered a severe setback with the onset of the First World War. Importing of French goods was made more difficult and then banned altogether. Rationing of all raw materials and foodstuffs made no exceptions for the distillery businesses. From spring 1917 production of high-proof alcohol was only allowed for medical purposes.

At the end of the war the conditions for peace were defined at the Treaty of Versailles in June 1919. Articles 274 and 275, the "champagne paragraphs," were concerned with unfair competition. Germany was obliged to respect French brand names, and German spirits distilled from wine were, from then on, no longer allowed to be marketed as cognac, a measure

4

enabling French winegrowers to defend their products against German imitations. On the other hand, the term "German brandy" didn't automatically mean that it contained distillations of only German wine. Hugo Asbach had registered his Asbach Uralt as a brand name in 1908 and marketed it as "real old brandy, cognac from the noblest selected wines." Even today the company uses wine from Charente, the heartland of cognac, as the basis for its brandy. The Italian equivalent, Vecchia Romagna, on the other hand, gets its character from ingredients from Gascony, the winegrowing region and center for armagnac. In accord with the Treaty of Versailles, "brandy" is now the official term and laid down in German wine laws. It has to be stored for at least six months, whereas "old brandy" has to be stored for a year. The base wines can come from any of the states of the European Union.

In the first decades of the twentieth century American bars appeared in Germany. Behind the bars, classic brandy drinks like SIDECAR, BRANDY ALEXANDER, and CHAMPAGNE COCK-TAILS with brandy were being mixed. In 1924 Hugo Asbach, ever active, presented a further novelty geared towards the ladies' market: the brandy praline. It was, at that time, still considered improper for well-bred ladies to drink hard liquor in public, and it was unusual to come across ladies in American bars, but nobody could deny them a couple of brandy pralines with their pot of coffee at an afternoon tea dance. In the wave of gluttony during the Economic Miracle, the brandy praline became the brandy bean, in which neat brandy was hidden in a coating of chocolate—a rather odd combination of eating and drinking.

Compared to the infinite storage periods of French cognac, German brandies are mostly still at the infant stage of their development. At least in the cocktail bars the connoisseurs are gradually shifting to imported cognacs and brandies. In the 1980s Asbach tried to buff up its outdated, almost stuffy German image with a campaign slogan of "guests throughout the world." It was intended to emphasize the internationality of the brand, which was exported to fifty-nine countries, and place good old Asbach in the world's leading hotels: the Peninsula in Hong Kong, Raffles in Singapore, the Copacabana Palace in Rio, the Waldorf Astoria in New York, and the Hotel de Paris in Monte Carlo.

Brandy is the best-selling spirit in Germany. Almost 90 percent of the German population know the brand name Asbach, and brandy cola could even be called the drug of the masses. The people of Berlin call this simple mixed drink a *Futschi*. In Wedding it is referred to as ABC (Asbach/cola) and comes in a regular short glass. A *Blond Futschi* is brandy and orangeade, and in Hesse they call it a *Hütchen*—a little hat.

The makers of the traditional brand Asbach strived to improve its rather lowly reputation among connoisseurs by introducing higher-quality grades in the 1980s, launching the Asbach Privatbrand and the even older Selection 21. A cautious modernization of the bottle and logo initiated a rejuvenation of the product; after all, in Rüdesheim they are looking back at a more than hundred-year-old tradition, and we shouldn't forget that German brandy really can be a worthy member of the respectable family of distilled wines.

Cognac and Armagnac: Rarities in Oak

IN ADDITION TO German brandy, the family of wine distillates includes Spanish brandy, the French products cognac and armagnac, and South American pisco. All are distilled from white wine, but that is where the similarity ends.

The stars of this noble group are without doubt the traditional French brands. Connoisseurs willingly pay US$125 and more for a good armagnac or cognac. As so often happens, a seemingly meaningless event long ago had crucial consequences on the shaping of a product and even the economic structure of whole regions many years later.

In 1494 a worried coachman pulled up his team of horses, dripping with sweat, at the little town of Cognac on the banks of the Charente. There were groans coming from inside the coach. Louise of Savoy and her husband were passing through when she was overcome by premature labor pains. A no-nonsense farmer's wife acted as midwife, and the birth, with the assistance of many helpers, took its course without complications. A baby boy saw the light of day in unfamiliar surroundings. Twenty-one years later he ascended the French throne as Francis I and gave his birthplace a generous present. The active and skilled inhabitants were relieved from paying all taxes and tolls on their products, which in turn gave them considerable advantages in the market. Francis I was a typical renaissance ruler with a distinct inclination to the fine arts. He owned works by Michelangelo, Titian, and Raphael and brought Leonardo da Vinci to France. Early in his reign he supported followers of the Reformation before later changing his mind. His successor, Henry II, canceled the privileges enjoyed by the people of Cognac and supported the Catholics in the religious war against the Calvinistic Huguenots. At the beginning of the first War of Religion, a battle was won by the Huguenots whose cause could be traced to the levying of a salt tax, which in the view of the population was unfair. As a result of this preliminary victory the region around today's Charente became the Protestant heartland of France. Many of the great cognac families like Hennessy, Martell, and Delamain come from this Calvinist tradition. They were successful producers and merchants who in the course of persecution had indeed lost their fortunes but not their contacts. Many of the bankers at this time were Huguenots who helped their brothers in faith and in doing so enabled the conti-nuity of cognac production. At the end of the Thirty Years' War, the winegrowing branch slowly began to recover. The Romans had already established winegrowing in the fertile, mild microclimate in the departments of Charente and Charente-Maritime, and the merchant fleets of the eager Dutch were the recipients of the barrels transported downstream.

Aqua Vitae

A CERTAIN CLOUDINESS surrounds the origins of distill-ing. Beer and wine were already known in the first city-states between the Tigris and Euphrates some six thousand years ago. But who got the most out of the ingredients? The ancient Egyptians distilled fruits, herbs, spices, and flowers, but they produced only pastes, creams, and ointments, not alcohol. The Chinese acted more purposefully, at around 1000 BC, by seal-ing bronze vessels in which a primitive form of brandy could have been produced. They also froze their wines, later remov-ing the ice and retaining the alcohol. The ancient Greeks got drunk on wine at open symposia and knew that somehow there was room for improvement—a problem known to have occu-pied Aristotle's mind. About a thousand years later Arabian high civilization was more advanced. They knew how to distill; the problem lying between them and brandy was Islam's prohi-bition of alcohol. Free from this stricture, the most prestigious centers of learning in Christendom were preoccupied with the production of gold and the successful production of high-proof wine distillate. In 1167 the time had come. In the auditorium of the University of Salerno, Magister Salernus demonstrated how it was done. Optimistically he called his brandy *Aqua vitae,* the water of life. Education at that time was a matter for the church, and the spread of monasteries throughout Europe

8

meant that the know-how of the high art of distillation slowly but surely reached this cultural area. In 1490 a doctor in Nürnberg warned, "In view of the fact that everyone at present has got into the habit of drinking *Aqua Vitae*, it is necessary to remember the quantity that one can permit oneself to drink and learn to drink it according to one's capacities, if one wishes to behave like a gentleman."[1] In subsequent centuries, and even to the present day, the definition of "acceptable amounts" has posed serious problems for Europe and the rest of the world.

Spirits and Tulips

BUT THE DUTCH were the first, in the seventeenth century, who distilled in grand style. The northern provinces of the Lowlands united under William of Orange against the might of Spain and the horrors of the Inquisition. The Eighty Years' War followed against an initially superior opponent, but in the end the newly created republic was victorious. But it was small, so small that it didn't have enough land to feed its population. Herring and mackerel were integral parts of the Dutch diet. By building dikes, they managed to reclaim further areas for cultivation. This revolutionary society was committed to religious tolerance as well as industriousness, both commercially and technically. Despite the long war against Spain, the Dutch managed, up to 1650, to build a merchant fleet of ten thousand ships, the largest in the world at that time. They also used this fleet for all kinds of smuggling, and the ferocity of Dutch corsairs became the stuff of legends. The Dutch loved unusual flowers, good food, and spirits. The republic's artists created still-life paintings of exotic foods, wine, meat, fruit, or flowers just for the sake of it, a novelty in art history.

Throughout Europe, the Dutch bought wine, at that time a perishable commodity. As a result of long and bumpy transport, the contents of some of the barrels turned to vinegar. To prevent this they sterilized the wooden barrels with sulfur and encouraged winegrowers to distill some of their wines as high-proof concentrates, thus reducing volumes to between a sixth and an eighth of their original quantities. Later these concentrates could be diluted with water. The Dutch were the first to distill wine on a large scale. They influenced the cultivation of grape types that were particularly suitable for the production of cognac brandy in forested areas like Gascony, the Charente, and even in Spain, the country of their old enemies. These were regions where originally no winegrowing was practiced but where abundant supplies of wood were available for the barrels. In the process it became apparent that the weaker wines from the region around Cognac were a better basis for the end product than the high-grade wines from other areas.

Behind High Walls

IN THE REGION around Cognac, an increasing number of winegrowers with their own plots and distilleries prospered. Growing in confidence, they hoarded their stocks in the knowledge of their merchants' dependency. "You keep your money, and I'll keep my barrels"—this form of negotiation became familiar in the area. The rural stubbornness of the farmers was exasperating for some of the urban dealers. The winegrowers lived in seclusion in isolated farmsteads. High walls, often with a single gateway, sealed the estates and protected them from the prying eyes of the outside world. An English visitor in 1815 declared in bewilderment:

Anyone who observed these people congregated together at the Cognac or Jarnac market or fair, would at once recognize them from their appearance as a class of men who, having had a difficulty in getting what wealth they possess, are determined to keep it.... Although in their best apparel, they are ill dressed and shabby-looking; the clothes they wear might at some time or other have been genteel.... The ill-fitted clothes show that the present wearers are not the original proprietors... one keen and subtle looking man, whose clothes would not have fetched five shillings, was pointed out to us as a man worth 80,000 pounds."[2]

Charles Albert Arnaud, an illustrator of Balzac's works, also made fun of the provincials in a letter to a friend. Invited to dinner by one of the most important winegrowers, M. Saunier, he described his host as "a small, grizzled man, completely tanned, baked and baked again by the sun; his face was wrinkled as a dried grape."[3]

The farmers brought their fresh or already distilled wines to the market where merchants bought them for processing. The Dutch government supported this import. In doing so the scarce supplies of grain for the basic provisions of the population could be spared instead of landing in the pot stills of the distillers. A shift from quantity to quality took place only in the middle of the eighteenth century. The English market had discovered cognac. Up until this time it had been drunk as light and as fresh as it had left the distilleries, but political rivalry between the English and French led, now and then, to punitive tariffs, harbor blockades, and trade embargoes, causing sales to come to a standstill. In Charente, rather reluctantly, they began storing their cognac in oak barrels as a temporary measure, and soon it was discovered how good the results tasted.

Smugglers, mostly from the Channel Island of Jersey, were also involved in bringing the coveted goods to British buyers.

One of them was John Martell, who later married into one of the great cognac families and, as Jean Martell, within a very short period became one of the most important dealers.

Phylloxera and the Consequences

LONG-STANDING PROSPERITY IN the hilly landscape was abruptly interrupted in the 1870s. Phylloxera, North American relatives of aphids, descended on the country like a biblical plague.

The pests first attacked the leaves of the grapevines, extracting the juices; they then laid eggs, several hundred per insect, out of which within eight days offspring hatched. Leaves that had been attacked turned brown and fell to the ground. Up to this point the damage from infestation resembled attacks from other parasites, so winegrowers were not overly concerned. But some of the pests managed to reach the roots of the vines and overwintered there. In spring, when the vines began to sprout, the nymphs perforated the roots seeking nourishment, laying eggs, and creating the next generation. At the end of the summer some of them grew wings and again infested the leaves or with favorable wind conditions could reach other plants within a range of up to twenty miles. As a general rule, once a winegrower discovered that leaves had been infected it was already too late, and many other vines had already been affected. No sprays were effective; even uprooting the vines was pointless. On the contrary, the insects and eggs spread farther afield on the tools and even under the footwear of the workers.

Vines, hundreds of years old, died within a few years either from the infestation or from subsequent fungal, viral, and bacterial infections. Within ten years 80 percent of the vines fell victim to the pests, and complete vineyards were devastated. The price of a hectare (about two and a half acres) of land in winegrowing areas plummeted from seven thousand to six hundred francs.

Salvation for the distressed French winegrowers came from far away—not from Italy, Spain, or Portugal, but from the small town of Denison, Texas, where in 1877 Thomas Volney Munson, horticulturist and breeder of grapes, discovered a phylloxera-resistant root stock that could be grafted onto other plants. He was made Chevalier du Mérite Agricole, and in 1988 Cognac was twinned with the small town in Texas.

But even today the dangers have not been completely eradicated. Not only have crossbreeding and refining processes improved; the insects have too, and evolution is on their side. In the meantime, even NASA scientists are busy saving the grape.

When the vineyards were restocked, only the best native grape species were used, making the expensive and work-intensive process of grafting worthwhile. In the long term this led to an enormous improvement in the quality of French wines. One further aspect of the phylloxera crisis turned out to be advantageous to cognac producers: the involuntary shortages strengthened the status of cognac as a luxury article.

On the Thirst of Angels Above Cognac

AS THE WINTER months approach in Charente, an aromatic haze seems to enshroud the gentle hills and isolated farmsteads. Light still comes from the windows of production plants—the distilling season has arrived. The young wine has until April 1 to be distilled if it is to mature to real cognac. Afterwards the pot stills cool down and are left for the rest of the year. Dust settles on the exteriors until the stills are reheated in December.

The selected grapes are pressed; the pips and stalks are not included, as the tannic acid affects the taste of wine. No sugar is added, and the fermentation process is not allowed to be stopped by sulfur. So, just as it is, together with fine yeast and sediment, it is distilled in copper stills and hand-forged flasks. Cognac production follows the alembic distillation process. The basis wine is preheated to about 140°F and fed into stills on an open fire. The rising alcohol vapors pass through a swan neck into the serpentine tube system of the condenser, cooling down and becoming liquid again. This initial distillate is distilled a second time, resulting in the refined distillate that the French term *bonne chauffe*.

Each distillation eliminates fusel alcohols, which affect the taste or cause headaches. But at the same time they are sources of flavoring, and adequate amounts should remain. For cognac these two cycles are enough. The refined distillate remains, to a large extent, true to its original winey character. Subsequently it disappears into oak barrels for at least thirty-six months. The wood doesn't come from any old oak; no, it has to be 70 to 150 years old and felled in Limousin or the Forêt de Tronçais. The wood is seasoned in the open air for years, the rain, wind, and sun mellowing its natural tannins before it is worked into barrels without resorting to glues, nails, or plastic. All cognacs are initially matured in new barrels to acquire color and taste from the residue tannins and then are decanted in used barrels, sometimes for decades.

From the outside, the places where, behind thick walls, the silent batteries of mighty oak barrels await their classification are easily recognizable. The escaping vapors react with the saltpeter in the stone, offering living conditions to a particular species of fungus. The walls and roofs of venerable storage depots are blackened by the spores of *Baudoinia compniacensis*.

The protracted maturing process leads to substantial losses. Four percent of the distillate evaporates per year, never to be seen again. It is referred to as the *part des anges*—"the angels' share." The total annual loss at all depots in Charente is 22 million bottles, thus making angels the second-largest world-wide market. The fact that losses are so large in the first place is linked to the immensely long storage times, sometimes up to a hundred years. The consequence is that there is more capital committed to the production of cognac than to the entire French automobile industry.

Almost all commercially available cognac is an assemblage. The skill of the cellar master, the *maître de chai*, is to create the same taste, year after year, from hundreds of wooden barrels full of distillate from a variety of depots that have come from diverse vintages decades ago. This task remains within the same family over generations. The apprenticeship of a *maître de chai* begins in childhood.

The stored refined distillate has an alcohol content of around 70 percent, much too strong for normal consumption. In stages over months a mixture of cognac and distilled water is reduced to a drinking strength of about 40 percent. A little sugar and some caramel can be added. Only then can the taste buds of the connoisseur appreciate the wood and wine aromas.

Armagnac, numerically not nearly as important as cognac but for some the superior product, is produced in neighboring Gascony. The first distillate was officially registered in 1461, thus making Armagnac the oldest official distilling region in the world. Unlike cognac, armagnac was originally distilled in a continuous process, but since 1972 the double-distillation method practiced in Charente is also permitted. Additional flavoring from plums, nuts, or herbs is allowed. Armagnac is also stored in oak barrels and, most importantly, for a long time. Cognac and armagnac are at the top of the league of wine distillates due to the particularly strict specifications ranging from designated growing regions and acceptable grape species to precisely defined distilling and storage times. The early founding of the authorities that regularly monitor all the requirements should also not be forgotten. Both regions, to a great extent, exist due to the production of these internationally renowned spirits. They provide a livelihood for tens of thousands, and the awareness that something unique is created from their labors is apparent at all levels. Last but not least, cognac and armagnac can thank this high degree of identification for their quality and fame.

"Rollin' with my Homies, Sippin' Yak all Night"

IN ADDITION TO England, still the best customers for cognac, America and the Far East have developed into important markets. In China, of all places, a bottle of French cognac has become the must-have present at weddings.

In America it was the hip-hop scene of the 1990s that discovered the pleasures of the noble French brandy, often shortening it to "yak," "gnac," or "Henny" for Hennessy. Humpty Hump from Digital Underground rapped, "I'll drink up all the Henny, you got on your shelf, so let me introduce myself." Coolio's favorite pastime was "rollin' with my homies, sippin' yak all night." And Snoop Dogg observed in "Gz Up, Hoes Down": "Cognac is the drink that's drank by G's." This affiliation between black Americans and the French noble brand already existed at the end of the Second World War. Many winegrowers in Charente gave their American liberators a bottle of cognac for the road. The black GIs, in their own army often considered second-class soldiers, were delighted that they, too, as a matter of course, should receive a customary present. In the 1950s Herbie Hancock and Wayne Shorter formed a jazz quintet and named it VSOP (Very Superior Old Pale), the official title of cognac that is at least four years old.

And yet again the black youth of America are doing a service to the small regions of France. Towards the end of the millennium, sales were declining. Enraged winegrowers barricaded the access roads to Cognac with burning tires. The large distilleries had canceled their orders for grapes; the depots were full. Then, in 2002, Busta Rhymes came along and demanded, "Give me the Henny, you can give me the Cris. You can pass me the Remy, but pass me the Courvoisier." And the homies did what they were told.

American demand for cognac continues to grow steadily. In 2013–14, 54.1 million bottles were delivered to the US, the top international market.[4]

The Flying Bird

PISCO IS MADE in a part of the world not normally considered linked to the distillation of wines. It is a green grape brandy produced in Chile, Peru, Bolivia, and Argentina. During production, the juice, skin, and pulp ferment for eight days in steel tanks. Afterwards this basis wine is distilled once, creating a strong-tasting product full of fusel alcohols, aldehydes, ethanols, and alkaloids, its taste resembling grappa. Traditionally it was stored in *botijas* (huge clay vessels), but nowadays these have largely been replaced by oak barrels. Already after six months, the light, slightly yellowish liquid reaches the market. The origin of its name could be traced to Quechua, an Inca language, where *pisquo* describes a bird in flight—a clear reference to the high-flying effects of alcohol, say the more poetic aficionados. A more likely origin is the small town of Pisco ninety miles south of Lima and the cradle of South American brandy. Its roots stretch back to the sixteenth century when it was an important harbor and outpost of Spanish colonizers. Being so far away and difficult for supply ships to reach, Pisco citizens were forced to take care of their own provisions for alcohol and other agricultural products. There are records of winegrowing in this region dating back to 1560 that indicate that they were so successful that by 1630 they were exporting 5.3 million gallons of wine and brandy. Today, however, it is no longer Peru that dominates wine and brandy production on the continent but Chile, with wines from over sixty estates covering a total area of some 300,000 acres. It was in the Chilean port of Iquique at the beginning of the twentieth century that the English barkeeper and former sailor Elliot Stubb discovered the PISCO SOUR. He mixed pisco with the local and extremely sour variety of lemon (*limón de pica*), rounding it off with sugar. The mixture quickly became a popular specialty of the house. We do not know who later crowned the Pisco Sour with whipped egg whites, thus taking some of the sharpness out of the alcohol, but the white topping is now an integral part of the recipe. Throughout the whole region the Pisco Sour is considered the national drink, and it is now served in places as diverse as the smallest of village bars, where under somewhat doubtful hygienic conditions the egg whites awaiting processing are kept in quarter-gallon jugs next to batteries of pisco bottles, and grand hotels, where it is served in voluminous crystal glasses. The extent of the country's identification with this refreshing cocktail was apparent in 2004 when February 8 was officially declared Pisco Sour Day. Fifteen thousand people lined the road to Pisco toasting each other at midnight and made it into the *Guinness World Records*.

Al-Andalus

THE ANDALUSIAN PROVINCE of Cádiz, deep in the south of Spain, is the region that produces Spain's best brands. The Sherry Triangle (*Marco de Jerez*) consists of the two coastal towns El Puerto de Santa Maria and Sanlúcar de Barrameda and, ten miles inland, the city of Jerez de la Frontera. It covers the strip of coast and the plain between the rivers of Guadalquivir and Guadalete. Here in the chalky soils flourish the Palomino, Moscatel, and Pedro Ximénez grape varieties grown for the production of sherry. The special climatic conditions near the Atlantic offer cooling winds, occasional moisture, and many hot, sunny days.

This is the home of flamenco, castanets, guitars, and *Gitanos* (Spanish Romani), of racing horses and bullfighting. In Jerez de la Frontera this wild and romantic image is carefully groomed. The largest bodega in Europe is based here. In this *catedral de vino*, Williams & Humbert stores hundreds of thousands of barrels of sherry patiently waiting delivery, mostly to the English market, as Dry Sack. Here, actually in all the bodegas, they are conscious of their heritage and not shy of their folklore. The butts (casks) rest in dimly lit, well-ventilated halls full of antiques and heavy furniture, the walls decorated with flags, banners, and coats of arms. Sometimes collections of vintage coaches or sumptuous bridles are displayed. Sometimes flamenco concerts are held, or even parades of thoroughbred horses going through their dressage routines in integrated riding arenas, all demonstrating an affinity with the cultural heritage of Andalusia. At González Byass, Spain's best-known sherry bodega, they have trained mice to climb a ladder propped against a *copita* (a tall-stemmed, tulip-shaped sherry glass) and genteelly drink the contents.

Even when Cádiz was a Roman province, considerable amounts of wine were exported to the capital of the empire. Only under the dominion of the Moors after around 700 AD did the region really begin to blossom as a cultural and economic center. Free from the dogma of the Catholic Church, which had stifled science in the rest of Europe, research and learning underwent a boom. The Moors developed new irrigation techniques for agriculture that also benefited winegrowers, although for religious reasons the new rulers did without the pleasures of wine. About a third of all grapes were uprooted; the rest were used for making raisins and to provide for the non-Muslim population. Historians believe that the art of distillation, for medical and cosmetic purposes, was cultivated and refined at the Arabian university at Córdoba.

In 1492 there was a bloody re-conquest of the area around Jerez by the Catholic Queen Isabella I and King Ferdinand II. Vast estates in the area seized were given to Spanish noblemen as rewards for military assistance. Guzmán the Good was one such recipient; despite heavy losses he managed to successfully defend Tarifa, and he founded the illustrious line from which the dukes of Medina Sidonia descend. Here too lie the origins of the feudal structures that were to shape Andalusia for centuries to come. Commercial and mercantile wealth made inroads in the towns and cities, while, unaffected by this, life in the country carried on in abject poverty. This discrepancy remained a characteristic of life in Andalusia up to and beyond the Spanish Civil War. In the sixteenth century Cádiz became a center of trade with newly discovered areas abroad. Unlike Seville, there was a harbor here with direct access to the Atlantic Ocean. The silver fleet was relocated to Cádiz, where ships were refitted and provisioned for voyages to the New World, with local dealers providing oil, wine, and ship biscuits. Continuous battles between the then super powers, England and France, involved alternating alliances and hostilities. Despite the Eighty Years' War with Holland, long and distinguished trade relations continued. The name of brandy is derived from the Dutch word *brandwijn*. Even today the results of the first distillation are referred to as *hollandas*, a clear clue as to the original consumers of this primitive form of brandy.

IN THE NAMES for their spirits the Spanish brandy producers display a somewhat unique historical awareness. Here are a few examples:

LEPANTO

NAMED AFTER A sea battle in 1571 in a Greek bay of the same name between the Holy League, mostly consisting of Spaniards and Venetians, and the main fleet of the Turks. It ended in the first defeat of Ottoman military forces, considered until then to be invincible. Thirty-eight thousand men died in this bloody battle. Strategically, however, the Holy League failed to exploit its victory, as it had no army to follow up on its naval success.

GRAN CAPITAN

A SOLERA GRAN Reserva from Bobadilla (Osborne) named for Francisco Pizarro, the conqueror of Peru. In 1531 the former swineherd crossed the Andes at the head of some two hundred troops searching for the legendary El Dorado, the Inca land reputedly rich in gold. In 1533 after the execution of the Inca sovereign, Atahualpa, Pizarro entered and plundered the Inca capital of Cuzco. Three years later after successfully defending Cuzco from an uprising, Pizarro quarreled about the sharing of bounty with his long-standing comrade-in-arms, Diego de Almagro, and had him executed. Four years later Pizarro was assassinated by Almagro's son.

CARDENAL MENDOZA

DON PEDRO GONZÁLEZ de Mendoza was a Spanish cardinal, statesman, and military strategist. In 1478 as a trusted advisor to Queen Isabella of Castile and King Ferdinand of Aragon, he was involved in the foundation of the Santo Oficio de la Inquisición, the Holy Office of the Inquisition. It was above all aimed at converted Jews, who allegedly continued to practice their old beliefs in secret. Confessions were extorted under torture and the victims then burned at the stake. In 1491 Cardinal Mendoza contributed to the conquest of Granada, which marked the end of the peaceful coexistence of Muslims, Jews, and Christians under innovative and tolerant caliphates. Although sworn to celibacy, the cardinal left a daughter and two sons, who were recognized by both the monarchy and the Vatican. Queen Isabella referred to his sons as his "two sweet sins."

GRAN DUQUE DE ALBA

NAMED AFTER FERNANDO Álvarez de Toledo y Pimentel, governor of Flanders from 1567 to 1573 and commanded to subdue the Protestant uprising there. His Court of Blood in Brussels cost the lives of six thousand supporters of independence. He persecuted printers in the belief that they were responsible for the spread of Reformism, either executing or exiling them. His men killed eighteen thousand inhabitants of Antwerp and Mechelen, a slaughter remembered as the Spanish Fury. His brutal regime provoked those who, until then, had been indifferent to independence into a readiness to revolt. In 1574 he was ordered home and temporarily sent into exile. Seven years later seven provinces formed a confederacy and the beginnings of what we now call Holland.

The English Consumer: A Family Affair

"Man, being reasonable must get drunk;
The best of life is but intoxication."
LORD BYRON, DON JUAN[5]

23

FRANCIS DRAKE, IN a preemptive strike on the Spanish Armada at Cádiz in 1587, also managed to capture 2,900 barrels of sherry, making him popular at the court of Elizabeth I back in England. Was this the beginning of England's enduring love of sherry and brandy? "Any time is sherry time," Queen Victoria was to inform her subjects three hundred years later. On researching the origins of Spanish brandy, time and again you stumble across English-sounding names among the producers.

Guzmán the Good, Duke of Medina Sidonia and Lord of Sanlúcar de Barrameda, had after liberating the region done everything within his powers to repopulate his lands and encourage trade. He first established contacts to the English court through the crown prince, who was passing through his lands. In 1527 his successor, in an edict, confirmed privileges for English merchants in what is today Andalusia. It allowed them to go about their business in Sanlúcar, not only during Feria—the annual trade fair after grape harvesting—but throughout the year and gave them a part of the town, Calle de los Bretons, "street of the Britons," to conduct business. Here an English colony was founded with its own administration that was even outside the jurisdiction of the Holy Inquisition. It became a port of call for merchants and early explorers.

SAMUEL PEPYS, WORKING for the Admiralty as provisioner for the Royal Navy, was a chronicler of wines and brandies from sunny Spain. He confided in his diary that on his way to a debate in Westminster, he had bolstered himself with a couple of glasses of sack and a dram of brandy. Thus fortified with "Dutch courage," he was able to present his case, uninhibited and freely, as if he were within his own four walls.

24   The Irishman William Garvey arrived in Spain in 1780 to purchase merino sheep on behalf of his father. His ship in distress, he was rescued by the captain of a Spanish fleet, who later invited him to his house in Puerto Real to recuperate. There he

fell under the charm of Sebastiana Jiminez, the daughter of his rescuer. He shipped the sheep to Ireland but remained in Spain, married, and joined the wine business. That, at least, is how the legend of the founding of Garvey goes, a company that still exists today.

In 1809 nineteen-year-old Lord George Byron visited relatives who had settled in Jerez in 1746 and were in the wine trade. He stayed the night in the family's generous accommodations, which had been built directly adjacent to their bodega. It is hard to imagine that the young man, who had just left his wild student days at Cambridge behind him, went to bed sober. In *Childe Harold's Pilgrimage*, a lengthy narrative poem that made him an overnight celebrity, are a number of stanzas about Cádiz, wild landscapes, and the fiery eyes of Spanish girls, so they must have left a lasting impression on the young poet.

In the middle of the eighteenth century there is ever-increasing evidence of Spanish–English cooperation. Wine-growers and large landowners joined up with financially powerful Englishmen who had good contacts to world markets. Osborne, Terry, Duff Gordon, Garvey, Williams & Humbert, and González Byass are all companies that began as wine dealers, exporting wine or sherry to England and later moving into brandy production. Brandy and sherry production were and are impossible to imagine without each other.

Over the centuries, sherry has demanded a consistent high quality in grapes, so sherry is taken as an indicator of the quality of brandy. At any rate, brandy, to acquire its specific characteristics while maturing, needs secondhand oak barrels from sherry production. Sherry, in turn, is pepped up by the wine distillate.

Brandy is often served for the family or for special occasions. Unlike French brandies, which from the very beginning have a stronger taste geared towards their English consumers, the brandies from Jerez have a wide and sometimes confusing diversity of tastes, although they are produced almost exclusively from the same Airén grapes. Peaches and other fruits and almonds or other nuts can be added to the basis wine before distillation.

Step by Step from Top to Bottom: Solera

EVEN IN SPAIN, the barrels sometimes piled up in the depots because embargoes prevented their delivery.

Bodegas are depots in spacious, well-ventilated, and shaded buildings. Their stone block vaults and pillars, the bast fiber hangings on the windows, and the continuous gloom have an almost church-like atmosphere. Here the barrels can await delivery and at the same time gain goodness.

The wine here is stored in butts stacked on top of each other in three or more rows. Butts on the bottommost row are termed the *soleras*, derived from *suelo* meaning "ground," "floor," or "base"; the remainder are called *criadas* from the Spanish word for "servant." Only one-third of the contents of the bottom row are bottled; the butts are refilled from topmost to bottommost. Thus the sherry or brandy undergoes a dynamic process of maturing and mixing, often lasting decades. One of the most expensive brandies is Conde de Garvey. A bottle of this two-hundred-year-old Solera, untouched for the last sixty years, will cost you about US$850.

The storage, following the *solera* method, is the crucial characteristic of Jerez brandies as they are produced today. Stipulations prescribed by the Consejo Regulador del Brandy de Jerez are, unlike cognac, concerned not with the origins of the basis wines but rather with the special conditions for storing and ageing—the *envejecimiento*. Primarily it is the butts, made from American oak, that previously contained sherry for at least three years and the temperature that give this brandy its unique properties. There are three quality grades: Solera, with a minimum storage of at least one year, Solera Reserva, with at least three years, and Solera Gran Reserva, which has aged at least ten years.

Jerez brandies are exclusively stored in bodegas in El Puerto de Santa María, Sanlúcar, and Jerez, producing about 80 million bottles a year, of which a quarter is bound for foreign markets.

Pedro Domecq, a *bodeguero* (winemaker) from Jerez, is thought to be the first to produce a Jerez brandy in 1874. He named it Fundador—"the founder." Apparently he had discovered a long-forgotten barrel of brandy for producing sherry in his bodega and found the contents to be delicious—a story almost too good to be true. This barrel, resting on a cushioned stand, still appears on his labels.

A hundred years later this brandy became the preferred drink of the reticent heroes of Ernest Hemingway's *Death in the Afternoon* and *The Sun Also Rises*. Wistfully he remembered the fresh prawns, the fishing trips, and a large swig of Fundador to wash away the dust of the Spanish roads. The brand's advertising slogan until well into the 1960s was "*Salud, dinero, y amor... y un largo de Fundador!*" (Health, wealth, and love... and a long Fundador!).

The Work of God and the Devil's Contribution: The Rumasa Affair

AT THE SAME time, the beginning of the 1960s, Spain took a new course in economic policy. While the Franco years had favored the self-sufficiency that had isolated the country after the Civil War, there was then a push for a cautious opening of the country, the expansion of mass tourism, particularly in Andalusia, and a liberalization of the economy. The architects of this transition were the new managers and ministers often moving in the circles of the Catholic Opus Dei—an organization dedicated to the belief that the whole purpose of life is to serve God. Then and still central to the belief are the terms "sin" and "guilt," met with frequent prayers, firm daily routines, absolute obedience to priests, and strict segregation of the sexes. "Mea culpa, mea culpa, mea maxima culpa..." is the litany accompanying the self-flagellation of Opus Dei devotees. As a reminder of the suffering of Christ and as a plea for forgiveness, they kneel and lash their backs with whips and rods. As a precautionary measure, devout members wear a penitential belt, a metal belt with inward-facing spikes. Priests are required to wear such belts.

The first mayor of Jerez under Franco, Don Álvaro Domecq, was also a member of this elite corps of God. They infiltrated the upper echelons of the universities and commerce. A businessman joining Opus Dei could find not only eternal salvation but also a great deal of earthly advantages. As long as you could convince the organization of your zealousness with large amounts of money for the grace of God, you could be certain of support from banks, law courts, and government bodies. In 1963 Zoilo Ruiz-Mateos also became a member of Opus Dei. In less than twenty years he had succeeded in establishing a group of companies made up of 245 individual businesses, including important bodegas and distilleries employing 245,000 people. Additionally he purchased the largest private estate on the continent. In 1969 the magnate became the main sherry producer in Spain. Just over a million bottles were stored in his bodegas, and one-third of all exports from the Sherry Triangle originated from his company. This led to a cartel-like concentration of the spirit business, and it was feared that the production processes and the quality of Spain's prestigious product, brandy, would be affected. Not only small businesses, worried about being taken over or sidelined, but also the opposition party began talking—not of the Opus Dei, but the "Octopus Dei."

In 1982, seven years after General Franco's death, the PSOE, a social-democratic party under Felipe González, won the elections. One of the first actions of the new socialist government was the nationalization of the Rumasa (Ruiz-Mateos Sociedad Anónima) concern. Ruiz-Mateos refused to allow financial auditing by the authorities and withheld or falsified documents. He was found guilty of fiscal irregularities and forging documents, and his business was broken up. One of the direct results of the Rumasa affair was the formation in 1987 of the Consejo Regulador de Denominación de Origen Jerez-Xérès-Sherry, which since then has monitored compliance to the quality standards of sherry and brandy production.

Manolo Prieto's Bull

THE CALL CAME late. They had driven through the night from Andalusia to Catalonia. Felix Tejada, a metalworker since 1946, had seen a lot, but the sight of nine thousand pounds of metal, collapsed props, and twisted metal plates strewn all over the hill of El Bruc made him speechless on this February morning in 2009. Persons unknown had brought down the iconic Osborne bull, and they had made a good job of it.

Over ninety of these forty-six-foot silhouettes can be seen all over Spain near the motorways, and time and again there are attacks on these quiet giants. Their enormous size of some 1,600 square feet offers an ideal projection surface for all sorts of protests. For some the bull is *the* symbol of capitalism; separatists see it as a sign of centralism; and for others it is proof of Spanish *machismo*. In Mallorca it was painted in the colors of the

29

rainbow and became "Toro Gay." Sometimes his *cojones* were sawn off, sometimes a horn or tail was taken as a trophy, and sometimes people just gave him some boots or painted faces.

Senor Tejada and his three sons always appear when one of his charges needs him. They bring damaged parts back to their workshop in El Puerto de Santa María and carefully repair them. Each bull consists of 150 different parts. Thousands of screws hold them together and they are supported by four props sunk into concrete.

The story of the bull started with a lucrative contract with the Azor advertising agency in Madrid. Osborne, one of the largest brandy and sherry producers, was looking for a new logo for its bottle labels and a launch in the Mexican market.

Manolo Prieto, artistic director of an advertising agency, designed the outline of the bold bull with his characteristic horns in 1956. The head of the bull is pointing to the left, giving a hint about Prieto's eventful past. Early on, as a member of a Communist propaganda corps, the qualified illustrator made posters and designs for a frontline newspaper. Eventually he landed at the front and was wounded by enemy gunfire. His stay in hospital saved him from being captured. At the end of the Civil War he moved to Madrid. In 1956 the students rebelling against compulsory membership in a student organization with links to Franco were brutally quelled by the authorities, and it was against this backdrop that Prieto created the iconic symbol of the Osborne company.

This Andalusian bull was not going to be yoked and would be of no use working in the fields. His destiny was to fight. Defiant, proud, and free, the bull represented a different Spain out of reach of the church, order, and the family, the maxims of Franco's cultural policies. A sign that could be easily interpreted by the informed.

Initially his client was not particularly impressed; nevertheless, in 1958 Osborne decided to display the new emblem for advertising. Thirteen-foot-high wooden bulls, together with the Osborne lettering, appeared on billboards. In 1961 Prieto ordered the first metal bull from his brother-in-law's workshop, where his nephew, Felix Tejada, also worked. It was to be twenty-three feet high, weatherproof, and, above all, robust. A little later it was displayed on the road to Madrid.

A law intending to improve road safety was then passed prohibiting advertising within 500 feet of the road. Osborne reacted by removing the company name, moving the bull farther away from the roads, and increasing the size to forty-six feet. The effect was impressive. With the advent of tourism in the 1960s, the bulls became famous beyond Spain's borders. The *New York Times* saw in the *toro de la carreteras*, featured on the cover of its supplement in 1974, a forerunner of the new, post-Franco Spain. When new traffic regulations in 1994 stipulated that the bulls had to be dismantled, a wave of outrage swept through the country, and resistance began to grow, above all in Catalonia. Huge protest movements involving people from all walks of life and supported by artists, cultural institutions, and journalists began to form, and sure enough, firstly in Andalusia, they succeeded in persuading the authorities that the silhouettes of wild bulls had become a significant feature of Spanish identity. Eventually the high court passed judgment and the black silhouettes were allowed to remain on Spanish hills, but Osborne lost exclusive rights to its logo.

The biography of its creator seems to have been forgotten. Only in his hometown of El Puerto de Santa María is there a museum dedicated to Prieto's memory. And the sons of the metalworker Felix Tejada still look after the metallic bulls of their great-uncle Manolo.

Learning by Traveling

TOURISM HAD BECOME a significant economic factor in Spain, and with it came an increase in demand for sherry and brandy. From the Costa del Sol, holidaymakers brought home foreign foods and drinks as souvenirs of long days on the beach. Even the coffee was different here. In the cafés of Spain there was always a bustle of people, whether mornings before work, during the lunch break, or after late-night dinners, enjoying a Carajillo or a Carajillo quemado, a strong and sweet espresso poured over a flaming brandy, and the tourists copied them gladly.

At the beginning of the 1960s in West Germany, another variation of a brandy-based drink became popular, the LUMUMBA, a tall drink of brandy and cocoa on ice. Patrice Lumumba was the first black president of the Republic of Congo. The country, rich in natural resources, became independent during the reign of King Baudouin in 1961 but economically remained under the control of Belgium. Only thirty Congolese gained university degrees, and the young country was lacking in qualified professionals and civil servants. Lumumba publicly criticized the arbitrary rule of the former colonial power. Initially he sought economic and development aid from the US, but they weren't interested. He then turned to Moscow, but before he and the Russians got to the details he was deposed at the instigation of the CIA and with the approval of the Belgian crown. He was imprisoned, tortured, and finally executed, his body cut into pieces and dissolved in battery acid. Today controversy rages as to whether the drink was named in honor of a campaigner for freedom or, as with the golliwog, it was a veiled form of racism. The Lumumba case was only reopened in 2012 in Belgium.

Tourism in Spain brought not only foreign currency but also a special kind of cultural clash. A society in which only virgins married, intercourse was solely for reproduction, and contraceptives were sold only under the counter, watched anxiously

32

as the first bikini-clad girls hit the beaches of Marbella to enjoy their holidays freely and the first hippies began to trickle into Torremolinos.

In the legendary Marbella Club, founded by Prince Alfonso of Hohenlohe, the Spanish aristocracy rubbed shoulders with Gunter Sachs, Brigitte Bardot, Audrey Hepburn, Omar Sharif, Aristotle Onassis, Saudi crown princes, and the Aga Khan. Also to be found there was Thomas Terry, owner of the brandy company bearing his name. In addition to the spirit business, he had a passion for horse breeding, in particular the preservation of the Cartujo, the Carthusian horse, deemed to be spirited but quick to learn and well suited to humans. His project was so successful that this breed is now called the "Terry horse."

Nico and the White Stallion

IN 1962 TERRY selected his finest stallion as the symbol of the brandy line Terry Centenario, sending multiple shock waves deep into the Spanish soul. The first spot for alcohol on television showed a man in a tux with a glass of Terry brandy in his hand against an impressive backdrop of barren Andalusian ridges. Up to now nothing particularly exciting, but what was happening in the background caused outrage throughout the country. None other than Nico, later a Warhol muse and Velvet Underground singer, was galloping, without a saddle, on the back of a prizewinning white stallion, Descarado II, blond hair flowing behind her and wearing nothing more than a loose-fitting white shirt. Why she was wearing this was obvious and an affront to the more sanctimonious Catholics. Horse and brandy lovers, on the other hand, were delighted. Young viewers proved to be lastingly impressed, and the erotic subtext caused a whole generation of growing *caballeros* to lose their minds and prevented a good night's sleep.

33

Second Semester

VODKA

*"I'm not a heavy drinker, I can sometimes go
for hours without touching a drop."*

NOËL COWARD[1]

———————

LAS VEGAS, 1955. The receptionist at the Sands Hotel could hardly believe his ears as he took the order from the thirteenth floor, and just to be sure, he repeated it. Humphrey Bogart was in residence together with Lauren Bacall, Frank Sinatra, Judy Garland, Swifty Lazar, the Romanoffs, and a few others. They had arrived in a private jet for the premiere of Noël Coward's cabaret show and had booked a row of adjoining suites. The after-show party was long and liquid. For breakfast the illustrious guests ordered a respectable three hundred Bloody Marys. In the following hours waiters shuttled back and forth through the carpeted corridors of the hotel with trays laden with clinking glasses.

Vodka was the drink of the moment. The colorless spirit from faraway Russia had become the new fashionable drink and had spread rapidly throughout Los Angeles. It first became truly acceptable after a legendary party thrown by Joan Crawford in 1947 for Hollywood's crème de la crème. At this party, for the first time, there was nothing else to drink but vodka and champagne, and the actress was setting the style for Hollywood. Many of her showbiz colleagues valued vodka because they could appear on set after a night on the town without smelling of booze. It then exemplified an easy, elegant way of life and drinking culture. The vodka company Smirnoff advertised it in the 1950s as "white whisky" with the slogan "It leaves you breathless."

BLOODY MARY

THE BLOODY MARY is the best-known representative of the corpse-reviver or hangover-cure group of drinks. A good shot of vodka (one and a half to two ounces) is poured into a large highball glass with three to four ice cubes, followed by a squirt of Worcestershire sauce, a dash of lemon juice, Tabasco, celery salt, and freshly ground black pepper. Top it up with tomato juice and stir vigorously. A crisp celery stick is recommended as garnish.

The drink was first served by Fernand "Pete" Petiot of the New York Bar in Paris in 1921. Vodka was already well known in France in the 1920s. Even before 1917 the Russian aristocracy had brought their favorite drink with them to their summer residences at French seaside resorts. Then the white Russian émigrés sitting in Parisian bars fought off homesickness and revolutionary hangovers with Bloody Marys. In tsarist Russia there was a similar if somewhat simpler version called red *Katjuschka*, consisting of vodka and tomato juice. There are a number of even more nutritious variations to the classic Bloody Mary, one of which, the now rarely found Bull Shot, replaces tomato juice with double concentrations of consommé. Another variant is called the Caesar, a popular drink

36

on the East Coast of America and in Canada that substitutes straight tomato juice with a mixture of clam broth and tomato juice concentrate called Clamato. A hybrid of the Bloody Mary and the Bull Shot, called the Bloody Bull of course, consists of vodka and half portions of tomato juice and consommé.

Their function in the everyday life of a practiced drinker is best described by a quotation from Hervé Chayette and Alain Weill's book *Cocktails*: "Seldom do we have the feeling of not exactly knowing whether we are eating or drinking. Whether it is good or bad, whether we should curse the excesses of the previous night or surrender to the delights and just carry on where we left off."[2]

But how did vodka manage to conquer the American market? In its homeland, the Bolsheviks declared war on the people's drink of old Russia. Exports collapsed, and the last privately owned distilleries were nationalized; the owners' assets were seized, and they were forced into exile.

As former purveyor to the court and one of the richest men in Russia, Pyotr Smirnov was in a particularly precarious position. He was thrown into jail on numerous occasions and even sentenced to death, but was always reprieved at the last moment. Eventually he succeeded, after an eventful detour through Poland, in reaching Constantinople and then on to Paris. In his hand luggage he had the know-how for the production of his excellent vodka and enough start-up capital to open a new distillery in Courbevoie near Paris. In the middle of the 1920s Rudolph Kunett, Smirnov's former grain supplier, also arrived in Paris. He too had fled revolutionary Russia and was on a trip to France as a representative of the American cosmetic company Helena Rubinstein.

Kunett bought the rights to use the name "Smirnov" for the American, Mexican, and Canadian markets. He was expecting an imminent end to Prohibition and was certain that he

37

could establish vodka in America. He had to wait nine long years. Prohibition ended on December 5, 1933, and already by the beginning of the next year, Rudolph Kunett had started production from the second floor of a warehouse in Bethel, Connecticut, under the name "Smirnoff and Sons." But the big break never came. At its peak the company had eight employees and produced no more than six thousand cases of vodka per year. Only after John G. Martin, co-owner of the originally Canadian company Heublein, which concentrated on the wine trade and the import of foreign spirits, offered Kunett US$14,000 and guaranteed him a seat on the board did the marketing of Smirnoff improve dramatically. Martin was a bustling businessman, and in his friend Jack Morgan he found a suitable partner to bring his product to the people. Morgan owned a successful restaurant in Los Angeles called the Cock 'n Bull. One of his sidelines was the production of soda drinks, and in England he had acquired the license to produce ginger beer, a drink based on fresh ginger root, lemon juice, sugar, and water. After the end of Prohibition the demand for the slightly alcoholic product had declined. In 1947 at the Cock 'n Bull, the two friends combined vodka and ginger beer, creating a cocktail with the intention of making a breakthrough for the former Russian spirit.

THE MOSCOW MULE

THE MOSCOW MULE is a drink from the early days of vodka in America and nowadays is often mistakenly made with ginger ale, a simple soft drink, instead of ginger beer. The taste of these products, however, differs considerably. The drink is rounded off with a dash of lemon juice, a slice of cucumber, and, if you like, a sliver of fresh ginger.

Martin and Morgan promoted their cocktail with a major advertising campaign. They designed a special copper mug with a handle, and on the posters were well-known movie stars like Woody Allen or Groucho Marx popping out from under a pile of copper mugs. Additionally, people working for Heublein promoted the drink in a highly personal and effective manner. Armed with a Polaroid camera, then a sensational novelty, they toured bars asking barkeepers to make them a Moscow Mule while photographing them twice in the process. One picture was given to the barkeeper and the other taken to the next bar to prove that every bar worth its salt served Moscow Mules.

> *"Why does man kill? He kills for food. And not only food:*
> *Frequently there must be a beverage."*
> WOODY ALLEN[3]

BUT BACK TO America of the early 1950s. The Cold War was somewhat cooling enthusiasm for the white whisky. The atmosphere during the McCarthy era and the House Committee on Un-American Activities was tense. Vodka? Doesn't it come directly from the enemy country?

In 1953 well-intentioned patriots led an anti-vodka demonstration in New York in which a delegation of the American Bartenders Union also participated. "We Don't Need Commie Drinks!", "Down with Moscow Mule!", and "Boycott Smirnoff!" could be seen on placards. Smirnoff reacted with full-page adverts in major newspapers stating that its vodka had absolutely nothing to do with Bolshevik-infected areas of the globe, but just the opposite: it was produced in Connecticut in the heart of conservative New England and made exclusively from American grain. The triumphal march of Russia's national drink in the homeland of the class enemy was not hindered by hysterical warnings about the supposedly communist alcohol. Its growing popularity was not only the result of shrewd marketing strategies but also the consequence of a historically rooted change in the structure of American society. Prohibition hadn't drained America, but it had abruptly interrupted the development of its alcohol industry. Consumption shifted to the black market and the profits landed in the pockets of organized crime. Spirit producers based in Canada and Cuba also managed to profit. They put aside large stocks and flooded the American market once the Prohibition laws were repealed on December 5, 1933. Entry of the US in the Second World War confronted American producers once more with state control, as the country's alcohol was needed for the production of goods like fuel and rubber, goods that were more important in times of war. After the war, 100,000 thirsty soldiers returned to their homeland and the demand for high-proof drinks soared, and vodka offered a quick solution to this problem. Vodka needed neither long storage times nor expensive barrels, and its straightforwardness and efficiency well matched the attitudes to life in the post-war years. In 1950 American producers sold forty thousand cases of vodka. Five years later it was already 1.1 million cases, and in 1956 consumption quadrupled within a single year.

A number of distilleries sprang up in the Corn Belt of the Midwest, in Kentucky, Tennessee, and Illinois. With Russian-sounding names like Bolshoi, Anatevka, Majorska, and Kalinka and folksy presentation, they tried to lend their products a semblance of authenticity. In the 1962 film *Dr. No*, when James Bond ordered his Martini with vodka instead of gin for the first time, an icon of American bar culture tumbled. In 1963 more vodka was drunk in the US than whiskey for the first time, and in 1976 it overtook gin. During the 1980s the Swedish brand Absolut made inroads into the market with fresh concepts. The purist bottle design became the object of an artistically ambitious advertising strategy. Working with Andy

Warhol and other distinguished artists, photographers, fashion designers, architects, and all sorts of other creative spirits gave Absolut cult status in the bars of young, urban professionals. Today vodka has become securely anchored in American drinking habits, and it is impossible to imagine bars without it. The market is growing, and it is estimated that every other bottle of spirits that passes over the counter of a liquor store is vodka.

"Every one that drinketh of this water shall thirst again:
but whosoever drinketh of the water that I shall give him
shall never thirst; but the water that I shall give him
shall become in him a well of water springing up unto eternal life."
JOHN 4:13-14[4]

SO HERE IT is, the famous water of life, *Aqua vitae* as it was then called. The experimenting Italian monks in the twelfth century derived the name for their creation from this quotation in the Bible. And it is still called water, as vodka is nothing other than the diminutive form of *voda*—"water." They understand that in Poland, but also in Russia, and both countries claim to be the place of origin of this drink. On the basis of documents that historian William Pokhlyobkin unearthed from a monastery near Moscow, Russia, can claim the first production of *Aqua vitae* from grain in 1430. Monks on a pilgrimage to Rome had witnessed the new art of distillation and brought the secrets home. For want of grapes or wine back at the Chudov Monastery, the returning monks fell back on grains as the basis for their spirits. For Russians this is seen as the hour of birth for vodka. Poland countered with an older chronicle from 1405, the first written evidence of the word "vodka" describing high-proof schnapps made from rye. Offended national pride, economic interests, and political tension eventually led to the dispute being submitted to the European Court of Justice. In 2003 the verdict was declared in favor of Russia, a decision that even today is only grudgingly accepted in Poland.

We too can't say with any certainty where the cradle of vodka actually was. It is a simple fact that Poland, even in the thirteenth century, was an important center of agricultural production. Its grain surpluses were transported down the Vistula to the Baltic coast and from there were shipped to all of central Europe. So the base materials for the production of vodka were available. If knowledge of the new distillation techniques really reached the northeast via monks returning from Italy, then it is entirely conceivable that they practiced and refined these techniques in Poland before moving on to Russia.

During the High Middle Ages vodka was mostly used in Poland as an elixir or a cosmetic tonic, and it is in this use that the Polish tradition of flavoring is probably rooted. From early times, flavored variations of vodka emerged with mountain ash, apple, sloe, juniper, honey, or nuts, of which a number still exist today, like Krupnik and Jarzebiak. The simple rye schnapps of the farmers is called *gorzalka*. Large-scale production of vodka was first recorded during the reign of King John I Albert, who shortly before his death declared that Poles had the right to distill and sell their vodka. In the sixteenth century, during its Golden Age, Poland became an aristocratic republic. Noblemen elected the king and were permitted to participate in the legislature. The first university was founded in Kraków and the Italian influences of the Renaissance touched artists and architects. Religious tolerance accompanied an upturn in economic life. After 1565 trade and the production of vodka began to be taxed, and in 1572 the rights of distillation were granted solely to the aristocracy. The main centers were Kraków and especially Poznań, with its fertile agricultural hinterland and central road networks. Here in 1580, for twenty thousand inhabitants, there were already forty-nine distilleries. By the middle of the eighteenth century vodka was being exported from Poznań via Danzig to St. Petersburg, via the Oder to Germany and Holland, and via Wroclaw to Silesia, Vienna, and beyond to Moldavia, Hungary, and all the way to the Black Sea.

In three stages in 1772, 1793, and 1795, Poland was split up between Russia, Austria, and Prussia. Austria received Galicia, Russia the eastern Polish regions up to the Bug River, and Prussia western Poland, including Poznań and parts of Silesia. In the Russian zones, Catherine the Great reaffirmed the rights of the Polish aristocracy to produce high-quality vodka. In Poznań, on the other hand, the population initially benefited from the moderate policies of Frederick William III. He founded the Grand Duchy of Poznań, in which 521,000 Poles together with 218,000 Germans and 50,000 Jews were to be peacefully united under the bilingual administration of Prussia. In these quiet years autonomy prevailed with Antoni Radziwiłł, a friend of Chopin and Goethe, as duke-governor. The abolition of serfdom in 1823 led to the establishment of a large number of economically viable medium-sized farmsteads. This was also the founding year of the largest distillery in Poland at that time. In a building complex that had previously housed the Polish cavalry, the new owner, Hartwig Kantorowicz, began producing particularly high-quality vodka. It was claimed that at its presentation during a vodka competition organized by a Poznań newspaper, the jurors unanimously exclaimed "*wyborowy!*" which means something like "extra-clear, fine vodka." Kantorowicz adopted this honorary title as the official name of his creation.

After the November Uprising of 1830 in Warsaw against Russian dominion, supported with romantic enthusiasm by 2,500 people from Poznań, including the brother of the duke-governor, the political climate also shifted in

Prussian-occupied western Poland. Poznań became a garrison and fortress city. German became the official language of administration and the school system. Vodka, however, was so firmly anchored in national culture that it survived the years of Prussian occupation intact. In 1919 the Treaty of Versailles reestablished the autonomous state of the country, which had been hard hit by the war, and its population began with reconstruction. That same year Poland established a state monopoly for alcohol. In 1927 the name "Wyborowa" was registered as an international trademark. Hitler's invasion in 1939 marked the end of this short phase of independence, and the region around Poznań became Wartheland. Poles and Jews were persecuted, and over 750,000 people were deported or abducted for forced labor in Germany. In 1940 Hitler confiscated all Polish property, bringing the country's economy to a standstill.

Even after the Second World War there was no peace in the country. For two years there was a situation similar to civil war, and then the Communist regime prevailed. Stalin was supposed to have said that it would be easier to saddle a cow than to impose Communism on Poland. The Polish economy was nationalized and centralized. The twenty-nine remaining distilleries were administered by Polmos, the head office of alcohol production, and managed according to a five-year plan; export sales were managed by Agros, the head office of foreign trade. As collectivization of agriculture was never really implemented in Poland (75 percent of the area under cultivation remained in private hands), a close link was maintained between individual distilleries and local rye producers, enabling Wyborowa to preserve its regional character. Vodka was exported to other friendly socialist countries but also to Western Europe, above all to England, where it became very popular in the 1960s.

After the collapse of the Communist system and the transition to a market economy, Polmos was dissolved and the individual distilleries were privatized. The Wyborowa brand, in partnership with Pernod Ricard, took over Polmos Poznań, and this cooperation enabled investment in modern bottling, filtration, and packaging plants. Nothing changed in the traditional relationship between the producers and the thirty-one small decentralized distilleries around Poznań that process the regional rye harvests on their premises and deliver the crude distillate to central producers in Poznań, where the grain distillate is then refined, diluted, filtered, and bottled—over 2.4 million gallons per year!

But back to the initial question of which country can claim to be the cradle of vodka. In Russia, vodka became popular only in the fifteenth century on the introduction of crop-rotation practices and the sudden availability of grain surpluses. Spirits were initially distilled and sold in monasteries, but later also at large farmsteads and private inns, the *kortschma*. The *kortschma* played a central role in rural life. Here in the village inn you could meet up with friends, celebrate, eat, and drink. In the yard outside the young gathered to sing and dance, and inside sat the rest of the families drinking beer, wine, and mead. In a darkened side room the seasoned drinkers met and drank vodka. The institution of the *kortschma* stretches way back to the Middle Ages in White Russia, the Novgorod Republic, and Ukraine.

Life in Russian rural communities offered many opportunities for ritualized drinking sessions. At *Brattschina* there were meetings in open fields, at the village inn, or at the home of the local priest. The clergy were successful in integrating the originally heathen festival in the church calendar. The gatherings were presided over by the oldest drinker in the community, who was responsible for the organization and the conduct of the feast and the passing round of a huge chalice filled with vodka or *kornwein*. Births, baptisms, engagements, marriages and deaths, name days and birthdays, Whitsun, Easter, Thanksgiving and Christmas, the tsar's birthday, saints' days, and business deals, just to name a few, were all celebrated. The vast number of village festivals caused considerable disruption to agriculture and from time to time led to crop failures. Sonja Margolina, in her book *Wodka*, published in 2004, calculated that the annual festival calendar of the rural population up until the abolition of serfdom in 1861 allowed for only 140 official working days.[5] A priest reporting back to the Imperial Geographical Society from Yaroslavl in 1840 noted:

> Even on days which are not festivals the peasants will try not to miss an opportunity of getting drunk.... On Sundays after service, the people drink, as they say, "to extinction".... Not one drinking session goes without a fight. Indeed if someone is badly beaten up, the victim will not go to court.... Sometimes it happens that rivals, after exchanging several full-blooded blows without understanding why, will ask each other: "What are you fighting about?", and "What are you on about?" and then drown their enmity in half a bottle of vodka.... Of the women, I must say that they will never go into the tavern but at home on feast days, they, too, will take the opportunity to take a drink.... They also teach their children to drink. One can hardly be surprised when a child who cannot yet walk or talk reaches out for vodka.... A four- or five-year-old will already drink a whole glass.... And even a young unmarried girl does not find it shameful on occasion to drink a good glass of vodka and another of beer.[6]

46   The local clergy were also involved in the festivities. Again it was reported from Yaroslavl that during the Easter procession from village to village, Mass always ended with traditional gifts and not inconsiderable amounts of vodka. Thus fortified, priest

and flock staggered for almost a week through the district and in the process lost the incense burners and even some valuable icons.

When in 1547 Ivan IV, better known as Ivan the Terrible, came to the throne, he waged a bloody war of conquest against the Tatars. From them he adopted the idea of state-owned taverns, called *kabaks*. The first one was established in Moscow on an island in the river close to the Kremlin for the dreaded bodyguards of the tsar, the *oprichniki*. Shortly after there was a network of *kabaks* throughout the country in which vodka was distilled and sold, but almost all the revenue flowed into the tsar's treasury. The idyllic image of the village community celebrating in the *kortschma* of old gave way to the dreariness of the austere state-run barrelhouses. Inside such *kabaks* was a huge barrel of vodka, filthy from the numerous clothes that had fallen into it. Their former owners had peddled them for more drinks before ending up unconscious outside on a bank of urine-soaked snow, some with blood on their faces, others missing a shoe.

Landlords were not allowed to decorate their inns or sell food. Nothing was supposed to interfere with the cash flows to the treasury. An English traveler recorded in 1591, "You shall have manie there that have drunk all away to the verie skinne, and so walk naked (whom they call *Naga*.) While they are in the *Caback*, none may call them foorth whatsoever cause there be, because he hindereth the Emperours revenue."[7]

The *kabak* system laid the foundations for excessive drunkenness for a large portion of the Russian population. With the revenues from the state-owned inns, Ivan IV financed not only military campaigns and his bodyguards but also his ambitious plans to build St. Basil's Cathedral in Red Square. They also financed the first Russian court apothecary, which produced medicinal vodka for the family of the tsar, considered to be good for the heart, stomach, eyes, and mind, for treatment of wounds, and as a compress for headaches. A later tsar, Alexei I, not only was gentle and warm-hearted but also had a good head for figures. In 1649 he forbade the buying and selling of vodka from anywhere other than the state *kabaks*. Distilleries were destroyed or given to the authorities to control. All in all, twenty-one laws governed the penalties for illicit distillation. The milder verdicts included confiscation of equipment or fines, but more often the draconian penalties involved prison sentences, public ridicule, assault in pillories, or forced labor camps in Siberia. At the end of the seventeenth century, vodka production was a matter for the state. During the reign of Peter the Great, whose court became a drinking club whose members were commanded to get drunk every day and never go to bed sober, revenues from the alcohol business increased from 350,000 rubles in 1680 to more than 2 million rubles by 1759. This amounted to more than 20 percent of state revenue. Later this figure evened out at about one-third of the national budget.

Peter the Great reorganized the army following the European model. This included, during peacetime, the regular distribution of beer and vodka to his army and navy. In a military statute, the daily ration of 17 percent *kornwein* was decreed to be one and a half quarts, which in times of war was switched to three quarts of beer and one-third of a quart of vodka. However, a soldier with so much alcohol in him was never allowed to show any signs of intoxication. Tsar Peter set up the first drying-out cells at his barracks for drunken, undutiful, or disobedient recruits. Those sentenced of serious offenses like absence without leave or insubordination were awarded the Order of Drunkenness, a fifteen-pound medal made of cast iron that they were forced to wear before being executed.

Not until the eighteenth century was the production of vodka moved away from the inns. New *kabaks* without their

own distilleries were established and leases awarded to the highest bidder. The landlords received alcohol at set prices from the state. At the swearing-in ceremony they had to kiss a cross, hence their name *zelowalniki*—"the kissers." They had to swear to honor the interests of the tsar, abide by the prices, and not adulterate their vodka, which of course they did. To increase their profit margins they began to dilute their wares. They tried to disguise the inferior quality by adding pepper, aniseed, honey, and berries, but also tobacco, arsenic, or salt. The then reigning tsarina, Catherine the Great, noted for her promiscuous love life, reacted with the introduction of a two-tier system: the aristocracy were granted the privilege of distilling vodka for their own requirements and those of the court, while the rest of the population would continue to be supplied with the lesser-quality vodkas offered by the innkeepers. Although not displaying any signs of a common touch, this decree gave the development of vodka a fresh boost. The large estates of the aristocracy supplied the best materials. They invested in modern pot stills and improved filtration systems and were soon producing vodka of excellent quality that was highly regarded in the highest circles of the court.

In 1836 the first Russian railway line was opened from St. Petersburg to the imperial residence at Tsarskoye Selo, the scene of countless excesses. The then minister of finance, Georg von Cancrin, mockingly remarked "that while elsewhere railways were built to industrial centres, Russia's first railway led to a tavern."[8] The Romanovs' fondness of high-proof spirits was common knowledge. The annual bill that Tsar Nicholas ran up for vodka far exceeded the costs of the exquisite Fabergé eggs that he presented to his wife and daughters every Christmas and Easter. But the population in general was beginning to demand better-quality vodka. In 1860 there were vodka protests throughout the country. The rural population stormed the *kabaks* and in some places destroyed the pot stills. There were calls to boycott the overpriced and bad hooch, and some people, for a while, practiced collective abstinence. With the assistance of military force, resistance was quashed and eight hundred members of the abstinence movement were sentenced, some of them exiled to Siberia. In the course of reforms during the reign of Alexander II, the revenue-leasing system for *kabaks* was abandoned and replaced by excise on all produced drinks. Thus it was possible, for the first time, for private companies to invest in alcohol. New distilleries were founded, and with the introduction of tax stamps for the now obligatory sale of vodka in bottles, a vodka market was created for the first time that won international accolades at world fairs.

One of the most important producers at that time was Pyotr Smirnov. He had been granted a coat of arms by the government in 1877, later even receiving Imperial Russia's highest honor, the Order of St. Andrew. With enormous expenditure he presented his products at an agricultural exhibition in Novgorod in 1886. He had a sumptuous marquee erected, festooned with ribbons and garlands. Behind the bar was a trained bear balancing a tray of glasses filled with his Sibirskaya range. It was sold in black, bear-shaped glass bottles from one of seven glassworks that annually produced 7 million bottles of all varieties exclusively for Smirnov. Waiters dressed in bear costumes greeted visitors in the restaurant area of the huge marquee, and after a certain time revelers were not really sure whether they were being served vodka by a real bear or someone dressed as one. The tsar was so impressed that there and then he declared that Smirnov would now supply his court with vodka and awarded him another medal.

When the numerically small upper class consisting of aristocrats, estate owners, wealthy entrepreneurs, and the upper echelons of the military met in the chic restaurants of St.

Petersburg for their opulent banquets, they drank imported champagne and cognac, but also the highest grade of vodka. At the other end of the social scale the situation had noticeably deteriorated. Time and again the aristocracy had blocked necessary social and land reforms. Workers in the industrial centers were prevented from forming unions. Working days in the factories lasted twelve to fourteen hours, and even then their wages were scarcely enough to feed their families. In the cities there were wildcat strikes. Serfdom had been abolished, but if a peasant wanted to work his own land, he had to purchase it, which meant decades of repayments. The parcels of land were too small and the yields too low to pay the interest, let alone the installments. Additionally, the majority of peasants were illiterate. They found themselves in a hopeless spiral of debt, and their yields from this small, fragmented rural economy were not enough to feed a growing population.

The war of 1904–5 against Japan revealed just how extensively alcoholism had spread among the sons of Russia. On the way to the front or in their barracks the recruits plundered the state-run liquor stores and railway-station restaurants. Foreign observers thought that the catastrophic defeat of the Russian troops could be traced back to the very obvious alcoholic psychoses of a large section of the officers' corps and the alcoholism of the rest of the troops.

"Who defeated the Russians? The Japanese did not conquer, but alcohol triumphed, alcohol, alcohol," stated a British war correspondent.[9] This debacle was probably on the mind of Tsar Nicholas II on Russia's entry to the First World War. He ordered the closure of all state-run liquor stores and inns, naturally with the exception of the high-class establishments, and even abolished alcohol rations to the troops. In doing so he hoped to improve the effectiveness of his army and restore order to the cities that were still being shaken by strikes and demonstrations. However, the result was just the opposite. He lost a third of his revenues, setting off a chain of events that would eventually lead to his abdication. The supply situation in the third winter of the war was disastrous. In the countryside, peasants were distilling vodka from their own grains rather than selling them at minimum prices. In St. Petersburg, bread was scarce. Soldiers in the garrison refused to take action against strikers. There were food riots. Soldiers were deserting en masse at the front and teaming up with the fighting workers, forcing the tsar to abdicate on March 2, 1917. The Russian Revolution had begun.

One of the early measures of the provisional government was the confiscation of all imperial alcohol stocks. There was plundering everywhere, with the mob shouting, "Let's do away with everything the Romanovs have left." Storerooms and cellars were stormed, and they gulped down vodka using pots, pans, buckets, and anything else they could lay their hands on. These riots, which went down in history as the "Petrograd wine pogroms," are thought to have cost more lives than the assumption of power by the Bolsheviks a few months later. When the situation in Petrograd, as St. Petersburg had by then been renamed, began to become untenable, Lev Davidovich Bronshtein, better known as Leon Trotsky, the first people's commissar for war and founder of the Red Army, proposed that all wine and vodka stocks be unceremoniously poured into the Neva River, though a declaration of martial law ultimately proved sufficient. After the Bolsheviks' victory, Russia remained dry. In 1920 the alcohol industry was nationalized and reorganized to produce industrial alcohol. It was the time of the diktat of sobriety. People running illicit stills were declared enemies of the people and counterrevolutionary and were dispossessed and transported to Siberia. Vladimir Ilyich Lenin, too, turned against alcoholism, which he considered

53

to be the greatest hurdle for Russia on its way to Communism. "The proletariat does not need intoxicants, the communist ideal is a good enough stimulant to power the class struggle. A model communist is a teetotaler, a model state does not deal in alcohol," he said during the eleventh congress of the Russian Communist Party.[10]

After Lenin's death in 1924 the laws were moderated. Wine and beer were once again deregulated, and Stalin, despite huge ideological concerns, eventually revived vodka production. With the revenues from the nationalized vodka monopoly he was able to finance the industrialization programs of the 1930s. Victorious troops at Stalingrad were rewarded with the usual ration of three ounces of vodka, and soon the general consumption of alcohol reached prerevolution levels; by 1940 there were more retail outlets for vodka than for fish, meat, and vegetables combined.

What Is Vodka?

VODKA IS A spirit that features in not one, but many, highly varying countries of origin. Can we even use the same term for these products? What actually is vodka? What is it made from and how is it produced?

By definition vodka is a spirit from ethanol of an agricultural origin. The agricultural crops used in its production vary according to the location. Poland and Russia traditionally use rye, a modest grain bringing high yields from medium soils in climatic conditions that are far from ideal. Poland, with 7 million acres of cultivated land, is the world's largest producer of rye. In the US wheat is more commonly cultivated and thus used for the distillation of vodka. But vodka can also be made from potatoes, which they use, even today, in Ukraine for a variety of vodkas. Potatoes do have a number of disadvantages

54

compared to grains, however. They are more difficult to transport and store, and during fermentation they develop more unwanted chemical by-products. On top of this, vodkas made from potatoes are about 30 percent less profitable than those made with grains. Vodka can also be made from molasses, a by-product of the sugar industry, as practiced in Spain.

Whatever the base ingredient, it is cleaned, crushed, mixed with water, and heated until the starches in the mixture turn to sugar, resulting in a mash. Yeast cultures are added to start the fermentation process, which takes about three or four days. Thick yellow foam covers the vat, and the alcohol content of this mash is around 8 percent. In the distillation process that follows, the mash is heated to about 176°F. Alcohol evaporates at 172°F, separating from the water and residues, and is collected in the middle section of the condenser. To avoid impurities it is redistilled a number of times. The result is a basis alcohol of 80 to 90 percent. This is then diluted with demineralized, deionized, or natural (spring) waters, depending on the brand, eventually reaching a drinking strength of between 35 and 55 percent.

The final stage is filtration. Here, too, all producers swear by their own particular methods. In the early days of vodka, impurities were eliminated by freezing and thawing. People experimented with egg whites, milk, sand, and porcelain. Nowadays the most common techniques involve filtering, initially through paper and then through activated charcoal, preferably from Russian birches, a process discovered in 1780 by a German apothecary in St. Petersburg. Today, for example, every drop of Smirnoff vodka has been pressed through 7.7 US tons of charcoal—a process that takes eight hours. Premium brands advertise the fact that they use gold, platinum, and diamond dust in their filtration systems. The now highly technical operation of distillation and filtration results in a very pure product that seldom contains more than 0.004 ounces per gallon of impurities or flavoring agents. By comparison, brandy and whisky can contain up to 0.3 ounces per gallon of these substances. Vodka is pure and clear, the prototype—or, to put it another way, the essence—of a spirit.

With its nondescript color and unobtrusive aroma that enable it to be combined with almost all other forms of alcohol, it has secured a top spot among alcoholic drinks. A superstition among barkeepers says that a bottle of vodka will never sit easy next to a bottle of gin. Countless cocktails, the most prominent being the Martini or the Gimlet, can be made using one or the other as a basis. Among bar staff, too, there seem to be very clear party lines. If you press your trusted barkeeper you will soon discover that, if not professionally then at least privately, preferences lie with one or the other clear spirit.

Step by Step: Moscow to the End of the Line

HEMINGWAY, BUKOWSKI, LOWRY? They are all second-raters compared to the Russian king of alcoholic literature, Venedikt Yerofeyev. With his *Moscow to the End of the Line*, he gave the world the most high-proof work of literature ever.

The prose poem follows his alter ego, Venya, on a suburban train journey from Moscow to the small town of Petushki and, by accident, all the way back again. During the trip through thirty-six train stations, he drinks to delirium with fellow travelers, fare dodgers, and train guards, not before giving his audience a vodka-laden analysis of his enjoyment and devotion to alcohol and socialist society.

Behind the Iron Curtain, naturally, vodka was still being produced. In 1936 and 1938 the recipes for Moskovskaya and Stolichnaya were stipulated, and with the founding of Soiuz-plodoimport a central authority was established for the export business. By the end of the 1950s Soviet vodka was being sold in fifty countries. In the 1970s the development of socialist society began to stagnate. In satellite towns and prefab housing estates, people withdrew to their private spheres and drank. Alcoholism was a problem for people of all walks of life. Workers, farmers, creative artists, and the *nomenklatura*, the Soviet elite, were all affected. Once more there were complaints about dramatic economic failures. Workplace absenteeism was constant at 33 percent, and workplace accidents were common. Five million workers were officially down in the statistics as alcoholics, and the economic losses caused by alcoholism were estimated at over 180 billion rubles.

For the second time, vodka had a crucial role at a turning point in Russian history as Mikhail Gorbachev became the general secretary of the Communist Party of the Soviet Union in 1985. A man of great vision took the helm and *glasnost* and *perestroika* secured the sympathies of much of the population. Less popular was his struggle against Russian alcoholism. In an open letter in *Pravda* he announced his anti-alcohol campaign with the headline "Let's stop poisoning the people..." Vodka production was reduced and sales were strictly limited. Large queues began forming outside retail outlets, which were then open only at special hours. A coupon system allowed citizens a ration of only one bottle of vodka a month. As compensation, the lemonade and mineral water industry was boosted, earning Gorbachev the nickname of "Mineral Secretary."

More about this from another Russian literary figure. In his essay *The Eros from Moscow*, Vladimir Sorokin described a visit with friends to the Golden Ear restaurant. They found the huge room almost empty due to Gorbachev's anti-alcohol campaign; the restaurant wasn't even serving beer. The waiter recommended in a friendly manner that they have a word with the doorman. Andrei, one of the friends, followed this advice. A few minutes later the slightly inebriated doorman brought a bottle of Borjomi mineral water to the table. A Western European member of the group asked whether it was vodka. The doorman nodded. Why was it in a mineral bottle then? she inquired. "That's too hard to explain," the doorman said and turned to leave.

INITIALLY GORBACHEV'S MEASURES seemed to be effective. It didn't take long, however, for workers and farmers to fill the gaps in supply with homemade schnapps (*samogon*). Suddenly there were shortages in eau de cologne, glass-cleaning liquid, and even brake fluid, and sugar for the homemade hooch disappeared from the shelves. In 1988 the anti-alcohol campaign was abandoned without so much as a murmur. Under Gorbachev's successor, Boris Yeltsin, there were to be no such worries about prohibition, as here was a man who was a flagrant drinker representing the home of vodka on the international stage. In Ireland he managed to miss a meeting with the Irish prime minister, Albert Reynolds, while fast asleep in the official plane, his bodyguards too afraid to wake him. At some stage the Irish dignitaries got tired of waiting, rolled up the red carpet, and took the rest of the day off. At a banquet with Pope John Paul II he proposed a toast to his boundless love of Italian women. He spontaneously conducted a German brass band, and on disembarking from his plane he was often at a loss as to which country he was visiting. But vodka could not always cheer him up. Alexander Korzhakov, head of the Presidential Security Service, reported two failed suicide attempts, during one of which Yeltsin had barricaded himself in a sauna. A bit of a loose cannon, Yeltsin taught the world to expect the unexpected.

In the first years after the dissolution of the Soviet Union and the abolition of the state's alcohol monopoly, the vodka market was close to anarchy. Low-quality imitations of the

58

traditional brands, Moskovskaya and Stolichnaya, and illegal imports, some of which were health hazards, flooded the market. Moskovskaya is still trying to recover from the damage to its image. Only in the last few years has the Russian national drink experienced a bit of a comeback on the world market with the establishment of new premium brands. The Russian Standard brand gets its name from Dmitri Mendeleev, who scientifically formulated new state standards for vodka with an optimum strength of 40 percent. Green Mark, another new vodka, refers to the historical green seal of quality of Soviet production. Both reflect the long tradition of Russia's link with the distillation of rye.

Third Semester

WHISKY

─ ✦ ─

"*The devil made me do it.*"

CARRIE AMELIA NATION AND THE "DEMON DRINK"

─────────

THE SETTING SUN was reflected in the windows of the elegant saloon of the Carey Hotel in Wichita. The last beams lit up *Cleopatra at the Bath*, a painting by John Noble, and a small group of early evening guests enjoyed its revealing charms while celebrating the end of a working day with a good glass of rye—genuine American rye whiskey. On December 27, 1900, the doors of one of the fanciest bars in the Midwest flew open, heralding in a new era that was to shake Kansas to its core. Carrie Amelia Nation entered the bar, or rather swept in like a woman possessed. She had been raging for a long time against the demon drink, her words fading into the wide prairies like the thunder of ghost buffalo herds. The production and selling of alcohol had long been forbidden, but nobody took any notice.

Carrie Amelia had lost faith in the power of words and had decided to take action. The first swing of her hatchet hit the shelves of whiskey bottles. The mirror behind the bar smashed, raining down a cloud of jingling glass splinters. The determined mid-fifty-year-old then turned her attentions to poor, defenseless *Cleopatra*, hurling glasses and ashtrays at the provocative painting. The barkeeper and guests cowered behind the bar as she continued, her hatchet swinging, on her path of destruction through the saloon. Only the arrival of the police managed to stop her. She was imprisoned for three weeks before being freed, and, with an ever-growing number of supporters, she continued attacking other establishments. She was one of six children of a Kentucky plantation owner. Neglected by her mother, who had a mental illness and who long believed that in the near future she was to give birth to the next queen of England, Carrie Amelia grew up in the care of slaves.

Her first marriage to an alcoholic doctor, with whom she had an intellectually disabled daughter, ended in divorce. A few months later the abandoned doctor died. Marriage number two, to a newspaper editor and lay preacher, was put to the hard test by Carrie Amelia's support of the poor and needy. Her husband and his children found a growing number of people unable to look after themselves accommodated in their home. Time and again the lady of this large household was imprisoned for vandalism. The church suggested that her troubled husband resign his post as preacher, as the public-spirited behavior of his wife was becoming too much of an issue. In the end he got a divorce, and Carrie Amelia was free to concentrate her struggle against the main enemy: alcohol. In 1911 she fell into a coma during a speech with the words "I did what I could," and died a few days later.

Carrie Amelia Nation· was one of the most colorful figures in the temperance movement, which was founded in the 1820s and had almost 1.5 million members. It was involved in the banning of alcohol and was against gambling, tobacco, and prostitution, but it was also behind social reforms and women's suffrage. It promoted a sober and pure world in accordance with the guidelines of evangelical Christianity. The Salvation Army, decked in uniforms and banging drums, stems from the spirit of the temperance movement.

In the New World, alcohol was becoming a problem. Women and children suffered from hunger because fathers, straight from work, were drinking their weekly wages in the nearest bars; domestic violence was often the result of complaints. The increasing use of machinery in the working environment led to a rise in serious injuries to workers whose reactions had been dulled by alcohol. The vehemence of the teetotalers nourished itself on this alcohol-fueled misery and can't alone be explained by religious fervor.

The Wild, Wild West and Whiskey

"Whiskey has killed more men than bullets, but most men would rather be full of whiskey than bullets."
LOGAN PEARSALL SMITH[1]

WHISKY ARRIVED IN the New World with the Irish and Scots who, fleeing poverty, epidemics, and starvation along with exorbitant taxes, dispossession of lands by the English crown, or persecution by the Anglican Church, had boarded ships to America. Included in their luggage were both the equipment and the knowledge of whisky distillation. They initially settled on the east coast, where shortly afterwards the first American whiskey was distilled using the traditional base grain, barley. Later, using rye, the first genuine American whiskey was produced. American whiskey is spelled, as in Ireland, with an *e* slipped in towards the end, unlike Scottish or Canadian whisky.

In the second half of the eighteenth century the covered-wagon trails started heading west. Legend has it that it was a Scottish Baptist preacher, Elijah Craig, who prepared the way for alcohol. For many he is still the creator of bourbon, the second of the true American whiskey sorts, although today it has been proven that he never lived in Bourbon but rather in Georgetown, another whiskey center. Even at this time, alcohol was not without controversy. Whiskey drinkers and producers needed a figurehead in the struggle against their religious opponents, and a man of God like Elijah Craig seemed the perfect candidate. But even God couldn't save his preacher from being sentenced for running an illicit still in 1795. No matter who discovered it, bourbon originated in the southern and midwestern states where corn, its main ingredient, thrived. Kentucky and Tennessee developed as centers of whiskey production and have remained so up until today—even though, curiously enough, there are no distilleries today in Bourbon County.

It was the first American president, George Washington, of all people—as before his political and military careers he was a farmer—who introduced measures to tax whiskey. Unlike later president Abraham Lincoln, George Washington had a decidedly positive relationship to alcohol, and he considered himself to be an experienced drinker. As much as he appreciated his whiskey he was completely wrong in believing that he could tax the water of life without any problems. The citizens of the young state were particularly outraged that the tax affected not only commercial alcohol production but also the widespread practice of private distilling. By 1794 so much resentment had built up that there was a whiskey rebellion in Pennsylvania. A horde of fifty enraged farmers and trappers tried to storm the fortified home of John Neville, whom they considered to be a particularly ambitious and resolute tax inspector. Only with the assistance of his slaves was he able to repel his attackers.

Reinforcements were sent to protect the tax inspector and many arrived, but, as it transpired, not enough. On the following day a strong force of some eight hundred rebels mustered, not only armed with pitchforks and machetes but also accompanied by drummers and a bagpipe player. As Neville caught sight of the wild horde, he fled. His fortified home, Bower Hill, was burned down. The settlers lived in an area that was still occupied by American Indians, and the struggle for land had not been fully resolved; all forms of trade were dangerous. One of the few opportunities to earn a few additional dollars was to be found in selling goods that were easy to transport, like fur or whiskey bottles that people could hide in their boots, hence our word "bootlegger" for a smuggler. The courts in the Wild West, presided over by understanding locals, gave lenient judgments for tax offenses. You could get away with the most ridiculous excuses as long as you conducted your business without attracting too much attention. Other courts openly declared solidarity with the accused and issued judgments that were against the guidelines stipulated by the capital.

The sharpest and most conscientious tax collectors were recruited from the Quaker—or their offshoot, the Shaker—communities. The Irish and Scots complained that one of them was worse than fifty Englishmen. On the east coast many of these fundamental Christians held important posts in the government or military services, which is why some people thought that an outbreak of civil war between East and West was more likely than one between North and South—a war between freedom-seeking settlers who simply wanted to be masters of their own destinies and the elite from the cities who sought to control the country by means of religiously motivated repression. In some areas of the West, tax collectors were pilloried and held to public ridicule before the very eyes of local sheriffs, sometimes even with their connivance. Their wigs were burned and their heads shaved. Tarring and feathering, adopted from the Apaches, was considered to be particularly humiliating, and even more painful was the practice of branding, usually reserved for cattle and horses.

George Washington could no longer afford to look on idly. He answered the defeat of his troops by raising an army of twelve thousand, almost twice as many as were needed for the decisive battle against the English. In the process he made the final push for defining American civilization by the puritan extremist spirit of a religious splinter group. This pacified the western provinces. Most of the tax revenues now flowing into the treasury were used to finance the war against the American Indians. Advances in civilization in the former Wild West also spurred on an improvement in the quality of whiskey production. Up until this time the quality of a whiskey was ascertained by burning it together with some gun powder. Good, pure whiskey produced a constant blue flame; the sort of whiskey that would make you blind produced a flickering yellow flame.

A number of today's brands have their origins in these times. In 1795 the German settler Jakob Böhm (later changing his name to Beam) applied for a license to distill, and he passed on this license to subsequent generations of his family. James "Jim" Beam, six generations later, was one of the heirs, and he enjoyed a considerable reputation in the world of whiskey. Only at the onset of Prohibition was his family forced to abandon the business. In 1933 as the opportunity arose for a fresh start, Jim was already seventy, and he joined forces with another businessman, Harry Blum. Shortly before Beam's death, the first bottles had reached maturity and were still being sold under the old brand name of Old Tub. Only after his death in 1947 was the whiskey named after him. Harry Blum bought the family out and built up the brand by means of clever marketing. Since then, the six heads of this whiskey dynasty have adorned the labels of the bottles from Frankfort, Kentucky. The family is still very much in the whiskey trade; the business is now run by Fred Noe, a direct descendant of Jakob Böhm, and Parker Beam and his son Craig are master distillers at Heaven Hill, another bourbon distillery with roots in the Wild West. The founder, Taylor Samuels, was related to Daniel Boone and Jesse James. I.W. Harper, one of the first brands to sell labeled bottles, which even then won awards, was also founded at a time when America's West was wild. As was the case with Old Tub, the man behind I.W. Harper was a German settler, Isaac Wolfe Bernheim. Bernheim is said to be the inventor of the hip flask and could afford being a philanthropist. He bequeathed Bernheim Forest to the nation, and his gift became one of the first national parks within his own lifetime.

Jack Daniel's life was also intimately linked to the Wild West, and legend has it that he was born during an American Indian raid. He ran away from home as a child because of problems with his stepmother. He was taken in by a local farmer and at an early age became acquainted with the art of distillation. At the age of fourteen he took on the equipment from his self-appointed stepfather, who had come to the realization that his distillery was no longer compatible with his lay-preaching activities. At the age of twenty Jack founded his own distillery near Lynchburg. He quickly rose to be a distinguished businessman and was often referred to as the "Little Gentleman," as he was shorter than five feet three inches. He always wore a black frock coat and a hat with a huge rim and had one of the mightiest moustaches in all of Tennessee. As he remained childless, he summoned his Russian-born nephew, Lem Motlow, to the business, who brought with him charcoal-filtering techniques used in vodka production. This method is now the hallmark of Jack Daniel's. The other great Tennessee whiskey,

George Dickel, is also filtered. Jack's death did not pass without a certain amount of tragicomedy. He died in 1911 from the results of a broken toe that never properly healed. He sustained the injury when kicking a jammed safe door. His nephew, then alone, thankfully succeeded in saving the business after Prohibition; however, visitors to the distillery today are still barred from taking a drop of whiskey. Although a law was passed in 1937 allowing whiskey to be made in Tennessee and sold in other states, Lynchburg, the home of Jack Daniel's, is within Moore County, which has remained dry since Prohibition.

Dry

IN THE EARLY hours of the morning of July 4, 1926, police stormed the 300 Club. Chinese lanterns bathed the surging mass on the dance floor in a red light. At the sight of the uniforms the forty scantily clad fan dancers flew like headless chickens through the throng, leaving a trail of feathers. The club owner, Texas Guinan, lounging on the piano dramatically, stretched out her hands for the officers to handcuff. She ordered the orchestra to play the "Chorus of the Hebrew Slaves" from the Verdi opera *Nabucco*. The operation brought an abrupt end to the victory celebrations of the British Open golf champion, Bobby Jones. Among the party were two senators, the ex-president of Cuba, and a host of other people, most of whom were able to flee through the emergency exits. Also present was Edward, Prince of Wales, who was whisked off to the kitchens and disguised as a dishwasher with an apron and towel to avoid the embarrassing controls. The whole festive party was transported to the police station in three police vans. Gossip columnists from the popular press who were also arrested gave detailed reports of Texas Guinan entertaining both night revelers and police with vaudeville songs and jokes. Eventually she was released on US$1,000 bail and spent the rest of the night in her own bed.

On the surface the US became a dry country on October 28, 1919, but beyond what was visible, huge wet areas developed, above all in the large cities. The teetotalers, despite President Woodrow Wilson's veto, had pushed through the Volstead Act, which penalized, throughout the country, the possession, consumption, or trade in alcohol—a resolution also known as the "Noble Experiment." For some states this did not change much. The law had previously been introduced in thirty-four of fifty states, and in the rest, implementation was slow. Representatives from New York, for instance, had voted unanimously against the act and, at least initially, were not particularly rigorous about complying.

So, (night) life in the beginning carried on much as before. Bars and liquor stores didn't immediately close or ban all alcoholic drinks from their range of products, but gradually the stocks disappeared and it became ever more difficult to organize replenishments. One by one bars were forced to close, and in their place, speakeasies began to appear. The rise of organized crime in the US began with these illegal establishments, which were mostly run by criminal gangs. Three personalities, each in their own way, embodied a facet of the spirit of that age.

The Singing Mayor

LET'S BEGIN WITH James Walker, the mayor of New York from 1926 to 1932. Coming from a family of politicians from Greenwich Village, he was one of the first representatives of the people to recognize that popular image could be more important than meticulous execution of official duties. On election, at age forty-five, he was still relatively young. He was handsome, quick-witted, and charming, and he dressed fashionably and brought a breath of fresh air to the city administration of this metropolis. His acting talents had been proven on Broadway, and in 1918 he had had a nationwide hit with his own composition, "Will You Love Me in December, As You Do in May?" He won the election campaign against his pious Republican opponent with statements like "It's no disgrace to miss the Sunday service by oversleeping but it is a real one to go to bed on the same day you got up" and "If you can't break ice how 'bout drowning it?"

New York was a prospering city; jazz ruled in Harlem, and the citizens of the Big Apple were very different to the provincials in the Bible Belt. You had to dodge Prohibition as well as you could, and Walker, by wanting to interfere as little as possible in the lives of his citizens, managed to hit the right note with his election promises. After his overwhelming victory, key positions in the city administration were given to his people, and soon nearly all office holders could be bought. Walker seldom arrived at the office before noon and never stayed longer than the aperitif before dinner. Afterwards he plunged into New York nightlife, always earning new nicknames in the press. They called him the night or jazz mayor and also Beau James. Affairs with various showgirls became known. There was no drop in his popularity—just the opposite. The city was doing well and the people celebrated the fact, and in the Roaring Twenties they freed themselves from outdated conventions. Walker was one of them. He structured the municipal transport systems and created a number of public parks.

Under his aegis the ban on cinema screenings and sporting events was lifted, and boxing became legal. At the peak of his powers Walker was able, from his booth in Club 21, to foil a major raid by federal state police by getting New York police to tow away their cars. After the Wall Street crash of 1929, however, the night mayor's fortunes began to wane. In 1932 James

Walker had to face a board of inquiry, and unable to convincingly explain his personal bank accounts, he resigned. He was put under pressure by Franklin D. Roosevelt, the prospective presidential candidate for the Democrats. The abolition of Prohibition was one of the central features of the party's campaign during Roosevelt's nomination, and he did not want to risk bungling his chances with any dubious characters. Walker set off for Europe, where he married one of his showgirls, Betty Compton. Once it was clear that the chances of criminal prosecution were remote, he returned to the US. He became the founder of Majestic Records, which had popular performing artists such as Louis Prima and Tommy Dorsey under contract. A biopic, *Beau James*, was made in 1961 with Bob Hope in the starring role.

The Queen of the Nightclubs

"Come in and leave your wallet on the bar."
TEXAS GUINAN[2]

TEXAS GUINAN, ACTRESS, dancer, and nightclub owner, was another colorful figure in the New York of the Roaring Twenties. Born in 1881 in Waco, Texas, she moved to Hollywood in the first decade of the last century, where she succeeded in landing roles as a cowgirl in a number of films. After her first divorce, she tried her luck on Broadway in New York. The roles there didn't really appeal to her, although she soon acquired a good reputation as an extremely funny and quick-witted entertainer. She was just one of hundreds of talented stage artists in the city. After she had incited a sluggish audience to collective singing and wild celebration at a trendy Broadway restaurant, the Café des Beaux Arts, the proprietor hired her as mistress of ceremonies. It was in this role that in the following years she rose to the heights of New York society and achieved fame throughout the country. The stars of Broadway productions submitted to the rough charms of her provocative appearances. At the end of the twenties she became acquainted with the aspiring gangster Larry Fay. Impressed by her performance he offered her a partnership in his club, the El Fey. We can picture Larry Fay as a real Harlem hustler with tailor-made suits, pink shirts, and opulent ties. His cufflinks were decorated with swastikas, his own personal good-luck symbol, which was also to be found as an emblem in his club. It is worth remembering that in the twenties Hitler was totally unknown in America.

Guinan was thrilled by the good stock of spirits at the El Fey and by the exorbitant prices paid for them. She hired a troupe of forty showgirls whose task on top of dancing was to encourage the guests to drink more alcohol and to distract them when the time had come to pay. With this concept and within a short period of time, the El Fey became *the* meeting place in New York in which the underworld and the financially secure high society gathered to be entertained. After almost a year of fun, the authorities forced its closure. Unperturbed, Guinan and Fay opened their next club, Club Intime, within a few days. Here, too, Guinan attracted more people and attention than a speakeasy could cope with. There were raids, and again the bar was closed. Her standard excuse at the police station was that she was selling only cola and soda; the guests must have brought their own spirits. The regular raids didn't really damage business—both partners are thought to have earned US$700,000 in a year. Nevertheless, Guinan decided to end the partnership. She was not shied by all the attempts to pressure her, as in the meantime she had more powerful friends than the Harlem rising star.

She opened the 300 Club, the most glamorous speakeasy of its time. Everybody who was somebody tried to get in there:

Rudolph Valentino, Mae West, Dorothy Parker, the mayor James Walker, and Babe Ruth, among many others, were regulars. Guinan directed affairs from a table on the stage where she could keep an eye on the proceedings. The arrival of an important guest was greeted with a blow of a police-issue whistle. She personally greeted every illustrious guest with a hearty "Hello, sucker!" She wore an ermine shawl, as all royalty do, and plenty of jewelry, and she changed her costumes a number of times each evening, particularly her extravagant hats. She announced the beginning of the showgirls' act with a lusty "Give the little girls a great big hand," which became a catchphrase throughout America. Naturally, all the gossip columnists of all the important newspapers were among her patrons. She even had her own column in the *New York Post*. Neither Guinan nor her guests had to worry about serious troubles. In 1927 a federal official complained that roughly three-quarters of the New York judiciary, from executive to legislature, were in cahoots with smugglers, dealers, or club owners. So, for example, the coastguards took care of escorting the illegal alcohol transporters under the auspices of whichever syndicate offered the most cash. Time and again pieces of evidence simply disappeared from New York police stations. If somehow there was still a prosecution, most of the accused could hope for acquittals or mitigating circumstances.

For a while Guinan's luck held. She opened two other clubs, the Diamond and the Argonaut, but the rising curve of her biography made an abrupt dip at the stock market crash of 1929. With her troupe she tried her luck in France but was refused permission to perform; returning to the us, she used her experiences to promote the "Too Hot for Paris" show throughout America. She died of peritonitis in 1945. Ten thousand of her former guests paid their final respects.

The Man with the Machine Gun

THE LAST CHARACTER in our history of Prohibition is Al Capone, the prototype of a gangster, who ensured that supplies of hard liquor were not interrupted during the thirteen dry years. Although he was born in New York, he goes down in history as the gangster boss of Chicago. In his youth he was a member of the notorious Five Points Gang. After he performed his second murder he had to disappear, and in 1919 he moved to Chicago. Even before Prohibition, Chicago had the highest crime rates in the US and was well known for its weak judiciary. In the 1920s the Windy City descended, more or less, into a state of lawlessness.

There Al Capone quickly became the protégé of the mobster Johnny Torrio and rose to be his right-hand man in the gambling business. The chance to really hit the big time only came with Prohibition. Torrio immediately recognized the potential of this black market and organized discreet transport of alcohol from Canada. On top of this he gained influence over the numerous breweries in the city. Closing them down despite Prohibition was unthinkable, as too many jobs depended on them. Officially, however, they were allowed to produce only beer with an alcohol content of 0.5 percent. Torrio and Capone managed to buy off the union representatives. After the barrels were delivered to the mobsters, the contents were upped to the desired drinking strength with the addition of neutral alcohol or ether. Over and above this, of course, all other beers that the market demanded were also being produced. Business boomed, and a veritable war over the profits cost the lives of more than one thousand victims.

One of the best-known episodes of this struggle was the Saint Valentine's Day Massacre that Al Capone organized in 1929. He ordered four men, two dressed as police officers, to drive in broad daylight in a police van to an illegal warehouse in the middle of Chicago. The seven mobsters guarding it were surprised, as raids were generally preannounced by cooperative police officers. With raised hands they lined up facing the wall and were mown down by 150 bullets from two Thompson submachine guns. The "police officers" put their two accomplices in handcuffs and, in front of numerous witnesses, escorted them to the Black Maria and drove off, never to be seen again. The police arrived at the scene a short time later and asked a dying mobster for the identities of the killers, but he refused to talk. In Chicago of the twenties, neither the press nor the justice system was able to differentiate between good and evil. In the underworld, brutal and ingenious crimes alike were immediately attributed to Capone, and so he rose to the top of the league of Chicago gangsters. Officially he acted as an antiques dealer with a modest income. Unofficially, with a network of stooges, he had an annual turnover of an estimated US$100 million and was one of the richest men in the US. He bought a number of hotels and other properties and owned shares in Sanitary Cleaning Shops, a large dry-cleaning chain; it is from this connection that we have the term "money laundering." He ensured the loyalty of his gang members with generous presents and nurtured his popularity with public appearances akin to a showbiz star. After the Wall Street crash of 1929 he organized soup kitchens for the poor and forced some of the businessmen that he protected to donate food and clothing.

But in 1927 a new man was appointed to head the Bureau of Prohibition in Chicago. Eliot Ness radically cut the number of employees at the corrupt offices from 150 to a solid core of 11 "Untouchables." With them the struggle against Al Capone began. They severely damaged his business ventures and officially declared him Public Enemy Number One. Capone relocated to Florida but was tracked down there and eventually indicted for tax evasion. Investigators from the FBI managed to connect high revenues from gambling to Capone. In concrete terms it was only US$215,180.17, but the laws had been previously tightened to put Scarface behind bars at long last. In 1932 he was given an eleven-year sentence and was committed to the most modern jail of the time in Atlanta. When some journalists, intending on reportage, went to visit him there, they discovered an abandoned cell. Capone, back to his old habits, had bribed the guards and was on day release and looking after his businesses. As a consequence of this incident he was transferred to the notorious high-security federal penitentiary on Alcatraz Island. There he remained inconspicuously for the rest of his sentence. On release he returned to his forty-room mansion in Florida, where he died in 1947 from the late effects of syphilis.

On December 5, 1933, after thirteen years, ten months, nineteen days, and seventeen hours, Prohibition in the US was lifted, almost at the same time as Capone's imprisonment ended. In the minds of most American citizens it had caused more problems than it had solved. The lost revenue to the American Treasury had been immense. It has been estimated that US$36 billion was spent by Americans on illegal alcohol, and a black market had been created. Organized crime had profited by maintaining supplies to the speakeasies and to private households. Also, in private life there had been a change that few would have reckoned with. According to the Ministry of Health, alcohol consumption among women had risen in the thirteen years by an estimated 37 percent.

While drinking had previously taken place mostly in public, there were strict limitations to women's alcohol consumption, if it was allowed at all. With the shift to the private sphere there was the chance for women to have free access to alcohol without being observed; it was to be found on sideboards, in home bars, and even in kitchen cabinets. It became the trusty companion of American housewives, and after legalization it was a staple that they didn't want to lose. So Prohibition contributed to the emancipation of women, even though it was in a different way than planned by Carrie Amelia Nation and her teetotalers.

> *"Always carry a flagon of whiskey in case of snakebite,*
> *and furthermore, always carry a small snake."*
> W. C. FIELDS[3]

Manhattan: The Height of Elegant Drinking

PROHIBITION HAD CHANGED the drinking habits of a nation. Every glass could be the last one; a bust or shortages could end that pleasure at any time. So people drank what they could get... and quickly. The quality of the spirits was secondary. For the development of cocktails, with their painstakingly calculated mixture of select ingredients, the dry years were a low point from which it would take a long time to recover.

Cocktails—as we understand them today, a generic term for mixed drinks—were up to the 1930s simply a subsection of all mixed drinks like punches, fizzes, flips, toddies, sangarees, and so on. The first definition of "cocktail" appeared in an article in the New York publication *The Balance and Columbian Repository* on May 13, 1806: "Cocktail, then is a stimulating liquor, composed of spirits of any kind, sugar, water and bitters."[4] This original version of a cocktail was renamed "Old-Fashioned Cocktail" in bar books appearing at the end of the nineteenth century. Shortened to OLD-FASHIONED and refined with the zest of lemons and oranges, this mixture has gone through a

77

renaissance in recent years. In the 1860s barmen had begun to round off the basis spirits not only with sugar and bitters but also with liqueurs like orange curaçao and maraschino or syrups like orgeat. These mixtures were called "improved cocktails," and included among them are the BRANDY CRUSTA with a sugared rim, the JAPANESE COCKTAIL, the EAST INDIA COCKTAIL, and the famous SAZERAC with absinthe, all of them being based on modified Old-Fashioned recipes.

Added to this new diversity of possibilities behind the bar in the second half of the nineteenth century was another freshly imported ingredient from America that was to revolutionize cocktail culture: vermouth. Red Italian vermouth not only served as a sweetening element to the original cocktail but also took the bite out of the mixture with its low alcohol content and lent it a welcome multidimensionality. And it was this that made it appealing to the broad spectrum of the bar crowd, which was beginning to include increasing numbers of women. With the spread of vermouth in America we are approaching the creation of one of the most elegant cocktails of all: the MANHATTAN.

The earliest mention of a recipe for the Manhattan, from Harry Johnson's *Bartenders' Manual*, describes it as being equal measures of whiskey and vermouth mixed with a dash of orange bitters.[5] Towards the turn of the twentieth century Manhattans became drier with an increased whiskey proportion, a mixture that resembles today's Manhattan. The exact recipe aside, it simply consists of a balance between a good whiskey and high-quality vermouth. Careful addition of a drop of angostura gives the drink depth. Originally rye whiskey was used, Canadian whisky being used only as a substitute during Prohibition because high-quality American whiskey disappeared until 1933. The rediscovery of pre-Prohibition cocktail culture at the beginning of this century brought a number of interesting Manhattan variations. In honor of the classic, they are named after New York neighborhoods in the borough of Brooklyn: GREENPOINT, BENSONHURST, and RED HOOK. Today connoisseurs are again drinking their Manhattans with rye whiskey.

Scotch and Irish

FOR THE MOTHER country of whiskey, that is to say Ireland, Prohibition had dire consequences. Even if, for many whisky drinkers, Scottish single malt is the crown of creation, the drink was first made, in all probability and to the annoyance of all Scots, in Ireland. The spread of Christianity began in the Emerald Isle before moving to Scotland, and it was Irish monks who brought the knowledge of how to create alcohol through heat and condensation north from Italy. Due to the lack of written testimonials, the origins of *Aqua vitae*, or the Celtic *uisge beatha*, remain shrouded in mystery.

One legend, in any case, tells of the Irish patron saint, St. Patrick, donating whiskey to his fellow countrymen. During his lifetime in the fifth century, the art of distillation was indeed known but had not yet been used for preparing alcohol. Another unknown is when whiskey production actually stopped being practiced solely for medicinal purposes and the skills moved away from monasteries to farms and on to private production. There is, however, a written document, which the Irish are still proud about today, proving that the oldest licensed distillery in the world was on Irish soil. The head office of Bushmills was built on the foundations of one of these early distilleries, which historians say date back to the thirteenth century.

In 1556 and again in 1620 the Irish government was forced to point out the health hazards associated with whiskey; *Aqua*

79

vitae was becoming *Aqua mortis*. In 1661, at Christmas of all times, a law was passed levying a tax on whiskey. Overnight it turned a nation of upright citizens into moonshiners. From then on the Irish had two kinds of whiskey: parliamentary whiskey and *poitín*, the illicit and real thing. A 150-year battle followed between the tax collectors and the moonshiners, who insisted on their rights to produce and sell their own whiskies. Tax collectors often encountered their drunken antagonists in remote areas—an easy job. On the black market in the cities, however, it was a different story. Here the whiskey lovers outnumbered the authorities, and prior alcohol consumption made them fearless and uninhibited; some of the battles between the *shillelagh* and bayonet ended in their favor.

> *"What whiskey will not cure, there is no cure for."*
> IRISH PROVERB[6]

IN AROUND 1760 the report of an English medical professor suggested a certain admiration of the properties of *uisge beatha*. It was the true savior of every doctor thanks to the diverse nature of its qualities. It was recommended for the treatment of moist hands, as a digestive, as a remedy for melancholia, to improve memory, and to delay the ageing processes. And what did the American musician Jerry Vale think of all this? "Whiskey is by far the most popular of all remedies that won't cure a cold."[7]

The Grain Determines Taste

IN THE 1820S both the Irish and Scottish whisky industries were based on firm legal foundations. Quality standards were set, especially for Irish whiskey production. Barley is used as the basis of the malt for the Irish and Scots alike. The grain is placed in a tank to absorb water—this stage is called steeping. Then in a controlled germination process lasting eight to ten days, the dampened grains activate enzymes, which the embryo plant uses to break down starch, firstly to dextrin and then to maltose, a water-soluble malt sugar. To prevent the seeds from using up the remaining starches for growth, the process has to be stopped by drying or kilning, as it is called in the trade. This happens in three stages, traditionally on perforated metal plates heated on an open fire. In the process, flavoring agents are created in addition to the enzymes that already exist, and it is the third and last stage of these drying processes that makes Scottish whisky different from Irish and all others. In Scotland the drying process takes place at a relatively cool 140°F and peat is added to the fire, thus preserving the phenols that give Scottish whisky its distinctive smoky aroma. The malt man is responsible for this process. Sprouts and roots are removed and the remaining malt crushed and again mixed with water to reactivate the enzymes that had been stopped by kilning. The remaining dextrin turns to malt sugar and becomes soluble once it is stirred in the water. This mixture of water and malt is called mash. Towards the end of the process, stirring is stopped to allow the grain husks or hulls to sink to the bottom and form a natural filter through which the remaining sweet wort has to pass through. This process is repeated twice, and both liquids, the worts, are transferred to washbacks, huge vessels made of Oregon pine or cypress wood. Yeast is then added and fermentation begins. The yeast bacteria break down the sugar of the wort to alcohol and carbon monoxide. The resulting wash, also called distiller's beer, has an alcohol strength of 8 to 9 percent and is then fed into copper pot stills.

81

Both Irish and Scottish whiskies are exclusively produced in pot stills, but the Irish ones are much larger. Whisky is always distilled three times, making it light in color and particularly pure. The big difference between the two sorts of whisky is that the mash of Irish whiskey is predominantly made of unmalted barley, to which a small amount of barley malt is added.

Scotch, Bourbon, Rye, Irish, and Canadian

"There's no such thing as bad whiskey. Some whiskies just happen to be better than others."
WILLIAM FAULKNER[8]

———————————

AT THIS STAGE we would like to go into the differences between European and American whiskies. Bourbon gets its name from a county in Kentucky that, in turn, is named after the French aristocratic dynasty, the Bourbons—a reminder that the French were also involved in the colonization of America. At least half of the grain used for bourbon comes from corn. The higher the proportion of corn, the sweeter the whiskey. All bourbons are made using the sour mash procedure, meaning that remains from previous distillation processes are added. Acids introduced during sour mash control the growth of yeast bacteria so that the fermentation process doesn't get out of control. The mash is then distilled twice. The result of the second distillation is termed "white dog" and normally has an alcohol content of 60 to 65 percent. The resulting clear spirit is stored in charred oak barrels from which it gets its typical vanilla and caramel aromas. The barrels are allowed to be used only once and, as a rule, are then sent to Ireland or Scotland. New barrels have a more intensive effect than used ones. The storage time for bourbon is at least two years, but is usually four to six years, and is rather short compared to Irish and Scottish whiskies.

82

Rye whiskey is made in a similar way but using rye instead of corn. The last of these whisky types is Canadian. It is not as intensive or full-bodied as the other whiskies. For many, Canadian is synonymous with rye, but this is wrong. Rye is indeed a component of all the great Canadian brands, but it is the blend of grains and corn that gives Canadian its distinguishing features, as opposed to the American straight ryes.

Nowhere in the world of whisky do the distillers have so much freedom as in Canada. They can mix in malted or unmalted grains, rye or barley, corn or wheat, as sole grain or in whatever combination they choose. The distillers produce straight ryes or straight bourbons or any other basis whiskies. Various possibilities are also allowed during distillation as well as during storage when new or old bourbon, sherry, or brandy barrels can be used. The minimum storage period is three years; higher-quality brands are stored for five years, but more than ten years is unusual. What they do all have in common are blending with neutral-tasting grain spirits and a relatively low proportion of basis whisky, which even in high-end brands does not exceed 10 percent. Flavoring with sherry or plum wine and even the use of non-Canadian whiskies are also permitted.

But back to the Irish. Its soft, slightly oily notes, drawing many comparisons with brandy, made it more popular in the eighteenth century than the heavier Scottish brands. John Powers, John Jameson (a Scotsman), and William Jameson were the owners of the three largest distilleries in the country and the authors of *Truths about Whisky*, which was first printed in 1879 and in which they warned of the dangers of bad and adulterated whiskies.[9] An early indication, perhaps, of the qualitative and economic decline of Irish whiskey that was to drag on for the next hundred years. There were four main reasons for this decline. First, the temperance movement was beginning to find a footing in Ireland. Father Mathew achieved dubious fame because he was able to vividly depict the consequences of the "demon drink"—so vividly, in fact, that during his six-year campaign against alcohol, the number of pubs declined from 21,000 to roughly half that number.

The second factor was the invention of the continuous still by Aeneas Coffey (an excise man in Dublin), which enabled large amounts of pure alcohol to be produced, and thus also grain whiskies and blends, that were considerably cheaper than those made in pure pot stills. The verdict in the famous "What Is Whisky?" case of 1909, by which all grain distillations were recognized as whiskies, was a serious setback not only for Scottish malt distilleries but also for Irish ones. The decision brought with it the final breakthrough for blending, forcing the Irish to mix their pot stills with cheap grain or, to put it less delicately, to adulterate it.

Finally, there were two events, one in 1916 and the other in 1920, from which the Irish still have not recovered. As reprisal for the half-won struggle for independence against England, a trade embargo was set up with the Commonwealth that remained in effect until Ireland joined the European Union in the 1970s. On top of this, with the introduction of Prohibition in the US, the Irish lost their most important market. Of the two thousand distilleries that once flourished, only about a dozen remain today, and they have had to combine in order to survive at all.

> "My God, so much I like to drink Scotch that sometimes
> I think my name is Igor Stra-whiskey."
> IGOR STRAVINSKY[10]

SCOTCH, FIRST AND foremost, is just a denomination of origin. Malt, a distillate from barley malt made in pot stills, is distinguished by the more or less intensive aroma of malt and smoky notes, which are of considerable importance to the taste. Malt whisky is not permitted to have any additives besides water and yeast. It is matured, as a rule, for eight to twelve years before being diluted with water to the desired strength for drinking and then bottled.

Single malt comes from a single distillery, whereas vatted malt is a blend of various single malts. Production of malt is an extremely protracted business and therefore very expensive. Scotch is also the term used for simple grain whisky, a clear grain spirit without long maturation or particular storage methods and correspondingly also without any special flavorful characteristics. Apart from a few exceptions it is produced industrially and used in blending. Most people, however, think of scotch as being one of the world-famous blends, a mixture of grain and malt whiskies. Generally these mixtures contain a blend of fifteen to fifty different whiskies. As grain whiskies are usually more or less colorless, the laws allow the addition of caramel for coloring. While the malts are there to give the blend character and taste, the grains are intended to ensure that this character doesn't become too independent and to harmonize the blend. The success of scotch is based on this moderating influence, which gives Scottish whisky its light body and keeps production costs down, ideal prerequisites for mass production. Nowadays 90 percent of Scottish whisky production consists of blends.

From the fourteenth century until the invention of continuous stills, scotch had only regional impact; it was hardly known south of the Scottish Lowlands. Since the first alcohol tax was levied in 1644, it became for most of Scotland, mostly

in its illicit form, a symbol of resistance to the English crown—
which for the avowed Scotsman, Sean Connery, it remains to
this day. In London of old, a trendsetting city even then, the
powerful smoky spirit was considered the drink of uncivilized
hillbillies. In the metropolis they drank brandy and cognac
and, from 1850 onwards, refined gin. All this changed dramatically when towards the end of the nineteenth century the
vine pest was raging in the vineyards around Cognac and in the
Mediterranean region, and supplies collapsed. Lack of alterna-
tives forced people to try out the native grain spirits.

Scottish entrepreneurs Alexander Walker, James Buchanan,
John Haig, and John Dewar developed brands that today are
household names. They used the art of blending to create constant and recognizable qualities. Additionally they bottled
using labels, a new concept at that time, and launched advertising campaigns. All four became immensely prosperous,
and as whisky barons they moved in the highest circles. They
became patrons of London's music and art scene, which in
turn reflected positively on their products. When the Distillers Company Limited, an early conglomeration of important
Scottish drinks companies, won the "What Is Whisky?" case,
the course was set for even greater successes in the future.
The court case was triggered, by the way, by an advertising
campaign for Cambus grain whisky that promised "Not One
Headache in a Gallon."

The malt distilleries from geographically remote Scotland
were badly affected and either on the edge of bankruptcy or
had already been bought out. At the beginning of the twentieth century it was the Irish who were the global market leaders.
But the struggle for independence against England then weak-
ened Ireland, enabling the Scots to gain the upper hand on the
whisky market. With the tacit consent of the British government (many people claim with its actual backing) the Scots

distinguished themselves as smugglers. They not only served the acute demand situation, but also paved the way for the time after the great drought.

Bogey and Vatted Malt

*"Logic, like whiskey, loses its beneficial effect
when taken in too large quantities."*
LORD DUNSANY[11]

HUMPHREY BOGART WAS one of the most famous lovers of scotch. Every day he drank not just one drink but a number of them. He loved scotch, Martinis, and Drambuie. If you were to ask for Mr. Bogart in his favorite restaurant, Romanoff's, the barkeeper would cast a discrete glance at the level of the Drambuie bottle before replying that Mr. Bogart had not yet returned from filming.

From the age of twenty-three he worked as an actor, firstly in the theatre and then in films. It took him eleven years to become a stage star and a further six years to conquer Hollywood. He acted in small and middling roles on Broadway but also in the provincial theatres and appeared in more or less mediocre films. He accepted all roles offered; he wanted to be an actor, and this was his concept of professionalism. No woman, no setback, not even alcohol, would hold him back.

With his third wife, Mayo Methot, he destroyed hotel rooms. They were dubbed "the Battling Bogarts" and threw anything close at hand—flowers, glasses, ice buckets—at each other. For a while they weren't allowed in the 21 Club together, only separately. Most of the scuffles were started by Methot. Once Bogart was stabbed in the back with a knife. Her ability to drink was just as renowned as her jealousy. All these theatrics didn't help a bit, and she lost him to Lauren Bacall, who, despite the twenty-five-year age difference with Bogart, still knew how to enjoy herself. But Bacall was also distinguished and dynamic and had an unshakable loyalty to her husband and to all projects he was involved in. "Baby's a real Joe" was how he introduced her to a friend. Bacall steered his life towards calmer waters and lowered his consumption of alcohol to still considerable but bearable levels.

During filming of *The African Queen* with Katharine Hepburn in the then Belgian Congo, a large number of the crew went down with one or another tropical disease. Only John Huston, Bogart, and Bacall were spared thanks to a strict diet of baked beans, tinned asparagus, and considerable amounts of scotch. Bogart claimed that any mosquito that had the misfortune to bite him would instantly drop dead.

The couple's last house on Mapleton Drive between Beverly Hills and Bel Air was huge but modestly furnished. The library, however, was furnished with a bar and comfortable chairs, and a film projector (located in the adjoining guests' washroom) screened his films onto a private screen. Here Frank Sinatra, John Huston, Judy Garland, Lana Turner, Bing Crosby, and a host of other stars made themselves at home.

Bogart couldn't stand the pretense of Hollywood. The passionate yachtsman started his weekends on Saturdays at 10 a.m. with an hour-long drive to Newport Harbor, where he boarded his yacht, hoisted the sails, poured himself a scotch, took a sip, and placed the glass in its holder next to the binnacle. Relaxation, freedom, and rest. The *Santana* was the boat with the largest number of mounted glass holders on the Californian coast.

He was one of the few Hollywood stars to have a real family life with his two children. In twenty-six years he starred in eighty-two films and had a reputation of always arriving on set punctually and knowing his lines. He drank, for sure, but in his later years he was in bed by 10 p.m. when shooting was planned the next day. He never slurred his speech, and nobody had ever seen him stagger. Throughout his life he did as he wanted and said what he thought. He died at the age of fifty-eight of cancer of the esophagus, and after the simple burial the severely shaken Lauren Bacall invited close friends to the library for drinks.

Fourth Semester

RUM

"Fifteen men on the dead man's chest
Yo-ho-ho, and a bottle of rum!
Drink and the devil had done for the rest
Yo-ho-ho, and a bottle of rum!"
ROBERT LOUIS STEVENSON, TREASURE ISLAND[1]

Rum and Seafaring

O N AUGUST 31, 1970, from the poles to the tropics, there was much muttering belowdecks on the ships of the Royal Navy. It was a black day in the annals of British seafaring history. At midday thousands of sailors wore black armbands as they stood in line aboard their ships to receive their last tot of rum. One last time, their aluminum beakers were filled with a one-to-two diluted rum mixture, and all that was left was to take leave of a tradition that had been part of the Royal Navy for 316 years and had given joy and satisfaction to countless crews. When on a cruiser near the international date line the hatless crew with moist eyes ceremoniously buried the Rum Tub at sea, the tot was history and a new memorial day was born: Black Tot Day, honored with a special stamp from the post office in Portsmouth and remembered with devotion by drinkers inside and outside the navy.

"It was one hell of a change," remembered Commander Allsop.[2] In 1970 the tot consisted of half a gill (about 2 ½ ounces) of neat rum for senior ratings and diluted with water for junior ratings—"a reasonably gentlemanly affair."[3] It was a social occasion for friends to come together to enjoy a tot; tots were used to repay favors; and a tot saved going to the bar for a pre-lunch drink at midday. Now drab soberness was supposed to enable the crew to cope with ever-more complex weapon systems and navigational tools. The ban on high-proof spirits, however, only affected the ratings; the officers' mess continued to have a well-stocked bar. In protest, many long-serving and highly decorated seamen handed in letters of resignation.

Whether or not an eighth of a pint of rum is an acceptable daily ration, the fact is that the tot of the 1970s was a relatively harmless measure. In 1731 when free drinks were introduced at the cost of His Majesty, a daily pint of rum was considered adequate to make the lot of a starving sailor bearable.

Life on board was harsh and the duties were grueling. Most people would consider it to be some form of torture; living in confined quarters, existing on bad food and foul water, trying to survive all the illnesses and diseases linked to these deprivations, and then, on top of all of this, strict military discipline and long journeys to unknown oceans beneath scorching sun or through violent storms.

But special circumstances require exceptional people. Pieter van der Merwe, general editor of the National Maritime Museum in Greenwich, had this to say about seamen in the seventeenth century:

They lived in conditions that nowadays would be considered intolerable. It [the rum ration] was the one thing that made life bearable. You cannot imagine how tough these people were. Seamen were a race apart. They walked differently, they talked differently, they dressed differently. They were built like oxen. They could take punishment, and they expected it. They knew if they got drunk they would be flogged, and they still got drunk. [But] you mustn't imagine that naval ships were sailed by crews of drunken sailors. Everybody drowns if sailors are drunk all the time.[4]

The tot was introduced on Admiral Penn's ships. In 1655 he conquered Jamaica for England and on the voyage home decided to substitute the daily ration of a gallon of beer for a pint of rum. The daily ration of rum actually led to a decline in deaths and illnesses on his ships. The food situation improved too, as fruits preserved in rum remained good for months. Above all, the water quality profited from being sterilized by the rum. Storage in wooden casks might lend qualities to many kinds of spirits, but a cask is not really the ideal place for storing water. The contents of these casks—thick with filaments as long as your finger—were more reminiscent of ink than water. "When a cask was opened, 'it stank between decks like Styx, Phlegethon and Cocytus all together,'" reported the author Johann Gottfried Seume after crossing the Atlantic in 1782.[5] Mixing it with rum provided a remedy.

In 1731 after Penn's successful trials, the Admiralty made the rum tot obligatory on all His Majesty's ships. Its issue at noon became the high point of the day. When the warrant officer ordered "up spirits" to be signaled on the bosun's call, the crew gathered on the deck. The ship's supply officer—the purser, or "pusser," as they were known—first carried out a simple test. The rum was mixed with a few grains of gunpowder and ignited. The English measure of proof is based on this ritual. If the rum and gunpowder mixture burned with a blue flame, the rum was strong enough and "proofed." One hundred percent proof corresponds to 57 percent alcohol volume. A yellow flame indicated an alcohol content of above 57 percent (overproof). If the mixture failed to ignite, the rum was underproof and suspicion grew among the crew.

"The King, God bless him"—the first sip was always a royal toast to the king or queen. For each day of the week these words were preceded by a different opening:

On Sundays: "To absent friends and those at sea and the King, God bless him."

On Mondays: "To our ships at sea and the King, God bless him."

On Tuesdays: "To our friends and the King, God bless him."

On Wednesdays: "To ourselves as no one else is liable to concern themselves with our welfare and the King, God bless him."

On Thursdays: "To a bloody war and a sickly season, to a bloody war and a quick promotion and the King, God bless him."

On Fridays: "To a willing foe and sea room and the King, God bless him."

On Saturdays: "To sweethearts and wives, may they never meet, and the King, God bless him."

Before a sea battle or an encounter with dreaded pirates, rations were doubled. Two pints of rum should have washed away any concerns about the imminent slaughter—an effective measure, but at the same time one that severely hindered discipline on board. Harmless disputes became bloody conflicts. If the crew saved up their rations for a couple of days with the specific purpose of drinking them all at once, intoxication brought hatred to the surface, and to the sounds of pipes, fiddle,

94

and accordion, the crew would sing songs mocking the upper ranks. Disciplinary measures were harsh, ranging from canceled rations or food to confinement and corporal punishment with the cat o' nine tails. On August 21, 1740, Admiral Vernon issued the famous Order 349, which was binding for all captains in the Royal Navy. The order stipulated that tots were to be reduced from a pint to half a pint and that they were to be mixed with a quart of water. This order brought many a ship's crew to the verge of mutiny.

The mixing of rum and water was to be executed on deck under the watchful eyes of the crew and in the presence of all officers. A wooden vat especially made for the purpose was filled with rum, water, lime juice, and sugar. Admiral Vernon in person drank the first cup of this mixture to convince the crew that it was drinkable. It soon came to be called GROG, derived from Vernon's nickname, "Old Grogram," which was, in turn, based on his preference for a waterproof grogram cloak he wore on board. The wooden vat became the grog tub.

Another British naval hero who made a valuable contribution to rum was Lord Horatio Nelson, who from 1779 was stationed on Jamaica for a number of years. The Saturday toast—"to sweethearts and wives, may they never meet"—in particular must have rung a bell. Successful in battle and an outstanding strategist, he led England to victory over the numerically superior French fleet. On the high seas he was much loved by his crew. He was considered to be a man of the people and modest, and he ensured better provisions, even for the junior ratings, and ordered fresh fruit, onions, and lamb for crew members in the sick bay. Considerately he ordered the rum rations to be heated in colder climes, and he dutifully sent home polite letters to his wife, Fanny. On land another side of his character was revealed. He was a charming and inspiring entertainer, but vain and narcissistic.

In 1793 he first met Sir William Hamilton, the British consul in Naples, and in 1798 while he was being entertained by the Hamiltons, Lady Emma Hamilton succumbed to his charms. She assumed responsibility for nursing the injured naval hero, who at this stage had already lost an eye and an arm, and she kindled a veritable cult to her prominent guest. Memorial coins were minted for the hero of the Battle of the Nile, glamorous evening parties were thrown in his honor, and fireworks celebrating his fame decorated the balmy night skies over southern Italy.

Around her neck Lady Hamilton wore a medallion with a portrait of her hero. She had her underwear embroidered with his initials and anchors. A scandal was unavoidable. Sir Hamilton silently came to terms with the dedication of his young wife to the maltreated hero. With muffled voices England's upper class whispered about bigamy or even bisexuality. What is certain is that Lady Hamilton bore her warrior a daughter, Horatia. The girl and her scandal-ridden mother were on Nelson's mind when he was fatally wounded during the Battle of Trafalgar on October 21, 1805. "Take care of Horatia" were among his last words as he lay dying. It was decided to transport his body back to England, where he was to be buried with full military honors. The body was placed in a wooden cask that was then filled with rum and lashed to the mainmast. A guard of honor was stationed on the deck next to the body, and after three days a rumbling noise started coming from the cask. The lid rose; was it Nelson's spirit? Decomposition had set in, forming gases in the cask. Before reaching Gibraltar they were forced to let the rum out of the bunghole and replace it with brandy. Legends persist that loyal sailors didn't let this last bequest of their commander go to waste. In sailor's language, "Nelson's Blood" is still a synonym for rum.

At the beginning of the nineteenth century the Admiralty made great efforts to improve the quality of naval rum and to

96

standardize it. Central supply depots were established at Port Royal on Jamaica, at Portsmouth, at Devonport on Tasmania, and on the Chatham Islands, nowadays part of the Andaman Islands, in the Bay of Bengal. Here rums from various West Indian colonies were blended according to defined recipes and stored before being distributed among the ships of the royal fleet. The result was a sharp, powerful blend with a fine aroma, a uniform quality, and a uniform drinking strength of 40 percent.

But complaints about alcohol abuse on board the Royal Navy's ships did not abate. Even during the Second World War there were dramatic scenes when in 1941 Hong Kong was under threat from Japan and in 1942 when Alexandria was surrounded by troops under General Rommel. In both cases the beleaguered British troops, at the very last moment, were forced to pour thousands of gallons of navy rum into the sea rather than let it fall into enemy hands.

Then came Black Tot Day and with it the end of imperial rum. The legendary sugarcane spirit was served once more at the wedding of Prince Andrew to Lady Sarah Ferguson. The prince had spent some time in the navy and was well acquainted with the customs. Six hundred and fifty gallons had survived seventeen years in a forgotten Jamaican depot, and apparently even today the very last stocks—the bottles in handwoven wicker baskets to protect the priceless contents—can be purchased for the princely sum of US$5,000.

The tradition-conscious Briton, Charles Tobias, succeeded in 1979 in gaining the rights to the name of British Navy Pusser's Rum, and he pays a considerable, and to date undisclosed, amount of money to the Royal Navy Sailors' Fund. This is a charitable foundation established by the navy after Black Tot Day with a share capital of £3 million to look after the social concerns of sailors. The Sailor's Fund owns leisure facilities, educational institutions, and retirement homes for members of the British Navy. Tobias founded the company Pusser's Rum on Tortola, a small island in the British Virgin Island group, and marketed a blend of six rums following the traditions of the original recipe. One or more glasses of rum at Pusser's Bar on Tortola is an integral part and an eagerly awaited climax to many Caribbean cruises. This bar is still a treasure trove of reminders of the glorious times when ships were made of wood and men of iron.

In the Service of His Majesty: Buccaneers in the Caribbean

ANOTHER GROUP OF seafarers cruised through the turquoise waters of the Caribbean between 1630 and 1690 and, armed with letters of marque from the English or French crown, fought a low-budget war against Spain. The pirates, or buccaneers as they were also known, were the freelancers of their time. They signed on when they were low on funds or just felt like a bit of slaughter. Although it was one hundred years before the French Revolution, this wild horde was astonishingly democratic and well organized. They elected their captains, and the crew, not the captain, decided whether or not to attack. A complicated system organized the distribution of booty, and even the loss of an eye or any other part of the body was compensated with a fixed reimbursement. Some buccaneers lived in lifelong male partnerships, the institution being termed *matelotage* and the partners *matelots. Matelots* shared beds, booty, and food with one another. If they weren't gay they would also share women, and they fought side by side in battle.

Pirates had smaller but more maneuverable ships than their opponents. They preferred to attack at night, climbing up the ship's side and killing the watch and all the officers. The rest of

98

the crew considered their options and often chose the free life of the buccaneer. One of the inducements must have been the pirates' unlimited access to rum. On the not-so-positive side the price of freedom was high. They were hung with or without letters of marque, which explains why it didn't really matter to the freebooters whether there was temporary peace between England, Spain, or France or whether the respective monarchs had managed to summon back their pirates.

One of the most successful and colorful representatives of this group was Captain Henry Morgan, who is today remembered by a rum brand of the same name. With the film series *Pirates of the Caribbean* there has been no stopping the marketing machinery. Pirate parties were organized at sponsored events with captains in costumes flanked by Morganettes in miniskirts serving Captain Morgan Original Spiced Gold with cola, a somewhat weak reflection of the debauched parties much loved by the real pirates of the seventeenth century. Nevertheless, the introduction of this drink, which at a modest 35 percent can hardly be called rum, was one of the most successful of recent years. Inexplicably the company withdrew the considerably more potent 78 percent Captain Morgan Overproof from the market. Since then it has been sadly missed at bars; for many drinkers, a half ounce of it was the perfect ingredient for a respectable Mai Tai.

Henry Morgan came from Wales to Barbados in 1655, where he was indentured for three years' labor on a sugarcane plantation. Afterwards he moved to Jamaica, the home of his influential uncle Edward Morgan (who would later become the deputy governor of the island), and married his cousin, Mary. Although he had no seafaring experience he signed up with the buccaneers, who at first specifically supported English interests in the Caribbean and nurtured close links to the navy through the exchange of officers. Slowly but surely he advanced through the hierarchy of the wild men. At the request of the new governor, Sir Thomas Modyford, Morgan seized the Caribbean island of Providencia from the Spanish and tried to establish a pirate government there. The Spanish troops, disciplined and well equipped, put an end to this experiment in no time at all. Modyford, fearing retaliation against his base at Port Royal, instructed Morgan to make a quick attack against another target to distract the Spanish from their original plan. Morgan dressed in red silks, wore golden chains around his neck, and decked his fingers in jewelry, the epitome of a successful pirate. He moved from one hideout to the next and recruited five hundred determined men for his next raid. The carefully prepared coup was successful. They seized Porto Bello in Panama, then the center of Spanish trade in the Caribbean. It was in the waters off Porto Bello that the English privateer, Sir Francis Drake, succumbed to fever during an unsuccessful attack in 1596. Both the raid and the fabulous booty made Henry Morgan the stuff of legends. The victory rum party after the raid cost him his ship. A drunken pirate accidently ignited the gunpowder magazine, triggering an explosion. Time and again Modyford was ordered to distance himself from the pirates and to stop issuing letters of marque, and each time he gave in to the lure of a share in the booty by claiming that his official residence in Port Royal was in acute danger. Eventually Henry Morgan was imprisoned and shipped to London, but instead of the expected death by hanging he was knighted for his services, and he returned to Port Royal. It had become one of the most prosperous towns in the Caribbean, not least through trade generated by the booty of the buccaneers. It had "more houses than New York, more ale-houses than London and more brothels than Paris," as one description of the renowned town attested. The satirical writer Ned Ward was somewhat more forthright:

The Dunghill of the Universe, the Refuse of the whole Creation, the Clippings of the Elements, a shapeless Pile of rubbish confused'ly jumbl'd in to an Emblem of the *Chaos*, neglected by Omnipotence when he form'd the World into its admirable Order... The Receptacle of Vagabonds, the Sanctuary of Bankrupts, and a Close-Stool for the Purges of our Prisons. As Sickly as an Hospital, as Dangerous as the Plague, as Hot as Hell and as Wicked as the Devil.[6]

Sir Henry Morgan acted as lieutenant governor of Jamaica three times, in 1674-75, 1678, and 1680-82. In 1688 the lifelong rum drinker died of edema, then called "dropsy." He was buried in the Palisadoes cemetery, which sank beneath the sea after the earthquake of 1692. It is said that the casket floated away and Henry Morgan's ghost haunts the waters of the Caribbean looking for his mortal remains.

The Spirit of Early Globalization

RUM IS INEXTRICABLY bound to one of the darkest chapters in European history: colonization of the West Indies and the Central American mainland. The sea powers of the Old World—Portugal, Spain, France, England, Holland, and Denmark—participated in seizing and exploiting these tropical paradises.

In the new colonies they dreamed of gold deposits in legendary El Dorado, and if not gold then at least some exotic spices. The colonists took advantage of the favorable climatic conditions to cultivate a plant that was to prove just as precious.

Sugarcane, *Saccharum officinarum*, an otherwise robust crop plant, makes a number of demands on its habitat. It thrives on the high temperatures and regular rainfall that can be found in open areas of tropical lowlands. The stems of sugarcane grow for eight to ten months to a height of up to sixteen feet and are covered by sharp-edged leaves. Sucrose is produced in all parts of the plant via photosynthesis and, unmodified, is stored in the cores of the stems. The juicy core can contain up to 20 percent of this sugar.

In 1493 on his second voyage across the Atlantic, Christopher Columbus transported sugarcane seedlings from the Canary Islands to Hispaniola, the island that today is shared by Haiti and the Dominican Republic. Also on board was a brigade of Arabian prisoners intended to be used as labor for the sugarcane plantations. Emaciated from the voyage and the drudgery, they soon succumbed to a diversity of tropical diseases. The sugarcane, however, flourished on the moist and warm island. The Spanish cultivated it in Puerto Rico, Jamaica, and Mexico, and the Portuguese introduced it to Brazil.

Sugar in Europe was a much-sought-after commodity. It was needed to accompany other recently imported colonial wares like coffee, tea, and cocoa, which in those days were customary to drink heavily sweetened. The new masters forced the native inhabitants to work on their plantations. The latter had no problems with the climate, but they did have problems with the diseases that the Europeans had brought with them. Equally, they were not used to such harsh, physical labor. In Africa the European dealers found a labor force who defied the climatic demands, the heavy physical labor, and the manifold diseases. A morally corrupt but economically immensely successful intercontinental trade was born.

Ships laden with beads, colorful cloths, and mirrors as well as livestock and tools sailed from the harbors of Europe for the west coast of Africa to exchange their goods for slaves. From 1514 to 1866 around 12.5 million men, women, and children were abducted from their African homes and transported to the West Indies or North America on one of the 27,000 transatlantic passages. During the passage they were crammed together belowdecks by the hundreds. Roughly 1.5 million of them died at sea. The survivors were sold at the slave markets of Curaçao, San Juan, Havana, Kingston, and Port-au-Prince. On board for the return journey were the products of the colonies: sugar, molasses, fruits, tobacco, and later rum, the liquid gold of the Caribbean, or "the spirit of early globalization," as the German journalist Martina Wimmer aptly described it.[7]

On the plantations the sugarcane grew to maturity under the constant attention of the slave workers. Once it had been cut it had to be processed in the sugar mills as soon as possible. The liquids were ground out of the stems in mills powered by the wind or working animals and then boiled in huge pans until crystallized. Centrifuges separated the solid from the liquid components. What remained were the coveted cane sugar and its side product, dark brown molasses.

Today we differentiate rums distilled from molasses regardless of color, strength, or storage conditions, from the *rhum agricole* made in the former French colonies. The latter is not made from molasses but from distilled fresh sugarcane juice, the aroma clearly indicating its botanical origins. A similar rum from sugarcane juice is the Brazilian *cachaça*.

The Cradle of Rum

IN 1609 A hurricane stranded the ship of the British captain Sir John Summers on Barbados.[8] Eighteen years later British colonists began to clear the land on this uninhabited island to make way for the cultivation of sugarcane. By the middle of the seventeenth century and with staggering speed, it had become one of the richest colonies of the kingdom. Seventy-five thousand people lived on the Caribbean island, most of them West African slaves. Here, in all probability, rum was discovered by the English, who were well-versed in anything involving alcohol. Captain J. Walduck summarized the premises of the colonial politics of competing European kingdoms in a letter to his nephew in 1708:

> Upon all the new settlements the Spanish make, the first thing they do is build a church, the first thing ye Dutch do upon a new colony is to build them a fort, but the first thing ye English do, be it in the most remote part of ye world, or among the most barbarous indians, is to set up a tavern or drinking house.[9]

More or less by chance the English had noticed that molasses, when mixed with water and residual fibers, began to ferment rapidly. Previously they would have thrown it in the river or used it as cattle fodder or fertilizer, but now they used this sugarcane "wine" as medicine and prescribed it as a reward to the slaves. Using primitive distillation apparatus, they improved its strength. The early precursors of rum were called *tafia* and "kill devil," from which the French derive *guildive*. In 1661 the term *rumbullion*, a modification of "rebellion," appears for the first time in a decree from the governor of Jamaica. In time it was shortened to "rum" as an appellation for the brown gold of the Caribbean.

Production developed quickly, and by 1655 they were already distilling 900,000 gallons of rum on Barbados, with the profits strictly reserved for the plantation owners. Without even taking the slaves into consideration, the majority of islanders, even the English settlers, were poor. The average life expectancy of a slave after arrival on the island was three whole years. Rum offered the slaves a means to combat diseases, despair, and homesickness. Richard Ligon, chronicler of the island, wrote from his prison cell while incarcerated for debts:

"The people drink much of it, indeed too much; for it often lays them asleep on the ground, and that is accounted a very unwholesome lodging."[10] Despite his words of warning he left the world a recipe for a calf's foot pie made with minced and spiced pigskin, which he recommended washing down with a "dramme cup of Kill-Devil."[11]

In the eighteenth century the volume of molasses accruing from sugar production was way beyond the capacity of local distilleries. Surpluses were at first exported to Europe, but the West Indies and Europe were not the only sites of rum production. Since 1620 puritan settlers had become established on the coastal regions of northeastern America, rich in both forests and fish. In bloody battles the pugnacious pilgrim fathers had driven the native inhabitants farther west. They traded salted fish for Caribbean rum but above all for molasses, which they distilled themselves. Rum production was not as well developed everywhere as it was on Barbados, and here was an opportunity for the sugar barons to sell only the raw materials of distillation to New England. The Caribbean islands, on the other hand, with mainly monocultures of sugarcane, were desperately dependant on the import of foodstuffs. In 1640 the first of a rapidly increasing number of distilleries began production in New England. Rum production became one of the largest industries, and rum became the colonists' most important export commodity on the slave markets of Africa, where it was exchanged for slaves to restock the quickly depleted supplies of plantation workers in the Caribbean.

The church supported these developments to the extent of leasing some of its properties as storerooms, and some men of God were engaged not only in spiritual affairs but also in actual spirits. A New Englander above the age of fifteen drank on average seven glasses of rum a day. Indeed, as the high-proof

105

alcohol doesn't freeze, the fishermen off the Grand Banks considered it to be a form of liquid energy crucial to surviving the harsh winters.

Besides its function as currency for the slave trade, rum also played a grim role in the displacement and eradication of the native American Indians. One of the founding fathers of America, Benjamin Franklin, illustrated the fact precisely in his autobiography: "If it be the design of Providence to extirpate these savages in order to make room for cultivators of the earth, it seems not improbable that rum may be the appointed means. It has already annihilated all the tribes who formerly inhabited the sea-coast."[12] American Indians who knew the fermented but not the high-powered distilled form of alcohol soon became addicted. They would sign peace treaties and cede territory without further ado as long as there was the prospect of sufficient supplies of rum.

Rum and Independence

NEW YORK AND Boston represented important trade centers for New England. The Navigation Acts starting in 1651 tried to obstruct, if not prohibit, trade between the American colonies and France, Holland, and other European countries.

Rum was actually very strong, twice the strength of cognac or brandy. The producers of these latter drinks in their mother countries were up in arms about this new form of alcohol from the colonies and forced through an import embargo on rum and molasses in 1713. This was why the French colonies in the Caribbean started delivering their molasses to New England. Prices fell, and the aspiring colonies of the New World could for the first time offer their own rum at cheaper prices on African slave markets, undercutting British slave traders for the coveted labor force.

England retaliated in 1733 by passing the Molasses Act, levying heavy duties on rum and molasses produced outside of the empire. With this act, England wanted to prevent trade between French colonies and the New World. The New Englanders protested, but the British sugar barons had secured influence in the Houses of Parliament. Rigorous legislation primarily effected a rise in smuggling and fraud. Of the 1 million gallons of molasses imported to Rhode Island, only 50,000 were taxed. In 1770 Saint Croix alone exported 539,000 gallons illegally.

New England from that time on officially supplied the mother country only with furs, and with a swift expansion of its industries and its own trade networks it made itself independent. Rum brought the necessary liquidity. It was, above all, restrictions to their rum trade that stoked an increasing anger in the North American colonies against the mother country, which eventually sparked the American War of Independence in 1775. The second president, John Adams, noted in his diary: "I know not why we should blush to confess that molasses was an essential ingredient in American independence."[13]

The preferred drinks of the landed gentry and plantation owners in Massachusetts, Pennsylvania, and New York were imports: cognac, brandy, sherry, and madeira as well as wine and champagne. The everyday drink, however, was rum. In 1739 there were no less than 159 distilleries, 30 of them in Boston alone, and rum production had become a dominant economic factor.

Even George Washington led the life of the landed gentry before becoming commander-in-chief of the Continental Army and later the first president of the United States. His half-brother, Lawrence, bequeathed him a manor house—named Mount Vernon in honor of Admiral Vernon, under whom Lawrence had served in the British Navy—as well as other estates in Virginia. He cultivated tobacco and sold the harvest on commission to trading houses in London, and in return he ordered the goods that, according to the patterns set by the English aristocracy, befitted someone of his social status. Glasses, punch bowls, and decanters, all at horrendous prices, were to be found on George Washington's order lists.

He had already become acquainted with rum, however, in 1751, while accompanying Lawrence to Barbados. He overcame smallpox there, and so he brought back from his journey immunity against future infection and a lifelong attraction to the golden rum of that island.

At an assembly in Williamsburg on the eve of the elections for the House of Burgesses, a legislative body, Washington invited his potential voters to beer, wine, punch, and twenty-six gallons of Barbados rum. He promptly won the election and was sent as representative for Virginia to the Continental Congress. He was then offered command of America's forces, which at that time consisted of a motley bunch of militiamen who were eventually to defeat the British in the Revolutionary War. Washington endeavored throughout the war to improve the poor arms and equipment and the food and medical attention provided for his men. He considered smallpox vaccinations to be just as important for morale and physical well-being as an alcohol allowance. He installed distilling paraphernalia at Mount Vernon, processing his own raw materials into whiskey and molasses into rum. With the production of considerable quantities, George Washington managed to demonstrate his personal independence from the mother country.

The Boston Molasses Disaster of January 15, 1919, illustrates once more the tragic consequences of too fast and too much, a combination that occurs regularly when the topic of alcohol is discussed. In this case a series of adverse circumstances occurred that even with hindsight seem almost inexplicable.

An eighty-nine-foot-long cast-iron tank exploded due to a sudden rise in temperature from 5˚F to 43˚F. A flood wave of 9.5 million gallons of raw molasses gushed onto Commercial Street, bending the steel supports of the Boston elevated railway and derailing a train. It tore buildings from their foundations, carrying the North End pier way out into the harbor and transforming North End Park into a sticky lake. Twenty-one people died, as well as numerous horses and dogs, and at least 150 people were seriously injured. Three hundred volunteers needed more than two weeks to clear the gooey mass, which in places was three feet deep, from the streets. The Boston Harbor basin was brown from molasses until the end of summer, and the sweet aroma remained in the area for years.

The Drink of Gods: Tiki

"The goddess made me a pot of tea—
a dash of rum including;
While she herself enjoyed the rum,
without the tea intruding.
HEINRICH HEINE, GERMANY: A WINTER'S TALE[14]

AT THE BEGINNING of the 1930s North America was still shuddering from the consequences of the economic crisis. It had led to the collapse of banks, which had massive ripple effects on individuals and industry. So the excuse for one or more drinks was there. Ernest Raymond Beaumont Gantt, who later changed his name to Donn Beach, had a good nose for business in the times of the Great Depression, and he sensed the general willingness for escapism when he placed the first plastic palms in Don's Beachcomber Café on McCadden Place not far from the

Hollywood Hills. His grandfather, a Southern plantation owner, had introduced him to the sea, the Caribbean islands, and rum at an early age. He was taken on early morning trips to the oyster beds where ice-cold JULEPS were served on fine silver platters. On hot nights in New Orleans he was shown that, even at seventy-five, his grandfather was able to angle a stunningly beautiful, young black lover. And he was shown how to avoid the coastguard patrols with a boatload of illegal rum. This libertarian, hedonistic upbringing gave Beach the time of his life.

Straw mats, orchids, and banana plants adorned the walls of his bar, guarded by the beady eyes of the Polynesian column deities: the tikis. The spirits of the South Seas that he evoked here came just at the right time to ease the troubled souls of his clientele. His drinks, outstanding creations based on Caribbean rums of various colors and strengths, did the rest. He is the father of the ZOMBIE, the SHARK'S TOOTH, and DR. FUNK. The Zombie was created when a hungover guest didn't want to keep a business appointment while sober, and instead, with the assistance of this now world-famous drink, was transformed to one of the living dead. Beach's dedicated service to his guest was soon repaid. In a short time, Hollywood's film crowd began to frequent his bar; Charlie Chaplin and Marlene Dietrich were soon to be seen sipping away at his high-proof rum drinks. Beach increased his staff with the addition of four Filipino barmen who became legendary under the name "the Four Boys." The increasing number of imitators of his cocktails prompted him to introduce what could be considered as a pretty paranoid system behind the bar: rather than display the spirits in their original labeled containers, he kept them in numbered bottles so that neither the guests nor the bar staff would know his recipes. The Second World War abruptly interrupted the series of happy evenings beneath the palms. Donn Beach was called up and served in Europe. In his absence his ex-wife Sunny Sund started a chain of sixteen new bar/restaurants called Don the Beachcomber. When war ended a court judgment prohibited Beach from opening a bar using his own name. He relocated to Waikiki Beach on Hawaii, where he ran a bar along the lines of his old formula. "Of all life's pleasures drink deeply, at every worry give a wink, it's much, much later than you think" was his motto.

THE COPYISTS DIDN'T wait long. The most successful was Victor J. Bergeron. After visiting Beach's bar/restaurant and being infected with the Polynesian bug, he returned to his bar, Hinky Dinks, in Oakland and dedicated it to the gods of the South Seas, renaming it, on the suggestion of his wife, Trader Vic's. Equally talented as Donn Beach behind the bar but with a better nose for business, he turned his bar into a franchise, selling recipes for his drinks and "Polynesian" dishes, plus his interior design concept, mostly to hoteliers throughout the world. Most cocktails were served in tiki mugs—ceramic beakers depicting the column idols—or in fresh pineapples or coconuts.

Trader Vic's guests were entertained from time to time by one of Bergeron's macabre performances. He would stagger around the restaurant with an ice ax sticking out of his leg, and with gritted teeth he would extract it before the horrified eyes of his guests. It wasn't too painful, as he had a wooden leg. The real one, he would explain to the distressed barflies, had been snapped off by a shark, and he would then make a quick toast with a Mai Tai. In actual fact his leg had been amputated when he was a child as a result of tuberculosis. While Don the Beachcomber served relatively simple Cantonese dishes, Trader Vic's cuisine was an American/Asian hybrid. According to Polynesian traditions, meals were served on opulent platters decorated with real orchids and fruits for the whole table,

111

not in individual portions. Some cocktails also were served in communal drinking vessels for four to eight people. The stylishly decorated, dark localities became institutions of the establishment. During an official visit to the US in 1959, the wife of Nikita Khrushchev managed to escape the full force of the obligatory lady's program: shopping at Sears followed by lunch at Trader Vic's. Richard Nixon was a regular at Trader Vic's in the Capital Hilton in Washington, and even in 1983 the Reagans invited Queen Elizabeth to Trader Vic's for rum and suckling pig.

Trader Vic's gave the world of drinks the SCORPION, SAMOAN FOG CUTTER, and MISSIONARY'S DOWNFALL. An old argument simmered between followers of the Beachcomber bar and Trader Vic's over who created the MAI TAI, a mixed drink based on preferably mature Jamaican rum, limes, orange curaçao, and a dash of orgeat syrup. *Maita'i Roa Ae* (roughly translated as "out of this world") became the focus of a very worldly court case. Eventually the two sides managed to settle the case out of court by agreeing that Beach was the creator of a drink of the same name, but that Bergeron had created the cocktail that the world still enjoys as the Mai Tai.

In 1963 Walt Disney opened the Enchanted Tiki Room, a show with 150 singing and talking robots in the form of tiki idols, exotic plants, and animals. Elvis filmed there for *Paradise, Hawaiian Style*, in which he emphatically warns his co-star of the dangers of the Mai Tai. In the 1970s the wave of enthusiasm for all things Polynesian that had flooded America with Hawaiian shirts, ukuleles, and straw skirts, slowly but surely began to ebb. In Martin Scorsese's Mafia epic *Goodfellas*, the usual suspects hang out in a tiki restaurant. Blond waiters wear flower garlands and Hawaiian shirts, and small table lamps with red straw-skirt shades project a sunset glow on the hardened faces of Robert De Niro, Joe Pesci, and Ray Liotta.

The carefully constructed contrast between the hopelessly over-the-top interior and the tough clientele escalates when the manager cautiously presents them with the check. With a punch and a kick Joe Pesci floors him, and with him falls the era of all things Polynesian. Tiki was out; the idol's days were numbered.

In the original tiki cocktails, lemons and limes carefully balanced the sweet tropical fruits. Various colors and strengths of rum added complexity and depth. Cinnamon and nutmeg rounded them off. Too many imitators transformed the strong rum drink into an oversweet rum and fruit punch, its origins lost in the shade of little paper umbrellas.

A Splendid Little War

IN CUBA IN the middle of the nineteenth century the calls for independence from Spanish colonial dominion became ever louder. In Cuba's Wild East, progressive plantation owners, entrepreneurs, peasants, and Creoles rebelled. Many liberated their slaves. Ill-equipped, often armed only with machetes, these *mambises* fought unswervingly alongside their former masters against the militarily superior Spanish. The black general Antonio Maceo advanced with his guerillas on Havana, and victory seemed within their grasp.

Only at this late stage did the US decide on all-out support for the rebels. When the armored cruiser the USS *Maine* exploded in Havana Harbor under mysterious circumstances, the press fanned public outrage with the headline "Remember the Maine—To Hell with Spain!" Three hundred thousand troops were ordered to Cuba under General Shafter, a man who during the Indian Campaigns was awarded high military honors but who also had the dubious reputation of being an outright racist. Also among the troops were Wood's Weary

113

Walkers under Lieutenant-Colonel Woods, who despite being a cavalry unit fought as infantry because of the lack of horses. Woods's deputy and later US president Theodore Roosevelt personally recruited American Indians, cowboys, college athletes, and professional competition riders as members of his Rough Riders—the unit's other nickname. Shafter, who was so overweight that he had to be driven in a buckboard,[15] noticed on his first encounter with the *mambises* that many of the rebels carried a bottle of rum attached to their saddles or belts. They willingly allowed the foreign general to try a drop. *Canchanchara*, a mixture of *aguardiente* (a coarse sugarcane spirit), lime juice, and honey, was the drink that this motley band of warriors used as a food substitute, to strengthen body and mind, and as a narcotic for the wounded. "The only missing ingredient is ice," was Shafter's laconic comment.[16] A prophetic remark, as we shall soon learn.

In 1898 the decisive battle took place at Santiago. The Rough Riders had taken San Juan Hill, and together with inland Cuban units they began to besiege Santiago. The American fleet had destroyed the Spanish Navy in a sea battle, isolating the town. When the Spanish troops surrendered, this first "splendid little war" had lasted exactly four months.

The Cubans were not involved in peace negotiations. Spain handed over Puerto Rico and the Philippines to the US, and Cuba was placed under American military authority until 1902. But even after this date America secured military bases for itself and occupied key positions in agriculture, transport, and mining. Many Cubans today feel that the US intervention in 1898 cheated them out of victory over Spain.

"Drinkin' Rum and Coca Cola"

THE ANDREWS SISTERS

INSTEAD OF THE Cubans' yearned-for independence, the Americans brought coca cola. This brand new soda, made by the pharmacist John Pemberton in 1885 from kola nuts, caffeine, and coca leaves, was originally meant as a remedy for headaches and nervous disorders. In 1907 Cubans were presented with their very own coca cola factory. The CUBA LIBRE, actually a refreshing mixture of rum, limes, cola, and ice, had for them the bitter taste of betrayal. For the US troops stationed in Cuba—who were not allowed to drink alcohol—coca cola served as a good way of disguising light-colored Cuban rum.

The American mining engineer Jennings S. Cox managed a nickel mine in the remote Sierra Maestra in the Wild East of Cuba. Generous wages and premiums, including free board, cigars, and a monthly gallon of Bacardi Carta Blanca Superior, were intended to make the employees' stay in the humid heat a little more bearable. The lonely but adventurous Cox combined the mixture of rum, lime juice, and ice much loved by the native Cubans and gave the world its most popular rum-based drink, the DAIQUIRI. The recipe spread rapidly.

When the US introduced nationwide Prohibition in 1920, Havana became a magnet for all Americans who liked their drink. "Fly with us to Havana, and you can bathe in Bacardi rum two hours from now" was the slogan used by Pan Am Airways to lure thirsty customers. In the luxury hotels and well-stocked bars around the old part of town it was easy to escape from the puritan mood back home. "First port of call— out where the wet begins" was how Jose Abeal y Otero, aka "Sloppy Joe," greeted guests streaming in daily from American cruise ships to his Sloppy Joe's Bar. Cuban barkeepers rose to be stars of the drinking scene. The most famous was Constantino Ribalaigua, nicknamed Constante, who managed the Floridita bar on Calle Monserrat from 1912 to 1952. His PAPA DOBLE came without sugar and a double portion of rum with a dash of grapefruit juice.

Two of his Daiquiri variations are immortalized in literature. The LA FLORIDITA DAIQUIRI consists of a dash of maraschino liqueur in the usual rum, sugar, and lemon mix, and after Constante had acquired an ice mill it was prepared in the shaker as a FROZEN DAIQUIRI. This machine was able to produce for the first time snow-powder-fine ice that enabled barkeepers to produce ice-cold drinks with a slushy consistency.

"He had drunk double frozen daiquiris, the great ones that Constante made, that had no taste of alcohol and felt, as you drank them, the way downhill glacier skiing feels running through powder snow and, after the sixth and eighth, felt like downhill glacier skiing feels when you're running unroped."[17] Ernest Hemingway was a regular at the Floridita. He would appear at midday as one of the first guests, study the newspapers, and observe the bar business, and with the help of one or more daiquiris would make notes. In *Islands in the Stream* he fills pages with the bar conversations between the main character and Honest Lil, an elderly prostitute, about the bewildering state of the world, the impossibility of love, the difficulties of life, and...

"Drinking. Not just drinking. Drinking these double frozens without sugar. If you drank that many with sugar it would make you sick."

"*Ya lo creo.* And if anybody else drank that many without sugar they would be dead."[18]

When Leopoldina Rodríguez, on whom Hemingway based Honest Lil, was seriously ill, Hemingway paid her medical check, and when she died he was the only one to pay his final respects, as recounted by Antonio Meilan, long-standing bar-keeper and Constante's successor, in his memoir *De los mas famosos cocteles Cubanos: El barman de Hemingway revela secretos.*[19]

Hemingway lived for twenty years in his Finca Vigía on the outskirts of Havana. Gary Cooper hung out on his veranda and Ava Gardner swam naked in his pool. It was a place of peace, with birds twittering and the scents of tropical flowers filling the air. The property—the house; the garden; his fishing boat, *Pilar*, now on dry land; and the graves of his four dogs—can still be visited. Hemingway has now become part of Cuban folklore, the Floridita bar a fixed item on every package tourist's agenda. Every hour, sweating groups of tourists enter the hallowed bar with four electronic mixers relentlessly buzzing to produce daiquiris. They are shown his bar stool, and a life-size statue of the great man leans casually on the bar, invitingly placed for snapshots. They reverently follow the footsteps of the perpetual drinker Hemingway like Catholic pilgrims walk the Stations of the Cross in Jerusalem. Only if you are very lucky can you find a quiet moment for a Papa Doble away from the hurly-burly.

Hemingway really was attached to the island. He even bequeathed his Nobel Medal for Literature for *The Old Man and the Sea* to the Shrine of Our Lady of Charity of El Cobre. During the Second World War the Finca Vigía became a spy center. The new US ambassador, Spruille Braden, an eloquent and elegant man, recruited the casually dressed world-famous author for the US Secret Service. Hemingway knew the island like no other and moved easily through all the different layers of society, from the Spanish aristocracy to petty thieves. According to Braden his spy ring included "a barkeeper, a couple of wharf rats, a number of pelota players down on their luck, an ex-matador, two Basque priests and various counts and dukes living in exile."[20] Supporters of the Spanish Republic, a couple of their Falangist opponents, and some pimps and prostitutes completed the unit. Martha Gellhorn, journalist, author, and third wife of Hemingway, felt that her work was being disturbed by the comings and goings of the illustrious crowd at Finca Vigía and huffily referred to them as "the Crook Factory."

Braden, however, valued Hemingway's reports as being well researched and accurate. The FBI felt duped by the new secret agents, and Hemingway, in turn, felt that the FBI under J. Edgar Hoover was pro-Fascist and its agents inexperienced and without imagination. After just one year the Crook Factory had to cease their work. Hemingway began scanning the coast for German U-boats with his fishing boat, *Pilar*, and his Cuban skipper, Gregorio Fuentes. Fuentes, a former fisherman, was the inspiration for Hemingway's novel *The Old Man and the Sea*.

Havana remained the preferred destination for the rum-drinking excursions of US tourists until 1959. Under the last dictator, Fulgencio Batista, American investment in the hotel and restaurant business was rewarded with tax incentives and gambling licenses. The Mafia, too, invested in building hotels in the elegant neighborhood of Vedado. The Hotel Nacional, the Riviera, and the Capri lured customers with modern comforts, opulent cabaret shows, and casinos. Pan Am even organized special flights on which passengers were put in the mood for a weekend in Havana with mambo bands, Daiquiris, and dancers from a Tropicana show. The Habana Hilton was to top all other hotels. Time and again its opening day was postponed, and when finally it opened in the winter of 1958, its fame was short-lived. On January 1, 1959, the decadent glory days of Havana as a tropical playground for American tourists ended. Fidel Castro took over the government with his bearded campaigners and set up his headquarters on the top floor of the Habana Hilton. When the management cautiously asked how they intended to settle the accumulating account, the rebels, without further ado, seized the rest of the building and renamed it the Habana Libre.

The Rumble of Rums

ON OCTOBER 4, 1960, a radio announcement informed surprised business owners that all large private concerns had been nationalized.

Bacardi was at this point one of the most important Cuban producers and exporters of rum. Since 1862 Bacardi had been making a light, elegant rum, Carta Blanca Superior, that, with charcoal filtration, long maturation times, and special strains of yeast for fermentation, had reached the quality of select brandy or cognac and had received international acclaim. Although the company had not greeted the rebels from the Sierra Maestra on the day of their triumph with a huge "Gracias Fidel" banner fluttering from the roof of its headquarters, it was prudent enough to have transferred sections of the business and the hallowed yeast strain before it was taken over. By the 1970s, with its headquarters in Puerto Rico, it had become the largest rum company in private hands, not least through its advertising campaigns stressing the three s's—sun, sea, and sand. Early on, the family had chosen the bat as the company emblem. It was considered to be a symbol of luck for Afro-Cuban followers of Santeria, a system of beliefs related to voodoo. The bat symbol generated, then as now, a high recognition factor. At a time when only a quarter of the urban population could read or write, the emblem made the decision to buy easier for illiterates.

Not all companies were farsighted enough to relocate at least some of their production capacities overseas before or just after the Cuban Revolution. The Arechabala family, who, like the Bacardis, were involved in the rum business for decades, had been producing reputable rum under the name Havana Club since 1934. They, too, lost ownership and production plants to the Cuban nation, but unlike the Bacardis, they had not protected any of their company assets beforehand. Taking a circuitous route via Spain, they eventually resettled in Miami. They turned their backs on the spirit business and in 1973 neglected to renew their rights to their brand name.

In Cuba after nationalization, the production and marketing of rum lay in the hands of the foreign commerce body Cubaexport. Three years later Cubaexport secured the rights to the name "Havana Club" and had it endorsed by eighty countries, including the US—though it was not allowed to sell rum there because of the embargo on the export of Cuban goods to that country since 1962. A joint venture between the French beverage company Pernod Ricard and Cubaexport in 1993 helped what was until then a rather minor brand get its footing. The French invested in new distilleries and could fall back on their excellent distribution network. Havana Club, with annual growth rates in the double digits, conquered the global market.

Bacardi, on the other hand, with a broad portfolio of rums and other spirits successful on the market, had already begun in the 1960s to plot Castro's downfall. The Colombian journalist Hernando Calvo Ospina reported in his book *Bacardi: The Hidden War* that José "Pepin" Bosch, a member of the Bacardi family and on the board of directors, had planned to bombard Cuban refineries and, during the inevitable chaos that would follow, put an end to Castro's control of the island.[21] Documents released in 1998 by the National Security Council record

121

that Bosch had also contacted Mafia hit men and had already paid two-thirds of the US$150,000 agreed upon to assassinate Che Guevara and Raúl and Fidel Castro.

But the company also pursued legal channels to isolate the new leaders in the old homeland. In 1995 it bought the trademark rights of Havana Club, which had expired years before, from the Arechabala family. Senator Jesse Helms, financially supported by Bacardi, was the main architect of the Helms-Burton Act, passed in 1996. It stipulated a catalog of measures to be undertaken by the Cuban government before it could be legitimized as democratic and put sanctions on all trade with the country. Foreign companies investing in expropriated businesses would be refused entry to the US.

A legal battle began, with Pernod Ricard and Cubaexport on one side and Bacardi on the other, over the rights for the popular brand Havana Club. Numerous proceedings—which have cost both sides hundreds of millions of dollars and still have not been finalized—are evidence of the persistent tug of war for the sales rights in the US. In 1998 the four-thousand-page Omnibus Consolidated and Emergency Appropriations Act was presented to US Congress. Section 211, also known as the Bacardi Bill, was drawn up by a lobbyist at a cost of US$600,000 to the rum producer and prohibits the registration and extension of trademark protection rights in the US of previously appropriated Cuban businesses. We have to remember that these appropriations took place almost fifty years ago by an enactment of Cuban law.

Globally unparalleled and legally extremely questionable, the new US law legitimized the alliance of foreign policy and private interests with international commercial law, which aroused criticism from the World Trade Organization (WTO). The WTO demanded the withdrawal of Section 211 by 2004, something that to this day has not happened.

The Bacardi Bill prevented Cubaexport and Pernod Ricard from extending their brand entry in the US. Bacardi launched its own product on the American market under the name "Havana Club," subtitled "Puerto Rican Rum." Fidel Castro had in the meantime lost his patience and let journalists know that he had ordered the production of a Cuban Bacardi—an imaginative response that demonstrated the absurdity of Section 211, but one that never saw the light of day.

Pernod Ricard, on the other hand, has registered the name "Havanista" for a time in the distant future when the embargo is history and real Cuban rum can once more be delivered to the US.

Rum remains, as it always was, inextricably linked to the errors and terrors of worldwide political and commercial relations.

Fifth Semester

— GIN —

ITALY, 1961. THE early morning sun catches a snow-white
villa on the shore of Lake Como. Palms stretch out their
glossy fronds against a towering backdrop of the Alps mas-
sif. Cypresses and agaves border spacious gardens. Marble lions
guard the entrances, their radiant white silhouettes cutting
into the azure sky. The lobby of the property still lies cloaked
in semidarkness. Enter the butler, Maurice. He finds his
employer, the American industrialist Robert L. Talbot (played
by Rock Hudson), not as usual on the terrace with a glass of
champagne but swirling a gin and ice in the lobby. The previous night had been hard and, for the visibly disheveled Talbot,
sleepless. Playboy Talbot, of all people, was supposed to have
been protecting the virtues of a group of teenage girls from the
testosterone-driven clutches of young men. He had danced
ecstatically in a bar, drank the up-and-coming Casanovas
under the table, lost his feisty mistress, Lisa (Gina Lollobrigida),
and fired his longtime friend and butler, who had landed him
in trouble in the first place. Maurice asks Talbot if he should

serve breakfast for the last time. Talbot initially declines, but after thinking it over, orders an olive. "Martini for breakfast?" says the butler, anxiously shaking his head. Talbot replies dryly, "It's perfect for the day after. Especially if there hasn't been a day before."

For many a barfly and barkeeper the Martini was and is the king of cocktails, the drink that in its cone-shaped and frozen glass has made it from simple drink to *the* symbol of bar culture, according to American critic William Grimes.[1] A dry Martini is certainly one of the most distinguished ways to intoxication. The movie scene described above, from Robert Mulligan's *Come September*, illustrates the distinguishing quality that seems to accompany this drink.

Hollywood was quick on the uptake for the decorative drink. In particular, the first of six *Thin Man* movies, based on a Dashiell Hammett novel, which were filmed from 1934 to 1947, can with hindsight almost be seen as an advertising campaign for the Martini. Whatever the time, day or night, hardly three minutes pass without the detective, Nick Charles, played by William Powell, or his wife, Nora, played by Myrna Loy, bolting down a Martini, with their fox-terrier, Asta, providing plenty of comic relief. They are rich, attractive, smart, and sexy. Untypically for a private detective, Nick has no ambitions whatsoever to take on a case. "It's putting me way behind in my drinking," is how he explains his reluctance, and he becomes involved only once an impressive number of bodies begin to pile up. The storyline revolves around the sharp-tongued war of words between the couple while consuming vast numbers of drinks. "Are you packing, dear?" "Yes, darling, I'm just putting away this liquor." Nora wins 240 Martinis from Nick in a wager on a turtle race. She meets him in a bar and lines up five Martinis so she can catch up with him as quickly as possible. "Darling, would you like a drink?" is her standard question, whether on waking up with a hangover or after receiving a blow to the head.

In 1950, James Stewart, as Elwood P. Dowd, sparkled in *Harvey* as a diligent Martini drinker alongside a six-foot-six-inch rabbit that only he can see or hear. Whether Harvey is a figment of his inebriated imagination or a *púca*, a fairy spirit in animal form, remains a secret to the end. The only place that Elwood's invisible friend tolerates is Charlie's Bar, where the barkeeper without further ado always serves two Martinis for the buddies. Elwood has become rich from a legacy but has decided against ambition and for friendship, style, and perfect manners, especially towards those of lower social status. With extreme politeness he hands out his calling cards to mailmen, doormen, and nurses, mostly followed by an invitation to dinner the same night. His family tries to have him committed to institutional care. Dr. Sanderson on Elwood's admission cautiously asks him if, like everyone, he likes to drink now and then. Elwood replies, "Yes, I do, doctor. As a matter of fact, I'd like one right now."

The Martini always stands for composure and the intention not to let the absurd impositions of everyday life steal your pleasures, not to surrender, not to become normal, boring, or hysterical. The great Martini drinkers of the past are characterized by a sense of style, sangfroid, and the ability to be just a bit above it all. When questioned about his excessive bar nights, Humphrey Bogart simply replied, "The higher the monkey crawls up the tree, the more it shows of its tail." Nondrinkers, according to him, were simply frightened of their own shallowness.

The earliest known recipe was published in 1904 in Paris in *American Bar—Recettes des Boissons Anglaises et Américanes*, by Frank P. Newman,[2] and recommended the same amounts of gin and dry vermouth and a drop of aromatic bitters. These ingredients are carefully mixed together over ice cubes with a bar spoon and strained into a precooled cocktail glass with a lemon twist and then served ice cold.

The strictly ritualized preparation, whereby every hand movement is executed with purposeful precision, swiftly but not too hastily, avoiding a rise in temperature, creates one of the most harmonious drinks of all when using the best ingredients.

Compared to the impact of other alcoholic drinks, we discover that this cocktail has earned its iconic status in bar culture not by chance or for purely aesthetic reasons, but since it represents, more or less, the ideal companion for public intoxication. Red wine, a fine malt whisky, brandy, or cognac lead, at best, to a dignified, intellectual, definitely relaxed private drunkenness, whereas rum, as all other sugarcane spirits, accentuates the more sensual aspects of an evening. Vodka, on the other hand, places escapism in the foreground. Gin alone can move us to a state of socially visionary high, not anesthetizing the mind or conversation but unfailingly finding new heights through most of the night.

The Drunken Dog: Buñuel and His Martinis

IT IS NOT always necessary to have a drinking companion. The classic Martini drinker, Humphrey Bogart—to mention one person mainly responsible for the mythmaking surrounding this drink—although moving within society has more of a role as a wry, analytical outsider than someone at the center of events. For filmmaker Luis Buñuel, too, the bar "is an exercise in solitude. Above all else, it must be quiet, dark, very comfortable—and, contrary to modern mores, no music of any kind, no matter how faint. In sum, there should be no more than a dozen tables, and a client that doesn't like to talk."[3] The bar was for him a place of meditation and composure that enabled him to sink into a flood of images, often for hours, that surprised not only him but also the moviegoing public. "To provoke, or sustain, a reverie in a bar, you have to drink English gin, especially in the form of the dry martini,"[4] and Buñuel insisted on a specific ritual: Shaker, gin, and glasses had to have been placed in the refrigerator for at least one day. For the preparation of his DRY MARTINI, angostura and Noilly Prat had to be poured on ice cubes, lightly stirred, and drained, keeping only the ice, which retains a faint taste of both. Straight gin was then poured over the ice in a precooled glass; a quick stir and the drink was immediately served.

In the 1940s Buñuel and two friends came up with the idea of a bar. It was to be called the Cannon Shot and scandalously expensive, the most expensive bar in the world, and would serve exquisite drinks. Next to the entrance would be an old cannon, hence the name, and when a guest's drinking check exceeded US$1,000 the bar would fire off a blank salvo. This could be seen as a provocative signal of the victory of extravagance over economy to those in the neighborhood. Buñuel himself referred to the project as "tempting if not exactly democratic," but permitted others to seize upon his idea. His own drinking habits he described as a subtle ritual, where the intention was not to reach a state of total drunkenness but rather effect a light inebriation, a gentle feeling of well-being. He lived for a few months in America during Prohibition, where his credo of moderate drinking was put to the test. Never in his life had he drunk as much as during that visit.

Mrs. Parker and the Vicious Circle

AT THE BEGINNING of the dry years, laws forbade the public sale of alcoholic drinks, but consumption of alcohol at home or in hotel rooms or suites was still allowed. At the Round Table of the Algonquin Hotel a number of rebellious intellectuals used to meet every day at noon. Among them were the playwright George Kaufman and the humorist Robert Benchley. The latter is said to have quipped, "I've got to get out of these wet clothes and into a dry Martini."[5] Also included in the group were Noël Coward and Dorothy Parker, who with her famous Martini homage illuminates another interesting aspect of gin consumption: "I like to have a Martini. Two at the most. After three I'm under the table, after four I'm under the host."[6]

Martini drinkers have even developed their own counting system: "One, two, three—door. Four, five, six—floor." The writer and comic actor W. C. Fields in his most productive days was said to have drunk two Martinis before breakfast. Groucho Marx claimed that Fields hoarded spirits worth several thousand dollars in his loft long after 1933, anxiously fearing the return of Prohibition. One story goes that comedian George Burns ran into Fields, who had just been put on the wagon by his doctor. Fields explained, "I don't drink anymore, on the other hand I don't drink any less."[7] Burns was more forthright in his admission: "I never go jogging, it makes me spill my Martini."[8] In an interview he was once asked whether, as a ninety-three-year-old, he ever had the feeling that he was slowing down. He replied, "When I blow smoke rings, I notice they're smaller and not as round as they used to be. When I drink a Martini, instead of two olives I'm down to one."[9]

The Crowning of the King

THE HISTORY OF this inspired and inspiring drink begins in France in the eighteenth century, where they strengthened white wine by mixing it with the essence of *genièvre*. Towards the end of the nineteenth century, on the other side of the channel, well-to-do families in England began mixing the native gin with the latest import from France and Italy— vermouth. This drink quickly gained popularity in adventurous London as GIN AND FRENCH or GIN AND IT. The Martini cocktail was classified as a short drink. A short drink, as a rule, consists of three components: the base, the modifier, and the flavoring agent. The base is the main liquor ingredient of the drink, modified by a harmonizing ingredient that gives the cocktail its character; the flavor is refined using a bar spoon or a few drops of a flavoring agent. At the beginning of the twentieth century Martinis were drunk in a ratio of 1:1 (i.e., one base to one modifier) or 2:1 when a flavoring agent such as angostura, orange bitters, absinthe, maraschino, or grenadine was added. With Prohibition, knowledge about and the value of this third ingredient fell into oblivion, as did many recipes. In the 1940s and '50s Martinis became so dry that even the vermouth seemed to be in the background. The trendsetting Martini drinkers of this age were the Rat Pack, centered on Humphrey Bogart, Frank Sinatra, Dean Martin, and Sammy Davis, Jr., with Peter Lawford, David Niven, Shirley MacLaine, Lauren Bacall, and others as peripheral members. They created a cult of an ever-drier, and therefore ever-stronger, Martini.

In Hemingway's *Across the River and into the Trees*, Colonel Cantwell orders "two very dry Martinis. Montgomerys. Fifteen to one."[10] The waiter, who has served in the desert, smiles and disappears behind the bar. Viscount Montgomery of Alamein was the commander-in-chief of the British Eighth Army during the North African Campaign of the Second World War. It is said of him that he would attack his adversary, Field Marshal Erwin Rommel, only when His Majesty's troops outnumbered the enemy by fifteen to one, hence the Montgomery Martini. Hemingway was a regular at Harry's Bar in Venice and was acquainted with Giuseppe Cipriani, the founder and owner of this fine bar and the creator of carpaccio and the Bellini cocktail. He bought the rights to the name of the famous watering hole in Paris from his former colleague Harry MacElhone. In Venice they serve the Hemingway Martini in honor of the author in the Montgomery version.

Olive or No Olive

IN HITCHCOCK'S MOVIE *North by Northwest*, Cary Grant orders a Gibson instead of the usual Martini in the dining car during his train journey. This variation was named after Charles Dana Gibson, a popular illustrator and creator of the feisty Gibson Girls. Gibson used to meet his friends regularly at the Players Club in New York. Sometimes, however, he wanted to leave these drinking sessions with a clear head to be able to continue working on his latest front-page illustrations. He consulted the barkeeper, Charlie Connolly, who instead of a Martini produced an iced water decorated with two pearl onions. In another story, however, there is no mention of the iced water or the two pearl onions, representing the physical attractions of the cover girls of early men's magazines. A regular of the Players Club once tried ordering a Gibson in Dublin, where the barman on finding no pearl onions cleverly improvised with radishes, and the Murphy Martini was born. In the Black and White a black-and-white-striped licorice candy is added to the Martini. The Oysterini comes with a smoked oyster, a Springtime Martini with a green asparagus tip, and a Shrimptini with a lightly cooked shrimp. But for purists a Martini remains a mixture of gin and vermouth. The drink can be garnished with strips of lemon zest or olives. The olive should have its pit; stuffed, marinated, or pitted olives are widespread, but ruin the flavor. The most extreme form of this reprehensible practice remains an olive that has been marinated in oil

132

and stuffed with a clove of garlic. As to the Garlic Martini, the suggestion published in *Esquire* in 1934 is perfectly understandable: "The man who first put an olive in the Martini should be shot!"[11]

A Spirit Crosses the Channel

THE MOST IMPORTANT component of the Martini, and the reason for its success, is the oscillating aroma of the gin. Parallel to its rapid ascent as the drug of the people, gin opened the most sinister abyss in the history of spirits.

Gin is considered the ugly duckling of distilled drinks, waiting to shed its feathers and become a white swan, or the Cinderella rising from the ashes of the hearth to aristocracy.

It's often told that gin began its life in the hands of the Dutch scholar Sylvius de la Boë, usually described as a professor of medicine at the University of Leiden. But the persona "Sylvius" is seemingly not a single character, but a condensed version of Sylvius de Bouve, an apothecary at the same university at the end of the sixteenth century, and François dele Boe Sylvius, professor of medicine at Leiden from 1658 to 1672. Both experimented with distillation and fermentation and both used juniper cordials. It seems that the idea of a juniper-based grain spirit was quite widespread in the Dutch Republic and that genever was the product of a tradition in flux rather than a single moment of inspiration.[12]

Juniper was well known for its disinfecting abilities. During the Plague of the Middle Ages the initiated wore masks filled with the dark berries as protection against the devastating Black Death. And genever, the new spirit, soon found its way out of the pharmacy right into the tavern.

In 1575 the Bulsius family had moved from Cologne to Amsterdam, changed their name to the more familiar-sounding

"Bols", and opened a distillery on the outskirts of Amsterdam. A distilling business within the city was considered to be too dangerous because of the risks of fire in an area of mainly wooden buildings. Bols was the first distillery to commercialize the new medicine under the name "Essence de Genièvre."

In England at the beginning of the seventeenth century, the production of juniper spirits had also begun as a remedy for digestive disorders and for its diuretic properties. In the Thirty Years' War, the new drink, by then called "jenever," was used for fortifying the Protestant troops, which included the English. The returning soldiers gave enthusiastic reports of the new miracle cure that had given them the proverbial Dutch courage.

When William of Orange, a Calvinist Dutchman, was crowned King of England in 1689 and subsequently governed with his wife, Mary, his lawful successor, hatred towards France was strengthened. During this time the famous Bill of Rights was passed, making way for the first constitutional monarchy in Europe. Competition between the two countries manifested itself a short time later in a worldwide embargo the British imposed on French goods. This particularly affected the import of wine and brandy, and being fully aware that these products couldn't disappear from the market without substitutes, the newly founded parliament, under the leadership of the monarch, issued a general license to distill jenever, which later legislation encouraged and expanded. Brandy, produced in southern Europe, which was loyal to the Pope, was forced to yield its position on the English market to jenever. Jenever was the official drink of the court, and its consumption was considered a symbol of Protestant patriotism—England was then drinking English spirits for England.

The new industry created increasing prosperity for all participants. A moderate tax financed the war against the Catholics. With the rising jenever production, demand for grain shot up dramatically and farmers were able to pay the high interest rates on their land to the landlords, who, in turn, were determining legislation in the Houses of Parliament. To begin with it seemed as if the relocation of jenever to England was a runaway success story. This was soon to prove a fallacy.

Ruin and Riot: The Gin Craze

IN 1694 ANOTHER war against the Catholic League forced the king to introduce new financial measures. The foundation of the Bank of England allowed the government to take out more credit to finance the war, secured by, among other things, a considerably high tax on beer. The low-proof barley juice was then more expensive than jenever and for a large proportion of the population no longer affordable. Parallel to this, the production of jenever, which required a smaller volume of agricultural inputs than beer, was once again boosted, and it soon replaced beer as the most important staple sustenance.

A clear indication of this was the rapid spread of the shortened name for the high-proof liquor; from around 1700 awkward "jenever" became known more simply as "gin."

Another, nowadays slightly strange, law in 1720 gave new impetus to distillers: license holders were released from the unpopular duty of accommodating soldiers in their houses. The intent of this law was to restrict soldiers' access to alcohol, but the measure proved to be shortsighted. Instead of stemming the huge scale of consumption, which was slowly becoming a more and more obvious problem, the flooding of the market with gin by an ever-increasing number of distilleries could then no longer be halted. By 1720 a sociological phenomenon had developed that went down in history as the Gin Craze.

The population of London at this time grew at an astounding rate. Impoverished country dwellers moved to the prosperous capital, whose numbers swelled in twenty years to 700,000, making it the largest metropolis in the world. The urban infrastructure was not able to keep up with this rapid growth. Unmanageable slum districts emerged just a few blocks away from the better-off neighborhoods. In the streets the number of poor, more-or-less drunken day laborers looking for possibilities to survive was growing by the day. In 1727 Lord Hervey noted:

> The drunkenness of the common people, was so universal by the retailing of a liquor called gin, with which they could get drunk for a groat, that the whole town of London, and many towns in the country swarmed with drunken people of both sexes from morning to night, and were more like a scene from a Bacchanal than the residence of a civil society.[13]

Today's annual consumption of gin per capita is estimated at 0.1 gallon, but in 1751 it was one gallon.[14] Gin was omnipresent. In St. Giles, for instance, one in four houses was a gin house and the whole city area had over six thousand gin outlets, not including the numerous market stalls and street vendors hawking their wares from wheelbarrows. When it rained, not an unknown phenomenon in London, the unpaved streets were transformed into cesspits of mud and human excrement, and with the constant traffic of hackney carriages and oxcarts, animal excrement was added to the mixture. The drunken rabble vomited in the streets next to the motionless body of an unconscious reveler lying in the mud. Some livers and cardiovascular systems were just not up to the unfortunate combination of too little food and too much alcohol. Deaths began to mount.

The time was ripe for criminals, and those who had a bit of money found themselves in constant danger on the neglected streets of London, not only of losing their wallets, but also their lives.

Through excessive consumption, the spread of gin that had initially seemed so successful became just the opposite. As women were equally involved in the binges, there was a drop in the birthrate due to alcohol-related premature or still-births. The juniper spirit was nicknamed "mother's ruin" or "Madame Geneva." With the increased consumption of gin, the work ethic of the proletariat sank to such an extent that whole branches of the economy and even the London Docks were seriously threatened. There were numerous calls from the judiciary, church, and industry demanding measures to remedy the situation. The borders between moral standards and economic interests became attuned.

In the opposite corner was the still powerful gin lobby consisting of the owners of the larger distilleries, the farmers supplying the corn, and the landlords, well represented in parliament and who, from the distance of their estates, profited mightily without being confronted by the problems of the Gin Craze.

It was the beginning of the conflict of interests that led in 1729 to the first of eight Sale of Spirits Acts, commonly known as the Gin Acts. Consumption was taxed at a slightly higher rate and a special license for production was introduced. These changes were exclusively reserved for gin, while brandy, port, and wine—which the upper classes, following old traditions, then favored—remained unaffected.

But the hesitant measures did little to change the relentless rise in gin consumption. In 1733 the government felt forced to pass a further Gin Act forbidding all sales by street merchants and retail outlets. Gin could be drunk only in taverns, believed to be easier to control. This law also missed the mark and led only to the opening of an immense number of new taverns that then saturated the already hard-pressed capital.

In 1734 the case of a single mother, Judith Defour, shocked even the most hardened souls. She had gathered her two-year-old daughter from the workhouse, which had caringly provided the girl with new clothes for the outing. Instead of going to the park with her, Defour strangled the poor creature, left her naked in a ditch, and sold her new clothes to buy gin. In a drunken state she confessed her crime to a work colleague who was sober enough to inform the police. The artist William Hogarth was perhaps inspired by the sad story to make his print *Gin Lane*. In the foreground of the print, a gin-sodden mother, oblivious, lets her baby slip from her arms and fall to its death in the stairwell while nonchalantly taking a pinch of snuff; an unscrupulous pawnbroker takes the last possessions of poor drinkers for a few pence to feed their habit; and a drunken mob fights outside the distillers. In the background a corpse hangs from a beam, suicide as a last act of desperation. Astonishingly the print now hangs in many pubs and a number of living rooms as a reminder of the good old days. Hogarth had intended the print as propaganda for more stringent anti-gin laws, and it contributed to a drastic increase in taxes, tighter production licenses, and, above all, the threat of higher fines in the next Gin Act.

The authorities planned to implement the law by using informers whose rewards were to be financed with money collected from fines. As most of those convicted were incapable of paying their fines, the financing of this denunciation system soon had deficits. A further provision, which didn't prove to be entirely successful, was based on encouraging citizens to assume responsibility by acting against distillers in their neighborhood.

Those affected by the new measures were mainly the merchants and producers who were operating on the surface. The

Gin Act could not be enforced in the squalid slum areas, which remained difficult to control. Informers had no say in these areas; often suspicion was enough for an alleged informer to meet a grisly end. Attempts by the authorities to regain control were met by gin riots.

The London underdogs proved to be extremely reluctant to forego the previously encouraged consumption of gin; after all, just a few years earlier it had been considered an expression of the highest form of patriotism. They drank to forget the misery of a society with firmly entrenched class structures that offered no opportunities of advancement. With the courage of despair they fought ever-bloodier street battles with the authorities. One of the most important proponents of gin prohibition, Dr. Joseph Jekyll, was the victim of an attempted assassination. The discontent of the masses reached a peak with the attempted storming of Westminster Hall, which only just avoided being set ablaze. Behind the battlefront the gin business slipped more and more into illegality. The quality sank, affecting both health and the national economy. The number of criminal offenses increased, and hardly a day passed without an opponent of gin or an informer becoming a victim of the mobs' lynch justice.

The kingdom was evidently no longer in the position to enforce its own laws. To weaken the illegal and uncontrollable market, another Gin Act was passed partially repealing some of the tougher trade and production conditions. A new war against Austria, however, demanded reliable tax revenues, which in turn led to strong legislation in 1751.

Finding no employment, returning soldiers formed ruthless gangs, and again crime rates increased. In the meantime alcohol tax was twelve times higher than on its introduction in the late-seventeenth century. Production, as far as possible, was under state control, and higher standards of quality had been introduced. At the same time, beer became cheaper and

139

was encouraged as a substitute. The early days of the Industrial Revolution provided the economy with an upswing. Next to the large number of workers, a numerically small middle class began to form who chose to shape their lives more productively and frugally in order to accelerate and safeguard their social advancement. In these circles moral beliefs were becoming established, solidly supported by the church, condemning gin abuse and all its consequences. Reforms were advanced in the course of general political enlightenment, bestowing improvements in education and better opportunities for upward mobility for the population as a whole. In addition to all this a series of failed harvests led to shortages in raw materials for the distillers. All these circumstances together led to the end of the Gin Craze towards the end of the eighteenth century. The low point in the history of gin had passed, and it could slowly develop from being the people's cheap drug to the drink enjoyed and beloved by many.

Due to the lack of fully developed rectification procedures, the gin of old was an acrid-tasting spirit. To modify this sharpness producers started to make it sweeter. This version was called Old Tom Gin, and Old Tom Cat was the apparatus through which gin-shop owners infamously sold gin to bypass the laws; the innkeepers were not selling gin, as the customers were "purchasing" it from a cat. The customer on the street outside placed a couple of pence in slits in the cat's eye and held a glass under the cat's paw; the landlord inside his tavern then poured the right amount of gin into the tube, and the hasty drinker on the street was "served" by the cat.

The Forerunners of the Cocktail Era

SOME INNOVATIONS IN the beverage market created the prerequisites for cocktail culture. Artificial carbonation of water—

enrichment with minerals and carbon dioxide—was discovered, and in 1767 Johann Jacob Schweppe, a jeweler and amateur chemist, developed a practical process to manufacture tonic water. In 1790 he moved to London and built a flourishing business around his product. In his Indian Tonic Water he mixed bitter quinine, a substance used in the treatment of malaria, with the more palatable soda. By 1831 the elixir had found its way into Queen Victoria's court and from there, furnished with a royal stamp of approval, to the fever-ridden British colonies throughout the world. It only finally prevailed, as the aspirin of the Victorian era, in perfect combination with the aniseed and juniper aromas of gin. "A gin and tonic a day keeps malaria away," was the saying that made life easier in India when it was 113°F in the shade and humidity was at 98 percent.

Frederic Tudor started providing ice for the catering trade around 1800, long before the first icemaking machine was patented in 1851. His ice blocks were prepared in areas that were frozen year-round, and new insulation techniques enabled relatively trouble-free transport all the way to the Caribbean, where ice was conserved in special storehouses.

From the Tropics and into Gin: Aromatic Bitters

IN 1806 THE first recorded definition of "cocktail" was published:

> Cocktail is a stimulating liquor composed of spirits of any kind, sugar, water, and bitters—it is vulgarly called a bittered sling and is supposed to be an excellent electioneering potion, inasmuch as it renders the heart stout and bold, at the same time that it fuddles the head. It is said, also to be of great use to a Democratic candidate: because a person, having swallowed a glass of it, is ready to swallow anything else.[15]

In addition to high-quality spirits, water, and sugar, what was important when making cocktails was another ingredient—bitters. This ingredient, originally stemming from medicinal practices, consisted of some 48 percent herbal extracts and was prescribed for stomach complaints, fever, gout, and tropical diseases. One of the best known is Angostura Aromatic Bitters.

In 1820 the German doctor Johann Gottlieb Benjamin Siegert, who had joined the South American liberation movement under Simón Bolívar in its struggle against the Spanish crown, began researching tropical plants for medical purposes in Angostura, Venezuela. He left the troops and founded a pharmacy and a civilian hospital. He also ran a private practice for mostly European patients. Angostura at that time was a collection of clay and brick huts wedged between the jungle and the Orinoco River, an area riddled with malaria, smallpox, and yellow fever. Alexander von Humboldt and the French botanist Aimé Bonpland had been stranded there for a month in the summer of 1800 when both of them suffered from bouts of fever. Siegert succeeded in curing the fevers using the bark of the angostura tree, *Cusparia angostura,* "in a spirituous tincture and in aqueous infusion."[16] Twenty-four years later, after four years of research, the German doctor launched his tonic, Dr. Siegert's Aromatic Bitters, later renamed Angostura Aromatic Bitters, a 48 percent potable alcohol, as a remedy for tropical diseases. In around 1850 he began exporting, firstly to Trinidad and then to the motherland of the Commonwealth—England.

Mercenaries returning from the South American war of liberation and, of course, sailors soon made Siegert's remedy famous worldwide. In 1858 he abandoned his profession and founded a company, Dr. J.G.B. Siegert & Sons. After the death of their father and because of the continuing political unrest in Venezuela after Simón Bolívar's resignation as president,

Siegert's sons moved the headquarters to Port of Spain on Trinidad, where they still produce excellent rums and Angostura Aromatic Bitters. As with coca cola, the recipe is one of the best-kept secrets of the beverage industry. It contains, along with other secret herbs and spices, cinchona, gentiana, ginger, bitter orange, cinnamon, lesser galangal, angelica roots, St. John's bread, raisins, and cardamom. *Cusparia angostura* bark is not thought to be one of the ingredients but it can be found in other bitters.

An anecdote from the Battle of Waterloo shows that gin had gained a reputation in military circles. Marshal Blücher, one of Lord Wellington's closest allies, was seriously injured in a riding accident, and he attributed his exceptionally fast recovery solely to the medical prescription of gin and onion massages. In 1816 a ration of Plymouth Gin, from the garrison city with the same name, was part of a British naval officer's salary. The medicinal properties of angostura bitters were soon also recognized and used by the British Navy. They are not only called bitters; they are bitter. A British officer mixed his gin ration with a few drops of angostura, and the mixture, known as PINK GIN, became one of the most popular drinks of this epoch. In time the medicinal aspects shifted more and more to the background. Instead, angostura bitters developed into one of the most important cocktail ingredients.

All That Glitters: The Gin Palace

ON LAND AND in civilian life, gin also went through a renaissance that paved the way to glamour. In the 1820s in the larger cities in England, new kinds of drinking establishments were emerging that had nothing in common with the low dives of the Gin Craze, with their austere to downright squalid taprooms and where the main object was getting drunk as cheaply as possible. The gin palaces, as they became known, lived up to the name. They were financed by the big distillers, who provided the landlords with rooms decorated with rich fabrics, brass, luxurious furniture, and mirrors and had plate-glass windows and gas lighting. Charles Dickens in his *Sketches by Boz* marveled that the effect was "perfectly dazzling when contrasted with the darkness and dirt we have just left."[17] The pubs were given names like the King's Head, the Prince Alfred, or the Royal Philharmonic Drinking Hall, and those still remaining are protected listed buildings. Not only did these gastronomic establishments have a completely different appearance; the bar staff were also in contrast to the shady characters of the past. Good manners and expertise were becoming important. In addition to the rise of these cultivated localities, the first grand hotels were beginning to appear. Besides accommodating traveling salesmen, who, although they had always existed, were then growing in number, they catered to a new group of guests who were traveling exclusively for pleasure: tourists. This development was not restricted to Europe but included countries beyond the Atlantic and the still numerous colonies.

All Corners of the World

IN 1831 CONTINUOUS still techniques were patented by Aeneas Coffey. For the first time it was possible to produce in an endless process, day and night, pure alcohol of consistent quality. The important distilleries that still exist today—Gordon's, Beefeater, Finsbury, and Booth's, all producers of London Dry Gin—were founded at this time.

London Dry Gin was considerably drier than Old Tom Gin and obtained its complex character from flavoring with juniper and other agents. The flavors were gained either at maceration, with the direct addition of agents to the mash, or during distillation when the alcohol fumes were channeled through receptacles and sieves with the appropriate herbal or spice mixtures. Since then, gin producers have refined their flavoring techniques, which we appreciate to this day. The colonies supplied the botanicals from all corners of the world. The most dominant flavor, the juniper, is supported by coriander, Guinea pepper, cardamom, ginger, blackcurrants, aniseed, lavender, tea, licorice, roses, gherkins, fennel, and elderberry, as well as the peel of oranges and other citrus fruits. Over a hundred different and finely dosed ingredients give the gins of today their subtle taste. As a general rule, ten to twenty different aromas are used for individual gin brands.

The Bar: An American Dream

PARALLEL TO EVENTS in the UK, changes were also happening in originally agricultural America. The extraction of natural resources like gold and oil, the completion of a railway network linking the huge country, and the rapid progress of industrialization enabled the swift rise, economically and socially, of individuals regardless of background but solely through hard work, luck, and economic aptitude. The American Dream was alluring compared to Europe's stiff social structures.

North America was overcome by this breakneck transformation. Small settlements became cities within a couple of decades, the buildings eventually reaching for the skies. Sumptuous clubs and luxury hotels were rising up whose opulent décor and size far outshone the hotels of the Old World.

Especially in the US there was one institution that had to feature in every upmarket hotel alongside the tearoom, restaurant, and the American bar. Behind the bars a new profession was developing: the barkeeper. He not only drew beers and poured wines but also created mixed drinks like punches, slings, sangarees, cobblers, and many more. It's safe to say that drinkers and barkeepers have always produced mixed drinks, but while in the past the main point was to make low-grade alcoholic drinks, to some extent, drinkable, people were now trying to create totally new worlds of taste. The most famous of this fraternity was Jerry Thomas, nicknamed "the Professor." He created numerous drinks and published one of the first bar books in 1862, *How to Mix Drinks*.[18]

His BLUE BLAZER cocktail introduced the showmanship element to mixing behind the bar. For this performance the Professor would pour blazing alcohol from two separate vessels, in an ever-growing arc of flames, into another receptacle. Less talented imitators of this show left guests with third-degree burns and burned-out bars. His book had a number of editions, and then for a long time it was out of print. In recent years it has been rediscovered and reprinted and is now part of the base knowledge of all those searching for the origins of cocktails.

In 1868 he opened the first American bar in Europe next to the London Stock Exchange. Cocktails, for many people the only serious American contribution to the world of cuisine, achieved international breakthrough at the very latest with the American pavilion at the World's Fair of 1889 in Paris.

GIN HAD REACHED the point of being considered a noble spirit at the beginning of the twentieth century, a development that would have been inconceivable at the time of the Gin Craze. It had become the symbol of a British way of life. The popular golf player Lord Westmorland refused to play on golf courses where the clubhouses didn't have his favorite gin, Booth's, as part of their selection. The auto racer Brian Lewis compared a party without gin to a car without wheels, and the Earl of Northesk, a successful winter sportsman, used to fortify himself with a glass of artificially flavored juniper juice before every descent on the ski slopes.

A drinks cabinet now belonged in every superior household. Art Deco artists designed cocktail shakers, hip flasks, glasses, and accessories like cuff links in the form of Martini glasses, which were also sold at reputable jewelers like Tiffany's and Cartier. Nowadays these articles are barely affordable collectors' items or are in display cases in museums of decorative arts. A ruby glass cocktail shaker in the form of a woman's leg and wearing a silver high heel, for instance, has achieved cult status. Other designers produced mixing beakers in the shape of binoculars, lighthouses, penguins, airplanes, tanks, bullets, and hand grenades. Tanqueray even markets its gins in bottles resembling a shaker. No official occasion, whether private or public, was imaginable without the accompaniment of a gin-based cocktail. It had become the expression of a sophisticated, modern lifestyle.

Even royalty were affected by the fashion. Lady Elizabeth Bowes-Lyon was the loyal and strong spouse at the side of the shy king, George VI, who introduced him to the unconventional speech therapist Lionel Logue for treatment for his stutter. After the death of her husband and the accession of their daughter Elizabeth II, she became known as the Queen Mum, the most popular member of the royal family. For decades, always armed with a GIN AND TONIC, she was considered among the drink-friendly British as the first ambassadress of her country and the living proof of the elegance and class of the national drink. In the 1930s she was a patron of the Windsor Wets' Club, an illustrious drinking society with the motto "*Aqua vitae non aqua pura.*" Even respectful sources mention her impressive capacity for alcohol. Her lunch parties at Clarence House are legend, ending with guests passed out under the trees after failing to match her heroic consumption. She reached the impressive age of 101, and one can only state, after Winston Churchill, that she obviously took more out of alcohol than it took out of her.[19]

Drinks and Politics

THERE WAS NO stopping the triumphal advance of gin even on the other side of the Atlantic. Franklin Delano Roosevelt was a popular president, on the one hand because of the social reforms of the New Deal he initiated and his warmhearted and open nature, but on the other hand because he was the one who revoked Prohibition in 1933 and mixed the first legal Martini. One of his political allies countered the temperance lobby's criticism of the repeal of Prohibition with the remark, "If the Lord hadn't intended us to have a three-Martini lunch, then why do you suppose He put all those olive trees in the Holy Land?"[20] Roosevelt was well known for his mixing skills. In his modest but stylishly furnished study in the White House were diverse bottles, various sizes of glasses, plates with nuts and olives, an ice bucket, a tray with lemons and a squeezer, a small bowl of brown sugar, two kinds of bitters, and an impressive silver shaker. The president could handle all these objects extremely skillfully, as witnessed by Noël Coward. During his term of office Roosevelt shook his shaker for numerous statesmen—at the summit meeting of the Allies with Joseph Stalin and Winston Churchill in Tehran in 1943, for instance, or at the Potsdam Conference. Roosevelt's favorite cocktails were an Old-Fashioned or a Dirty Martini, sometimes called FDR's Martini. This variation includes a bar spoon of olive brine on top of gin and vermouth.

Another of Roosevelt's wartime allies is indelibly associated with the history of the Martini. The driest variant is named

after him: the Churchill Martini, also known as the Naked or
v Martini, half of which consists of alcohol and the other half
the performance of the barkeeper. The gin is poured into an ice-
filled glass and stirred until it is ice cold. Just the shadow of a
bottle of Noilly Prat above the glass counts as the second ingredient as the barkeeper makes a *V* for Victory sign with middle
and index fingers and bows briefly towards France.

> *"My religion prescribed as an absolute sacred ritual*
> *smoking cigars and drinking alcohol before, after and if need*
> *be during all meals and the intervals between them."*
>
> WINSTON CHURCHILL WHILE VISITING
> KING IBN SAUD IN SAUDI ARABIA[21]

ALMOST BEFORE THE future prime minister had grown out of
diapers, cocktails were an integral part of Churchill family life,
and they were to remain so. His whole life through he despised
all teetotalers, and the spats with his parliamentary opponent
Lady Astor provide us with a number of anecdotes. Lady Astor:
"If you were my husband, I would poison your drink." Churchill: "And if I were your husband, I'd drink it!" Renowned
for his ability to drink, the prime minister would often loosen
his tongue with a few stiff Martinis before entering into a battle of words with Lady Astor. On another occasion Lady Astor
was reported to have said, "Winston, you are drunk." To which
Churchill responded, "And you, Madam, are ugly. But I shall be
sober in the morning."

In a number of Churchill biographies are references to
dozens of Martinis being consumed in meetings of the senior
military staff during the Second World War.

Risking the Impossible

AFTER ENGLISH FORCES halted the advances of German troops on the eastern front in the winter of 1942–43, it was time to organize an offensive. German troops controlled all English Channel ports on the mainland coast, so an Allied invasion was possible only via the sea. But how could hundreds of thousands of soldiers and complex war machinery be transported to the continent without anywhere to land? Winston Churchill was the main proponent of the idea of landing Allied troops at a place where Hitler would least expect them—in the shallow waters off the Normandy beaches. After test operations with floating pontoon bridges and amphibian vehicles in Dieppe, North Africa, and Sicily, Operation Overlord—although extremely costly in lives—successfully landed Allied troops on the Normandy coast.[22] Some of the preparations seem with hindsight to be slightly odd.

A British special unit dressed in German uniforms was dispatched to bars in Normandy, where rewards of chocolate were given to the French for pinpointing German positions on a map.

Tons of tinsel were dropped from the air on D-day, intended to confuse enemy radars into thinking that the landing was taking place at another location. The same intention was behind the dummy landing craft meant to be photographed by German reconnaissance missions. They even dreamed up a fictional British Fourth Army, together with faked radio signals and trumped-up military mail services, to give the impression that Norway was the intended bridgehead. That is how the liberation of Europe from the Nazis began.

We will leave you to decide how drunk you have to be to avoid the power of facts. We, at least, would like to support the theory that Operation Overlord was a late-night crackpot idea.

In any case, in times of war the cigar-fueled Martini diplomacy of Churchill and Roosevelt was clearly superior to the hysterical abstinence of Himmler and Hitler.

Clear Drinks in a Dark Series

" 'A dry Martini will do.'
'A Martini. Dry. Veddy, veddy, dry.'
'Okay.'
'Will you eat it with a spoon or a knife and fork?'
'Cut it into strips, I'll just nibble it.' "
Raymond Chandler, The High Window[23]

THE SECOND WORLD War didn't just change the face of Europe, it also left deep-rooted scars in the minds of returning soldiers. Fear and alienation didn't disappear with the surrender of the Nazis but were reflected in the deep pessimism of film noir. The genre's locations are expressionistic, darkened urban jungles, their disillusioned dwellers shining with a ready wit and explosions of sexual innuendo. They chain-smoke and down Martinis in every other scene, with the borders between good and evil becoming blurred. In the end evil is exposed, but the triumph and survival of good remain in doubt. Raymond Chandler, whose books were important influences on this genre, sought his inspiration, and that of his tight-lipped hero, Marlowe, in another gin variant, the GIMLET.

In the budding optimism of the 1960s, the Martini was still prominent on the big screen. Until well into the 1970s, according to William Grimes, the Martini was "the capitalist cocktail, bar none. The official drink of the American Business Class, the high octane gas that powers businesses on Wall Street

151

and Madison Avenue—then the age of Perrier and lemon slices dawned."[24] It was a bleak time for our distinguished drink. The sixties and early seventies brought deliverance from the conventions of previous generations. Rock concerts were not settings for cocktails; you drank beer, smoked hash, took acid—anything but cocktails, which were old-fashioned and square. One famous and constant exception throughout these decades was Special Agent 007, James Bond. Grimes described Bond as "the first Transatlantic Man... perfectly at home with advanced technology, flashy gadgets, and foreign languages."[25] Her Majesty's secret agent's foible for Martinis comes across as modern and, in fact, something like an American. In the first Bond novel, *Casino Royale*, published in 1953, author Ian Fleming, who was said to have a daily ration of a bottle of vodka, gets his hero to order a shaken Martini—actually an incorrect mixing technique as, first, it is unnecessary because the ingredients can be easily stirred; second, the drink becomes cloudy if shaken when it really should be clear; and third, shaking could fragment the ice cubes and dilute the drink with their greater surface areas. Another, albeit intuitive, reason for not shaking is that the whirlpool created in the stirring movements gives the drink extra air to breathe and releases more aromas. Besides rather questionable advice on Martinis, Ian Fleming did come up with a recommended recipe: three measures of gin, one measure of vodka, and a half measure of Kina Lillet. James Bond names the drink VESPER in honor of the double agent Vesper Lynd. After her suicide, Bond of the novels never orders another Martini. The movie Bond, however, orders at least one Martini, "shaken, not stirred," in every movie; he's a stubborn fellow. Nevertheless, 007 epitomizes class, taste, cleverness, and masculinity. Thanks to his unconventional shaken drink, the Martini myth survived the macrobiotic 1980s.

Cosmic Sex in Martini City

IN THE 1990s bars made a comeback. But the yuppies in search of luxuries favored tropical and definitely light drinks. Martinis were again fashionable, although the ladies and gentlemen spent the whole evening with a cocktail glass in hand without being really interested in the contents. It just served as an accessory; the mixtures were evidently too strong. Matching the "light" society, drinks were diluted with juices made on an industrial scale. After the strawberry wave that flooded the bars in the 1980s came the passion-fruit nectar craze. Then in the nineties, cranberries conquered the bars. The Vodka Sour variation, the KAMIKAZE, becomes bright purple when diluted with cranberry juice and was given the contemporary name of COSMOPOLITAN. The series *Sex and the City* made it the fuel of the quirky, erotic sitcom and its protagonist famous throughout the world. The Martini experienced a new upswing with countless variations. The majority of these neotinis, however, contain neither gin nor vermouth. Only the glass remains to remind us of the origins. Curiously enough it is thanks to this re-Martini-ization of drinking habits that allows the connoisseur to enjoy the original cold lubricant in peace without being pestered about what exactly is in the glass. The essential cultural aspect of the Martini, whether myth, symbol, or just plain old drink, lies in its sophistication. As has often been said, a Martini is civilization in a cocktail glass.

Sixth Semester

TEQUILA

"WHERE IS THE gringo son of a bitch?" The fisherman El Mocho had a drawn pistol and was peering through bloodshot eyes into the darkened Beachcomber Bar of the Hotel Casablanca. The sounds from the swing band died away in chaotic discord. The musicians grabbed their instruments and scampered behind the curtain.

One shot to the ceiling and the ladies in colorful cocktail dresses shrieked and scuttled out into the balmy Mexican night. Waiters froze with trays loaded with Margaritas in their hands. El Mocho let loose another fusillade and finally found the gringo he was looking for. It was Teddy Stauffer—"Señor Teddy" as he was called in Acapulco in the 1940s. El Mocho tottered, aimed, and fired, but luckily for the King of Swing the tequila had blurred his vision and given him shaky hands.

Only one of the five shots caused a slight graze before the enraged fisherman could be overpowered. The previous evening, El Mocho, delirious from tequila, had gone on a rampage. Bottles, glasses, and tables had been demolished before Stauffer, as manager of the establishment, had kicked him out. Now El

Mocho was looking to avenge his wounded masculine pride. Only after a public embrace, organized by the controversial but locally extremely influential chief of police, was Stauffer protected from further confrontations with the Mocho clan.

Tequila and Swing

THE SWISS SWING musician, who had lived in the then tiny fishing village since 1944, became "Mr. Acapulco" for the Americans. He attracted Frank Sinatra, Gary Cooper, and, of course, his own wife, Hedy Lamarr, to the Mexican beaches. John Wayne was there too. The museum of Sauza Tequila is still proud of the framed letter from the old gunslinger: "Your special product has become as necessary in our household as air and water."

During the filming of *The Lady from Shanghai*, Teddy Stauffer, without further ado, whisked the lovely Rita Hayworth, at that time the most coveted woman in the world, away from her ranting husband, Orson Welles, and off to Paris. In the 1970s he opened the first discotheque in Acapulco along American lines, which he aptly named The Tequila a Go-Go. Until his death he resided in a tower with a drawbridge on the grounds of the luxury hotel Villa Vera, high above the sweep of the bay.

The Hotel Plaza Las Glorias was another hot spot and the stomping ground of the notoriously broke Errol Flynn. When the alimony for his first ex-wife threatened to ruin him financially, he managed to settle his debts by modeling for advertising campaign posters and doing radio jingles for the tequila distiller Herradura. That shouldn't have been too difficult for him as he was a great admirer of their product.

Even in the 1940s, large amounts of Herradura were exported to the US thanks to the initiative of the businessman/ bandleader Phil Harris and the musician Bing Crosby, both of whom had not only financial interests but also an affinity for the subject of their endeavors. The horseshoe on the label of the bottle refers to a find by Aurelio, son of the owner of the company, Felix Lopez, when the company was formally founded in 1870. While looking at land he was thinking of buying, Aurelio saw something metallic glinting in the sun; on closer inspection he discovered that it was a horseshoe. As horseshoes are symbols of luck worldwide, he felt inspired to name his family's tequila after his find. Gabriela Romo de la Peña, a renowned philanthropist, successfully managed the long-established company from 1953 to 1994. When she died she was buried in a tomb on the grounds of the classical hacienda that is still in the family's possession and where she is still regularly honored by locals. The family's book collection is also still at the hacienda and with 25,000 items is one of the largest private libraries in Latin America. The Romo family still has a special position among tequila dynasties; they are often at odds with the large suppliers, defending traditional values against market interests. Their independence is based on the fact that they use agaves exclusively from their own stocks.

Fun in Acapulco

TEQUILA HAS DEVELOPED from being the drink of the fashionable entertainment crowd at a famous beach to being one of the most important export products for the Mexican economy. The first exports at the beginning of the twentieth century, organized by the distiller Sauza, exclusively supplied Mexican immigrants in New Mexico, Texas, and California, but then Prohibition brought tequila its first boom. Those with cars drove down to Tijuana, where a red-light district had sprouted right on the border and where, in addition to prostitution, tequila and mezcal were legal. So as not to confuse the

Yankees these spirits were labeled "Mexican whiskey." The Hollywood set preferred Acapulco, which within a few years advanced from being a sleepy fishing village to a chic resort. A frequent guest was Johnny Weissmuller, five-time Olympic gold medalist and Tarzan actor. The idyllic beaches bordered by picturesque cliffs and the fact that he could legally enjoy Mexico's national drink induced him to stay. By the time his career ended, Weissmuller was an alcoholic. When he was admitted to a sanatorium he was released after a short stay because he kept disturbing the peace with his yodeling jungle calls. The impoverished Hollywood star was also buried in Acapulco. Prominent on his gravestone are the words "Tarzan Johnny Weissmuller."

Elvis also made his way to Mexico, for the filming of *Fun in Acapulco*. It is no coincidence that while serenading his co-star, Ursula Andress, with "Marguerita," she is unmistakably sipping a cocktail of the same name from a goblet with a salted rim.

Margarita and the Milkman

THE MARGARITA, THE fresh short drink made from tequila, orange liqueur, and lemon juice, became the holiday drink of the 1950s and contributed in no small way to the international breakthrough of tequila.

For the creation of this drink we can probably thank a barkeeper named Francisco Pancho Morales. A written document was found among his estate that was published by the Consejo Regulador del Tequila, and in it he had written that he named his cocktail after the dancer Margarita De Rosas in the hope of conquering her heart, unfortunately to no avail. The beauty had indeed enjoyed his drink, but it didn't amount to more. The barman didn't seem wealthy enough and there were no signs that would change. She was right. If he had patented his drink, though, Morales would have been a rich man. His son, Gabriel Morales, related that his father had never boasted about his flash of inspiration; he didn't even like the drink. Later emigrating to the US, he worked as a milkman for twenty-five years.

Liz Taylor and Richard Burton had owned property in Puerto Vallarta since filming *The Night of the Iguana*. Burton, after a hefty night of tequila, was in the habit of reciting Shakespeare naked on the beach in front of their house. Passing yachtsmen used to drop anchor in the bay, the moonlight illuminating the actor while Macbeth's lament rang out over the sands.

Pancho Villa: A Mexican Hero

AS WELL AS American screen stars, Acapulco accommodated actors from the Mexican movie industry, who specialized in running through variations on stories from the Mexican War of Independence and the Mexican Revolution. Driven on by bottles of tequila, the intrepid mustachioed screen desperados liberate the oppressed peasants from the clutches of landowners. Once on the screen, tequila was inextricably linked to Mexican machismo and the myths and legends of the revolution.

The inspiration for many of these epics was the swashbuckling biography of Doroteo Arango Arámbula, better known as Pancho Villa. Today in every Mexican schoolbook he is celebrated as a national hero. His name also adorns a brand of tequila, and even his horse, the stallion Siete Leguas, has been similarly immortalized.

From a lowly background, Villa, together with Emiliano Zapata and Álvaro Obregón, was the most prominent representative of a socialist revolutionary wing of insurgents. At the tender age of sixteen Villa shot the son of the owner of a large hacienda where his family worked. The son had raped Villa's sister, a serious offense, but at that time often at the lower end of the crime scale. Probably Villa was just coming to terms with his own trauma, as he was thought to be the fruit of *prima noche*—the then common practice for the lord of the manor/hacienda to spend the first night with the virgin bride as recompense for the costs of financing the wedding celebrations of his servants. Anyway, Villa was then forced to live the life of an outlaw. Initially he made a living as a miner before switching to the lucrative business of cattle rustling on the borderlands, which in his official biographies is often referred to euphemistically as "working in the meat business."

The country was governed by General Porfirio Díaz, a corrupt dictator who mainly served the interests of wealthy landowners and major American companies that had invested in the mining and oil industries and the railway networks. The motto of the government was *"orden y progreso"* (order and progress). In around 1900, 97 percent of land was in the hands of 1 percent of the population. *Indios* and *mestizos* were second-class citizens and weren't, for instance, even allowed to use the pavement. The later folk hero, Villa, extended his field of activities to include robbing banks. Human life was not worth much.

He was considered a Mexican Robin Hood among the simple peasants with whom he shared some of his booty in return for their support. Villa came into contact with the revolutionaries who were gathering ever-increasing numbers of supporters. The liberal Francisco Ignacio Madero, living in exile in Texas and who, by the way, came from a distiller dynasty, called for an armed revolution to begin at 6 p.m. on Sunday, November 20, 1910. People came in droves to rallies, and after a battle in which many ordinary soldiers joined forces with the revolutionaries, Díaz got cold feet and fled to Paris.

After these rapid initial successes the revolutionary zeal began to wane. Pancho Villa, due to his lack of formal education, didn't feel confident in taking up a government post, and the moderate government initially hired him to dispose of political opponents, only later to sentence him to death once he had become an unwanted and troublesome accomplice. His former patron, Madero, who had in the meantime been elected president, reduced the sentence to life imprisonment. While Christmas carols were being sung, Villa managed to saw through the bars of his cell with a file that had been smuggled in, and he fled to El Paso, Texas. Madero, who had been able to implement only a few of his objectives because of the power of an unreformed army, became a victim of circumstances, and after being arrested was shot while trying to escape—or so went the new government's version of the story . Shortly afterwards there was a putsch, in which Félix Díaz, nephew of the ex-dictator Porfirio Díaz, figured as a contender to be president. But the leader of the putsch, Victoriana Huerta, became president instead and dispatched Díaz to Japan as ambassador.

The Wild Bunch: War and Cinema

PANCHO VILLA HAD returned and expanded his wild bunch of one to a serious military force and was ready to compete with the hated new dictator in some style. Since the cattle-rustling times on the borderlands to New Mexico, he had kept in contact with a number of hardened Americans, who now became members of his troops. The legendary American soldiers of fortune, a hodgepodge of former soldiers, cowboys, and other desperados from the southern US, shared with Pancho Villa an aversion to the establishment represented by landowners of large estates, bankers, and railroad barons. These outlaws were interested not only in the booty, but even more so in the honor of participating in a David and Goliath battle. The movie director Sam Peckinpah paid tribute to them in his blood and bullets-ridden Western epic *The Wild Bunch*. Villa was famous both sides of the border. His views on financing his activities were just as revolutionary as those on the sharing of the riches of his country. After seeing a silent movie in 1913 his enthusiasm for the new medium was not limited to that of a spectator. He played himself in a total of four films with titles like *Following the Flag in Mexico* and *The Life of General Villa*, and he offered Hollywood the chance to film real action scenes in the Mexican revolutionary wars, which the filmmakers were only too happy to accept. This man who could hardly read or write had his fees paid in gold and weapons. Soon Villa's men had at their disposal cannons, machine guns, a hospital train, and even four airplanes. Suitably equipped, Villa's División del Norte attacked the Mexican Army. The revolutionary troops were eventually successful on all fronts and the revolution was triumphant for a second time, but there were quarrels about which troops and which of the leaders were to be the first to enter the capital. President Venustiano Carranza blocked coal supplies for the trains of the División del Norte, which then ran out of fuel halfway to the capital, while General Álvaro Obregón's troops were the first to march into Mexico City, celebrating with barrels of tequila they had confiscated en route. As a result of this, Pancho Villa terminated the military alliance. In 1914 there was a final attempt to unify the diverse revolutionary strains, but this too failed.

Carranza was forced to transfer his provisional government to Veracruz, while Villa and his old comrade-in-arms Emiliano Zapata, much to the consternation of the industrialists, aristocracy, and financiers, appeared for another victory parade in Mexico City. The people, on the other hand, feted the heroes. Villa had reached the peak of his powers. He was made governor of Chihuahua and printed his own banknotes with portraits of his former campaigners. The ex-bank robber arrested anyone who disrespected the new notes or refused to accept the unusual currency as payment.

But this period of peace was also short-lived. The Americans supported the conservative wing of the revolutionaries, and Villa and Zapata's men were edged out. Frustrated by this development, Villa decided, in a moment of megalomania, to attack the US; in 1916 he raided the border town of Columbus, killing ten US civilians and eight US soldiers, plundering the town, and finally setting fire to it. Just a week later the US sent out a punitive expedition under General John "Black Jack" Pershing. This was the last time that the US Cavalry was mobilized for a war that was fought mostly on horseback. The Americans marched into Mexico, scattering Villa's troops, but failed to capture him.

Mexican federalists bought Villa a hacienda and gave him the pension of a general. In the following years he was a model employer on his farm. He established cooperatives for skilled craftsmen and founded a school for the children of peasants. In 1923 he was ambushed by followers of President Obregón, who suspected his candidacy at the next election. On the morning of July 20 he was hit by dozens of bullets, the corpse photographed, and the pictures published throughout the country. Obregón was reelected but was assassinated before resuming office.

There were rumors that Villa's skull was stolen during the night of February 25, 1926, on behalf of Skull and Bones, a secret society at Yale University, and that it still remains hidden within Yale's grounds. There have been petitions to try to persuade the Mexican government to officially press for the return of Villa's skull, but no presiding head of government has dared to raise the matter at the highest level.

163

The curator of the Francisco Villa Museum in Hidalgo del Parral recounted another story. According to him the people's hero received a neat grave well cared for by the locals, but that unfortunately a short time later it was desecrated. A confused peasant believed that with the skull of Villa he could claim the US$5,000 reward from the American government. Villa's appalled relatives then reburied the mortal remains that were left in a plain grave, known only to close family members. Municipal leaders, in turn, didn't want the official original gravesite without any remains and quickly organized the burial of some unclaimed bones with full ceremony. In 1976 the then president sent a delegation to Parral to escort the bones of Pancho Villa to the Monument to the Revolution in Mexico City. A doctor, present at the exhumation, recognized that the bones must have belonged to a woman, but was sworn, as were the others, to absolute secrecy. Since then those in the know from Parral, on passing the monument, utter a curt "¡Hola, señora!" while the body of the hero rests next to the graves of his twenty-six wives back in his old homeland... and his head, according to the curator, now lies under the asphalt of a street in Chihuahua.

Under the Volcano

UNDER THE SPELL of the agave spirit fell not only actors and musicians, but the literati too. The chronically alcoholic author Malcolm Lowry worked for ten years on his novel *Under the Volcano*. The main character, the recalled consul Geoffrey Firmin, is in a late stage of alcoholism, and the last day of his life up to his violent death in a Mexican province is depicted from this delirious perspective. Associative scraps, repetition and loops, broken trains of thought, and sudden and arbitrary changes of direction reflect the effects of continuous alcohol consumption on the fragile psyche of the consul. It made the novel one of the most important examples of modern literature and gave its author a global reputation.

How many bottles since then? In how many glasses, how many bottles had he hidden himself, since then alone?... and now he saw them, smelt them, all, from the very beginning— bottles, bottles, bottles, and glasses, glasses, glasses, of bitter, of Dubonnet, of Falstaff, Rye, Johnny Walker, Vieux Whisky, blanc Canadien, the aperitifs, the digestifs, the demis, the dobles, the noch ein Herr Obers, the et glas Araks, the tusen taks, the bottles, the bottles, the beautiful bottles of tequila, and the gourds, gourds, gourds, the millions of gourds of beautiful mescal... The Consul sat very still. His conscience sounded muffled with the roar of water. It whacked and whined round the wooden frame-house with the spasmodic breeze, massed, with the thunderclouds over the trees, seen through the windows, its factions. How indeed could he hope to find himself to begin again when, somewhere, perhaps, in one of those lost or broken bottles, in one of those glasses, lay, for ever, the solitary clue to his identity? How could he go back and look now, scrabble among the broken glass, under the eternal bars, under the oceans?[1]

The Weberian "Wonder Plant" or the Secret of the Blue Agave

THE "BEAUTIFUL MEZCAL," the favorite drink of Lowry's delirious consul, is mainly produced from espadin agave (*Agave angustifolia* Haw.) but can also be made from other species. Traditionally, in the making of mezcal, the *piñas* (the succulent cores of the agave that resemble pineapples, hence their name) are placed in *palenques*, cone-shaped pits lined with stones and covered with woven palm leaves and earth, and then baked. The agave hearts remain there for a number of days until they are soft from baking and have absorbed the aromas of the earth and smoke.

The basis of tequila, which is closely related to mezcal, is the blue agave, botanically termed *Agave tequilana* F. A. C. Weber, a succulent plant of the lily family and not, as commonly believed, a member of the cactus family. Blue agaves grow to the desired size and quality at five thousand feet above sea level. When untended, the flowering stalk from which the agave heart ascends can reach heights of up to sixteen feet. Agave farmers have to be patient, as the plant has its first and last light yellow blossom only after five years. A native bat species with specially adapted proboscis takes care of pollination. Once this occurs the agave produces up to five thousand seeds and then dies. Cultivated plants are harvested after six to ten years. The stalks are cut off commercial plants to encourage growth in the lower part of the plant.

After a long period of ripening, the plants are unearthed. Herradura, a tequila producer, uses only fruits that have ripened for ten years, because the riper the fruit, the higher the sugar content. This relatively long maturation period is the reason for the recurrent supply shortfalls that still occur today. Agaves can be harvested at any time of year, as they are not subject to seasonal ripening cycles. A *jimador*, a Mexican agave farmer, separates the roughly two hundred spiky, fleshy leaves from the core using a *coa*, a flat-bladed knife at the end of a long pole resembling a hoe. After the leaves have been removed, the heart, the *piña*, is revealed. At harvest the *piñas* weigh between 100 and 250 pounds. An experienced *jimador* can harvest up to a ton of *piñas* a day; it is a dangerous job requiring much skill and is usually passed down from one generation to the next. The *piñas* are then transported to the distillery, where they are cut into halves or quarters and baked. Traditionally this took place in special ovens called *hornos*, taking up to three days of slow baking and just as long for cooling. Nowadays this is only practiced by smaller distilleries, while larger ones use autoclaves, which operate in a similar way to pressure cookers. Using autoclaves, distillers achieve similar results within twelve hours; the cooling process is also accelerated industrially.

After the procedure the *piñas* taste like sweet potatoes or yams but with a slight tequila note. In the next stage the giant hearts are shredded and mashed in a heavy mortar-like container, the *tahona*, which weighs up to two tons. The extracted juices, the *aguamiel* (honey water), are separated from the fibrous matter, the *bagasse*, by filtration and centrifugation, mixed with water and yeast, and left to ferment in large steel tanks. Traditionally this process takes twelve days, but it can be reduced to two to three days by the addition of chemicals. The resulting wort is allowed to rest a while before being distilled twice in pot stills or modern column stills. The first distillation produced after roughly one and a half hours is called *ordinario* and contains about 20 percent alcohol. The subsequent three- to four-hour distillation raises the alcohol content to something like 55 percent. Only the main portion of the distillate, the *corazón* (heart), is used for further processing. The *cabeza* (head) and *cola* (tail) are separated off. After distillation, tequila, like all distillates, is initially transparent. After blending with demineralized water it is reduced to the desired drinking strength of around 40 percent.

White tequila is stored in steel tanks for a further two days for homogenization before being bottled. Optional coloring results from storage either in new, unused barrels or in barrels from whisky, cognac, or sherry production up to fifty years old. These so-called *barricas* considerably influence the taste of

167

the drink. The barrels are then stored in *bodegas*, spacious and well-ventilated depots. The best-known and simplest form of tequila, the *blanco* (silver), is bottled directly after distillation or a little while later. The same applies for the *joven u oro*, the unaged and golden tequilas colored by caramel, sugar syrup, or oak extracts. The *reposado* (rested) tequilas age at least two months in wooden barrels and the *gran reposado* between two months and a year. The highest-quality tequilas, the *añejo* (aged or vintage), mature for one to five years. Storage times of more than five years do not lead to an increase in quality and are therefore uncommon.

The 100 percent *agave azul* (blue agave) always has to have been *hecho en México*, "made in Mexico." The highest grade is Tequila Añejo 100% Agave Azul, and the production process is subject to the strictest controls supervised by an authority especially established for this purpose, *Consejo Regulador del Tequila*.

Many of the less expensive tequilas are *mixtos*. They use no less than 51 percent blue agave with other agave species or sugarcane making up the remainder. They can be blended and bottled outside of Mexico, and the coloring comes from caramel.

How the Worm Got into the Bottle

ODDLY ENOUGH, IN some bottles of tequila you can find a worm, which strictly speaking is not a worm but the larva of a moth. These little creatures prefer to live in agave groves and are considered by the locals as a delicacy rich in protein; they can be found on the menus of upmarket restaurants either grilled or boiled. The practice of placing the insect in the tequila bottle can be traced back to a marketing gimmick by the bottler Jacobo Lozano Páez, and other producers followed his example. There are even bottles of mezcal containing scorpions and snakes, adding a further kick to the intoxicant. In Mexico these excesses of exuberant marketing fantasies are greeted with smiles, but it is standard practice to enjoy the pleasures of mezcal with slices of lime, salt, and chili powder or powdered moth larvae.

Everything Under One Sombrero

THE 1968 SUMMER Olympics and the 1970 FIFA World Cup in Mexico were two major events that attracted worldwide attention to the tequila industry. Acapulco became a target of American mass tourism, while students and hippies valued the country for its low prices. The supply of quality tequila, however, couldn't accommodate the rapidly rising demand, and it was increasingly considered as a cheap pleasure and not treated as a particular specialty of the country. Demand rose so quickly that the overexploited agave plantations ran out of usable agaves. Official purity standards were relaxed and *mixtos* of questionable quality flooded the market.

Tequila, in the form of *mixtos*, had also fallen into disrepute in Europe, serving only as the preferred fuel for adolescent alcohol excesses. Bought at moderate prices at twenty-four-hour filling stations, it reliably provided hospitals' emergency departments with comatose teenager admissions, and for those who managed to make it home, blurred recollections of the time between losing control and collapsing on their parents' sofas. The sharp and sweet aroma of the agave distillate was firmly engraved on the still-suffering subconscious the next day, causing the young to reject further experiments with the drink. Older and wiser, the majority of the younger generation of drinkers turned to other forms of alcohol.

In Mexico tequila is sold as a souvenir in a vast array of novelty bottle shapes: rattlesnakes, pistols, cow horns, or intricately decorated cowboy boots, to name just a few. The advertising line of the Sierra Tequila company—whose bottles are topped with a sombrero—"Everything under one sombrero," is a jest to this affinity to folklore. Producers of premium-quality tequila also have a penchant for elaborate bottle designs. The Mexican producer Ley .925 is well known for exclusive products; special-edition bottles for its Pasión Azteca series, the most expensive tequila in the world, are made of platinum, gold, or silver and filled with six-year-old agave tequila. The most expensive bottle consists of almost four and a half pounds of white gold and platinum, and this model would cost you US$225,000. For those who can't afford this there is the less expensive silver and gold version, which will only set you back a paltry US$25,000. Both the embarrassing effects on teenage newcomers to drinking and these excesses in design production are partially responsible for tequila's slightly dubious reputation in Europe.

Today some 253 million blue agave plants grow in the Tequila region. They produced, in 2010, 68 million gallons of tequila, of which 40.2 million gallons were exported. The production of 100 percent agave tequilas, in particular, has grown from 6.6 million gallons in 2000 to 26.2 million gallons in 2013.[2] The most important foreign market is still North America.

Americans, who became familiar with "Mexican whiskey" during Prohibition, cultivate a slightly more dignified association with the drink. Good 100 percent agave tequilas are sipped from sherry glasses in the US and Mexico, even the *reposado* and the *añejo* are swirled around in cognac glasses at room temperature to release the aromas. Since the 1980s there has been heavy demand in the US for premium brands. Whereas in

America a good tequila has a similar status to cognac or scotch, and in Mexico it is part of the cultural heritage, Europe, despite all the efforts of tequila producers, still remains, in this respect, a backwater.

The Tree of Wonders

THE FAMOUS SALT-AND-LEMON ritual is reserved only for ordinary and young tequilas. Those in the know don't down it in one, but drink it with deliberation—after all it is a spirit with over four hundred years of history, and long before the Spanish *conquistadores* distilled the first tequila from the hearts of the blue agave in the sixteenth century, the plant was an integral part of the everyday lives of indigenous people. The local population of the Hñähñu in the Valle del Mezquital thus refers to it as *el árbol de las maravillas*, "the tree of wonders."[3] It belongs to the succulent family, one of the oldest plants on our planet. The roughly two hundred species of agave that thrive in Mexico serve the population after some form of processing as materials for mats, hats, fans, and fences; the fibers are used to produce clothing, paper, and rope. On account of their high sugar content, agave hearts can be chewed for pleasure. The juice has healing properties and can be used in ointments. Fermented it becomes *pulque*, the alcoholic drink of Mexico's original native population that is still the preferred drink of the rural population in cultivated agave regions. *Pulque* has a cloudy, milky consistency and, being rich in vitamins and having a low fat content, is considered beneficial to health. Despite globalization it remains a regional product as it is difficult to conserve and is virtually unobtainable outside Mexico.

There are testimonies of the agave's use as an intoxicant in various cultures in Central America, such as the use of fermented agave juices in religious ceremonies. The pleasures, however, were initially confined to the ruling class and priests. The two most important cultures of Central and South America were the Mayas and the Aztecs. The earliest artifacts of the Maya culture date to about 2000 BC. The Mayas believed that the world was balanced on the back of a giant crocodile in a huge pool and that the movements of the crocodile were the cause of the earthquakes, volcano eruptions, flooding, and hurricanes that were continuous threats to their existence. Like the Aztecs, the Mayas practiced human sacrifices, though not quite as excessively.

The Olmecs, Mayas, and Aztecs played a Mesoamerican ball game considered a precursor of soccer, although the idea was to keep the ball moving without using hands or feet. Goal kicks and throw-ins were conducted with some form of racquet. Claims to power or the destinies of prisoners of war were decided in stadiums, mostly part of the temple complex as at Chichen Itza, with room for twenty thousand people. Sometimes a match was played to resolve conflicts as a substitute for genuine warfare. Bets were placed on the outcome of matches, which were often the climax of public festivities. The victors were rewarded with high social prestige, and the losers paid with their lives. At major sporting events the losers were usually sacrificed—a death, however, that promised immediate ascension to the gods.

From Conquista to Tequila

WHEN THE SPANISH arrived on April 21, 1519, the Maya civilization had been extinct for three hundred years and the Aztecs were the dominant power in Mexico. They built huge pyramids to study the heavens and established the city of Tenochtitlan on the site of present-day Mexico City. Tenochtitlan, on a high plateau between two volcanoes, had at the time of the Spanish conquest 200,000 inhabitants and was situated around a huge network of lagoons. Seeing the city's floating gardens, temples, and palaces, the Spaniards couldn't believe their eyes and initially thought they must be delirious. Hernán Cortés and Díaz del Castillo described in their journals the beauty of this paradise they had discovered before proceeding to occupy and plunder it, driving its architects and inhabitants to the verge of extinction and finally destroying it. With hindsight one wonders how, despite numerical inferiority, the Spanish were able to do this. The fact that the Aztecs believed that the *conquistadores* were gods returning to their people certainly must have played a role.

Whether we like it or not, it was the Spanish who brought to Mexico not only firearms, influenza, whooping cough, and syphilis, but also the know-how of distillation and thus the prerequisite for producing the national drink. Before the emergence of tequila there was *pulque*, the fermented agave juice, which was widespread before the arrival of the Spanish in the sixteenth century. There was a relatively well-developed market with sales distribution and production systems that went way beyond fulfilling the needs of the villagers' own requirements. *Pulque* was sold in towns just as other foodstuffs were. The Spanish soon discovered this and used it as the source product for distillation, as alcohol played an important role in the provisions of the *conquistadores*. As drinking water was often contaminated with parasites, by 1546 the soldiers were obliged to mix their water with agave wine or mezcal brandy, as they called the new drink. For official meals, by the way, only beer, wine, and milk were served.

The first Spaniard to bring together the art of distillation and *pulque* with any degree of ambition was Don Pedro Sánchez de Tagle, Marquis of Altamira, considered to be the father of tequila. Even though he didn't come directly from the area of cultivation, he was active in the region of today's tequila state, Jalisco. He founded his mezcal wine distillery and cultivated agaves on his hacienda specifically with the purpose of processing them into alcohol. The levying of taxes is evidence of the emergence of mezcal brandy as a beverage. The governor of Nueva Galicia introduced taxation on alcohol as early as 1608, and from 1636 producers had to buy licenses to distill mezcal wine. The success of the new drink was reflected in the ever-rising taxes in subsequent decades, which didn't seem to perturb the *aficionados* of the agave spirit.

The revenues, in a historic exception, were used not to finance a military campaign but for the building of roads and bridges and later for founding churches and universities. At the same time reports about the medical applications began to appear, for example in the treatment of rheumatism. In around 1700 mezcal had become an export product. Even then the mezcal wine from the region around Tequila was reputed to be the best; furthermore the town lay on the road to the port of San Blas. But before production could be fully developed and expanded, politics intervened. In 1785 the Spanish king, Charles III, banned the production of all Mexican spirits to promote the import of Spanish wines and brandies. The ban, naturally, was circumvented as much as possible, and ten years later the laws were changed again when King Charles IV decided that taxation on alcohol was more important than protecting the winegrowers back in the mother country, and distilling in Mexico was again legalized. From about 1850 tequila slowly became the accepted name for good mezcal brandy.

In 1795 an ambitious agave farmer, Jose Antonio de Cuervo, bought a license to produce mezcal and in doing so laid the foundations of a company that today is one of the most influential tequila suppliers and still remains in the family. It is fairly safe to assume that Jose Cuervo was distilling spirits before he acquired the license; he had bought the land thirty-seven years prior to getting the license and had in the meantime become prosperous. The headquarters of his *taberna*, as the Mexicans call their distilleries, was the small town of Tequila. At that time Tequila was nothing more than an impoverished backwater, and it was only the success of the eponymous drink that brought the community paved streets, churches, schools, a hospital, and finally world fame.

The Mexican War of Independence began in 1810. The predominantly Mexican population, fortified by a sip or two of tequila, took up arms against Spanish authority. One of their leaders was the parish priest of Dolores, Miguel Hidalgo, a hard-drinking servant of God. With an image of the Holy Virgin of Guadalupe in his hand, the priest impelled an army of peasants, and after a few months of military successes he was finally crushingly defeated in June 1811. Hidalgo's head was skewered on a lance and displayed at the marketplace of Guanajuato as a warning to others until the flies and maggots put an end to the horror. A soccer stadium, a federal state, and an asteroid have been named in his honor, ensuring that the name of the valiant man of God is not forgotten.

In 1821 Mexico bought its freedom from the Spanish and was afterwards financially ruined. There followed a succession of dictators, a war with the US—which forced Mexico to sell Arizona, California, New Mexico, and Texas, which had already been annexed, for the sum of US$15 million—and a French invasion, which brought the Mexicans Emperor Maximilian I, a member of the House of Habsburg and not a particularly bright character, whom Napoleon III installed as a puppet. Towards the middle of the nineteenth century the name "tequila" became the accepted term for agave spirits from the federal state of Jalisco and, similar to the terms "cognac" or "champagne," represented spirits from a clearly defined cultivation

175

area together with particular quality criteria. The Industrial Revolution brought the building of railway networks, and the distilleries invested in better stills and improved hygienic standards. The spirit that today bears the name "tequila" developed, more or less, from the stipulations set down at that time.

A Gift of the Gods

A LEGEND OF the indigenous population from pre-Columbian times illustrates the connection between the miraculous juices of the blue agave and their brutal gods.

Once, many years ago, the gods in heaven became bored. Below on earth the people were hardworking, god-fearing, and resigned to their destinies. They regularly sacrificed animals and humans on altars to the gods. But the gods were only moderately interested in the streams of blood and still-beating hearts offered up to them. They began to quarrel among themselves about how to proceed with their worshipers. Their strife darkened the skies and caused earthquakes. Thunder rolled and lightning streaked. One thunderbolt struck the heart of an agave, and after smoldering it gave mankind alcohol. Immediately the people began neglecting their duties; they turned their backs on work and celebrated this gift of the gods. They fell deeply in love, sang lustily, and danced wildly. Things ended in disputes and fights and finally peace and quiet. Delighted at being entertained at long last the gods congratulated themselves on their cleverness.

CHAMPAGNE

The Height of Decadence

"Ce champagne est prêt à partir;
Dans sa prison il fume,
Impatient de te couvrir
De sa brillante écume."

"This champagne is ready to fly;
In its prison it fumes,
Impatient to cover you
With its shining foam."

CARDINAL DE BERNIS[1]

"THE DEVIL'S WINE!" cursed the cellar master. He had just brought one of his workers with bloody gashes in his face up from the chalky cellar to the light of day and could now look in horror at the damaged eye. It was doubtful whether the man would ever see again. This was the third time one of his workers had been blinded by flying splinters of glass. The cellar master's own hands were studded with scars. He had organized masks and helmets to protect the faces of his men and heavy leather aprons to protect their bodies, but still almost every day there were accidents. In fall they had bottled the champagne and almost immediately it had begun to ferment; during the cooler temperatures of winter it hibernated and gave some respite, but after the March moon it had begun again to work, and now in summer it was bubbling away *en furie*. Every day explosions signaled the bursting of new bottles, with evil projectiles of glass flying everywhere. The floor was a foaming quagmire. Every exploding bottle wreaked havoc on the other bottles on the shelves. The cellar master had tried cooling the bottles with water to no avail. In the end he had sloped the cellar floor in an attempt to drain off the sludge. Every day he had to look on helplessly and watch a year's work literally fly through the air.

Depending on the temperature, the quality of the glass, and the skills of the cellarer, up to 90 percent of stored bottles were destroyed during the second fermentation—heavy losses for the troubled winegrowers. And yet they clung to their volatile product. The Champagne region around 1750 produced three kinds of wine: an excellent still white wine, a heavy red wine that had a relatively small share of the market of 5 percent, and the product that was to make it the noblest of all cultivated regions, the sparkling white wine, champagne. The heavier the losses and more difficult the production, the more delicious and more sought-after the end product was.

Wine Ascending

THE WINEGROWER CLAUDE Moët had in the mid-eighteenth
century managed to gain access to the court of Louis XV. One of Moët's ancestors had fought alongside Joan of Arc against the English, and this had helped open doors at Versailles for the ambitious descendant. And there, in one of the most

magnificent courts of Europe, he met one of the illustrious characters of the time: Madame de Pompadour, long-standing and official mistress of the king. She had lived for a long time in Champagne, both her father and brother owned estates there, and she had observed the development of the region's wines from the highly rated white wines and red wines to the champagnes. The charming and witty marquise became a loyal customer and made sure that champagne continued to be *the* drink for festive occasions at the court. According to legend, she maintained her beauty by bathing in champagne. She was also of the opinion that it was the only wine that leaves a woman's beauty intact.

Cardinal de Bernis knew of her weakness and wooed her with the following lines:

> This Champagne is ready to fly;
> In its prison it fumes,
> Impatient to cover you
> With its shining foam.
> Do you know why this charming Wine,
> When your hand does shake it so,
> Does like lightening [sic]
> Fly and hurry forth?
> Bacchus in vain in his flask
> Holds back the rebel Love;
> For Love always escapes from prison
> At the hand of a Belle.[2]

Louis xv's great-uncle, Philippe II, Duke of Orléans, reigned as regent for eight years until Louis xv reached the age of maturity, and during this time he heralded in "one of the most frivolous, extravagant, rip-roaring decades in [France's] history," in the words of one observer.[3] Versailles was almost closed down overnight and court life relocated to the Palais-Royal in Paris. Philippe was a man for whom "all the vices competed for first place." His *petits-soupers* (exclusive dinner gatherings) were legendary and peopled by bon viveurs, women of easy virtue, powdered dandies, and abbots in love. Uncorking bottles of champagne was mostly performed by the tender hands of women, and delight in the erotic symbolism of a popping cork and the gush of sparkling wine fueled many a regal orgy. The fashion of *petits-soupers* was not confined to France; other European courts quickly followed suit. In England a provincial newspaper reported an aristocratic binge in which the participants toasted and downed champagne from the shoe of a well-known courtesan, then proceeded to have the shoe wrapped in dough, baked, and served in a ragout.

Eighteen hundred bottles of champagne were drunk at a masked ball at the Hôtel de Ville in Paris on August 30, 1739. This was the first written record of a champagne-drinking bout that was to have further ramifications. The myth of champagne as the drink of licentious revelry and exclusive but fleeting love was born. The *vin gris* (ordinary still white wines) from the Champagne region already had a long association with the French court. Geographically at the heart of Europe, Champagne developed in the early Middle Ages into a pulsating economic center. In 816, Louis the Pious was the first of a long line of French kings crowned at Reims. The festivities accompanying these ceremonies spread the reputation of the high-quality wines way beyond the French border. The oldest wine-house still in existence, Gosset, was established in Aÿ in 1584.

It was said that the grandfather of Henri IV, the first Bourbon on the French throne, put a garlic clove in Henri's mouth and gave him a few drops of champagne on the day of his birth; as intended, he developed into one of the greatest gourmets of the time. He also had a reputation as a tireless lover, later proudly declaring, "Until I was forty, I thought it was a bone!"[4]

Louis XIV made the still white wines of Champagne his wines of choice. This was also the time of Charles de Marguetel de Saint-Denis, seigneur de Saint-Évremond. Although nowadays his name is seldom mentioned, among wine connoisseurs well-versed in history he is one of the people chiefly responsible for the success of champagne.

Saint-Évremond was a well-known author, philosopher, and satirist who in his younger days had a reputation for bravery on the battlefield. He served in the Régiment Royal-Champagne, whose motto on their standard was "Je m'en fous." This roughly translates as "I don't give a damn," which could well be seen as a motto for the later life of Saint-Évremond. This was a time when, on account of climatic factors, campaigns were fought only in the summer. In the cold winter months gentlemen could distinguish themselves on other fronts. It was a Paris of duels, which although officially strictly forbidden had a yearly death toll of around 1,500, but it was also a Paris of loose morals, excesses, and amorous adventures.

Described as "tall and well-formed," Saint-Évremond was a favorite with the ladies. At the salon of the Marquis de Sablé, the intellectual center of Paris at that time, he excelled in wit and intellect and taught his contemporaries about the most important properties of great wines and great cuisine. Saint-Évremond propagated balance, delicacy, lightness, and wholesomeness, what today we think of as core ideas of *nouvelle cuisine*. The Champagne wines were preferred to the heavier wines of Bordeaux and Spain.

Saint-Évremond, the Comte d'Olonne, and the Marquis de Bois-Dauphin became known as "Les Frères des Trois Coteaux" (Brothers of the Three Hills) because they drank wine only from Hautvillers, Aÿ, and Avenay.[5] Saint-Évremond, famous for his considerable intellect and blunt, often satirical discourses, fell out with Louis XIV after publishing a pamphlet criticizing the king's politics. On account of this he chose exile in England rather than the damp confines of the Bastille. In England he became a welcome guest at the court of Charles II, himself half French with eleven years of exile in France. The king shared with Saint-Évremond not only a weakness for the fairer sex but also a fondness for a cultured lifestyle to which the wines of Champagne belonged. The friendship was honored by the king, who appointed Saint-Évremond the first governor of Duck Island in St James's Park, a post that brought with it a generous pension for life.

By 1730 champagne had conquered the courts of Europe. From London to Vienna and Berlin to Madrid, the little bubbles fizzed at all the finest addresses of the capitals.

Frederick the Great ordered scientists at the Prussian Academy of Sciences to reveal the secrets of the bubbly drink but refused to provide one single bottle for research purposes. He would rather have died ignorant than sacrifice his precious champagne. Beau Brummell—who, like Oscar Wilde in the following century, was the epitome of the British dandy—spent a number of hours changing his clothes up to three times a day and had his boots cleaned with champagne.

Edward VII, who as son of the highly moral and long-living Queen Victoria was condemned to a life of perpetual heir to the throne, was also a genuine playboy. He compensated for this tragic destiny with the daily consumption of sparkling wine, which for him meant exclusively Gosset champagne. When as Prince of Wales he went hunting, he exasperated other hunters and beaters by calling for his boy in a thundering voice at regular intervals. The unfortunate servant had to follow the prince through all sorts of terrain with a little trolley laden with a full ice bucket, sufficient supplies of champagne, and all the necessary accessories. In the most exclusive clubs of London a "bottle of the boy" is still a synonym for a bottle of champagne with brunch.

Louis XVI drank champagne before ascending the steps to the guillotine. Napoleon Bonaparte, himself from a family of winegrowers, had a close friendship to Jean-Rémy Moët, who facilitated the building of a private hotel in Épernay for Bonaparte's family, which became a welcome refuge on many of his campaigns. The emperor personally accelerated the development of beet sugar, a local sugarcane and cheap product that was very important for the making of *liqueur de tirage* and necessary in the production of champagne. "I cannot live without champagne. In victory I deserve it; in defeat I need it."

The Vienna Party:
"The Congress Doesn't Advance; It Dances"

IT IS SAID that the Russian court had a very special affinity to the crown jewel of the French winemakers. Tsar Peter the Great enjoyed four bottles of it every night. His daughter Elizabeth substituted the usual Tokaj wine with champagne for toasting at official functions. Catherine the Great plied her consorts, whom she recruited from the officers' corps, with it. And Tsar Alexander I used champagne in a unique display of military might. On September 10, 1815, at sunrise, 300,000 Russian soldiers rose from their quarters in the area around Mont Aimé, France, not far from Vertus. By 7 a.m., an almighty jumble of Cossacks, hussars, grenadiers, foot soldiers, cannons, muskets, horses, and wagons had become an organized assembly of the most powerful army in Europe, and a group of riders split away and headed up the hill of Mont Aimé. From this viewpoint Alexander gave the signal, and the 300,000 troops formed a huge square. Accompanying Alexander were the Austrian emperor, the Prussian king, the Crown Prince of Bavaria, the Fürst von Wrede, and the Duke of Wellington. With serious faces they strode along the lines reviewing the endless phalanxes of bearded Russian soldiers. It was a colossal gesture of intimidation aimed at Austria and Prussia, who would have liked to have divided up defeated France to reduce her influence. Tsar Alexander, on the other hand, was interested in an influential France to keep her powerful neighbors in check. For Champagne, this summit meeting of the crowned heads of Europe was the greatest promotional event that any winegrowing area could ever wish for.

Negotiations at the Congress of Vienna had already been going on for a year. One hundred and forty-three delegates, representing most branches of European aristocracy, met to decide on the future form of European states among the debris left in the wake of the Napoleonic campaigns. The most important figures of this legendary meeting were the representatives of Austria, Graf von Metternich, of France, Charles Maurice de Talleyrand, and of Russia, Tsar Alexander I. One of the police spies noted of the tsar, "He rarely sits at his desk. Usually he spends his day attending the exercises and maneuvers of his soldiers, going out on horseback or in a carriage, in hunting or in making visits, the evenings he spends dancing until way past midnight. Through all this, champagne is his constant companion."[6] In another even more detailed report dated November 21, 1814, we learn that "at the ball given by the Count Francis Palffy, Alexander (I of Russia), who deeply admires the beauty of Countess Szechenyi-Guilford, said to her: 'Your husband is absent. It would be very pleasant to take his place temporarily.' The Countess replied: 'Does Your Majesty take me for a province?'"[7]

Talleyrand brought with him no armies to buffer France's claims, but he did bring Antoine Carême, France's most celebrated chef de cuisine. For artillery he presented champagne. Among his delegation he also included the intelligent and capricious Duchess of Périgord, the wife of his nephew, who was to take care of what we would now call public relations. Her liaisons with Talleyrand, thirty-nine years her senior, have been passed on to posterity by the letters and notes that survive.

Receptions and feasts greeted every arrival and departure. The Prince of Ligne wittily observed, "The Congress doesn't advance; it dances." The most important of all the social events was the Imperial Court Ball. Three thousand guests, including almost all crowned heads of state, danced the whole night in the light of 100,000 candles. The French delegation donated 1,500 magnums of champagne, a costly but ingenious advertising strategy contrived by Jean-Rémy Moët, who reasoned that it was easier to conquer Europe with good wines than with military force. Talleyrand toasted him with the words "My dear sir, you are assured of immortality... and I predict that, thanks to this coupe and its contents, your name will sparkle far longer than mine."[8] And he was right. After the Congress of Vienna, which might just as well have been called the Vienna Party and which lasted almost a year, champagne had indeed finally become established as the drink of the rich and powerful. Historians have seen the hedonism of the participants as a necessary valve to release the pressures and tensions of momentous decisions made at the conference table. Another explanation is that the European aristocracy just wanted to celebrate its existence one last time in grand style, with all the pomp and decadence of the *ancien régime*, knowing full well that the time of their political and cultural dominance was drawing to an end.

The influence of the aristocracy dwindled, but champagne became the drink of the upwardly mobile bourgeoisie. It has always been rare and expensive, making it all the more desirable—rare because it comes from a confined growing region and expensive because its production is an extremely complex and labor-intensive process, at the end of which it has to be stored for a year.

From Vin Gris to Sparkling Wine

"How sweet and airy sparkles the bubble
The widow Clicko in the glass."
WILHELM BUSCH, THE PIOUS HELENE (1872)[9]

THE FATHER OF champagne is still erroneously considered to be a man who did indeed make a great contribution to the wines of this region but who was not interested in bubbles at all—in fact the complete opposite; his efforts were aimed at eliminating the fine carbon dioxide bubbles. The Benedictine monk Dom (Pierre) Pérignon came from a well-to-do family. At the age of eighteen, instead of managing the family estate as the eldest son, he joined the Benedictine monastery in Saint-Vanne known for its high spiritual standards, strict rules, and absolute obedience. "Idleness is the enemy of the soul; and therefore the brethren ought to be employed in manual labor at certain times, at others, in devout reading."[10] That is how Benedict of Nursia, the founder of the order, expressed one of his rules to the brotherhood. At age thirty Dom Pérignon took over the administration of Saint-Pierre Abbey in Hautvillers, a once-famous and rich monastery that had been destroyed by homecoming crusaders time and again and burned to its foundations four times. The monks rebuilt the monastery over a period of thirty years, but first Dom Pérignon reestablished farming and winegrowing on the monastery's ravaged land. From 1668 to 1715, under his supervision were not only the highly valuable vineyards of the abbey but also the neighboring ones. The diversity of grape varietals, growing sites, and quality must have been quite a challenge for Dom Pérignon.

He busied himself with the attributes of the different wines, climates, and soil compositions and succeeded in creating an accomplished blend that warranted, year for year, an almost constant high quality. The concept of "cuvée" was born, which even today represents the reliable quality of Champagne wines. The still wines of Hautvillers Abbey, which admirers simply termed "Pérignon" wine, became the most famous in France. A barrel of this wine in 1700 would have been almost double the price of other contemporary wines. The Benedictine monk preferred red grapes in making his white wines; he rejected the use of white grapes, as they required secondary fermentation. He pruned back the grapevines to roughly three feet, which diminished the yields but improved the quality of the grapes. Only healthy grapes were pressed. All squashed or rotten grapes and the foliage were separated out, and the yields from multiple pressings were stored separately. Dom Pérignon was a perfectionist who during harvesting worked his wine presses to their limits and can rightfully be named one of the first enologists.

Another pioneer at this time was the lesser-known Brother Jean Oudart, cellarer of the Saint-Pierre-aux-Monts Abbey at Châlons. This abbey was not far away from Dom Pérignon's workplace. Although there is only one surviving account of Dom Pérignon visiting Jean Oudart's abbey, we can safely assume that the two monks exchanged ideas about methods and kept each other up-to-date. Oudart worked, like Pérignon, on perfecting production procedures, and the wines from his abbey, as far as quality was concerned, were often held in the same esteem as Dom Pérignon's wines. Brother Jean Oudart was sixteen years younger than Dom Pérignon and outlived him by twenty-seven years. As far as development goes these were very important years for champagne. Oudart experimented with sparkling wines, which turned out to be crucial for the future of this winegrowing region. Claude Taittinger divided the Benedictine monks of this time into conservatives and revolutionaries. He included Brother Jean Oudart in the latter group because he was the first Champagne cellarer to use *liqueur de tirage*, a blend of wine yeast and a little sugar. The reasons for this evolution were, first, the fierce competition of excellent wines from Burgundy and Bordeaux and, second, the increased demand for sparkling wines at this time, particularly from England. The progressive monk was also behind the trend of selling his wine in bottles instead of barrels. But the natural and chancy process of secondary fermentation evaded all forms of control for a long time. Another 150 years were to pass before the *méthode champenoise* was perfected.

The Mechanical Wine

THE BEGINNING OF the eighteenth century was the threshold between still *vin gris* and champagne as we know it today. Saint-Évremond, an ambassador of good taste, had introduced the still white wines of Champagne to England as early as 1661. He was appalled to discover that English wine merchants added a *liqueur de dosage* of cinnamon, cloves, sugar, and molasses to wines on decanting them from barrels to bottles. The English had discovered that when a *liqueur de dosage* was added to Champagne wines, which had a tendency to light effervescence anyway, the wines could be safely relied upon to produce the bubbles much loved in England, even after long storage periods. One of the most important prerequisites for this was sturdy bottles able to withstand the extreme forces of the secondary fermentation. In 1615 Admiral Sir Robert Mansell, concerned about timber supplies for shipbuilding, obtained a monopoly on the manufacture of glass.[11] In his factories coal was used instead of wood, which enabled furnaces to reach higher temperatures and produce glass that was stronger and more robust.[12] Between 1660 and 1670 the English succeeded in making a thick brown or green bottle glass from quartz sand. These bottles, made of *verre anglais*, "English glass," were just as essential to the production of sparkling wines as the stoppers made of Spanish or Portuguese cork, which were already common in England. The problem of bursting bottles, however, was not solved solely by stronger glass. In around 1840 the production of champagne was still a costly and, at times, dangerous business; breakages of 30 to 40 percent were by no means unusual.

To produce champagne you need a precisely calculated amount of sugar to get the desired carbon dioxide pressure during the secondary fermentation in the bottle. Today an enologist knows that 3.4 ounces of sugar in a gallon of wine creates a pressure of six atmospheres. However, these dependable figures were arrived at only in 1836—over one hundred years after Dom Pérignon's death—by a chemist named M. François from Châlons-sur-Marne. He succeeded in accurately determining the amount of sugar to add to the wine to achieve the *prise de mousse*, "effervescence." This procedure was first applied by Jean-Remy Moët. Eight years later Adolphe Jacquesson patented *muselet*, the wire muzzle that holds the cork in place.

Champagne bottles now contained monitored amounts of carbon dioxide and were firmly sealed, but the problem of what to do about the unwanted deposits of yeast that formed during the secondary fermentation, which could make champagne cloudy or even totally ruin it, still remained only partially solved. This sediment had initially been removed by decanting the contents several times—but there was a corresponding loss of liquids and fizz. The problem was then more effectively tackled with the development of *remuage*, "riddling," in 1816, thanks to the input of the Bavarian Antoine de Müller, who was on the staff of an almost legendary figure, Barbe-Nicole Ponsardin, a widow from the age of twenty-seven. Under the long-time direction of her husband and his father, the company had mainly been involved in banking and the wool trade, with the production of champagne as a small sideline. But after the sudden death of her husband the young widow had managed to persuade her father-in-law to sign over the company, even though she had never worked there. As her first official act she had renamed it Veuve ("widow" in French) Clicquot-Ponsardin and concentrated its activities on champagne production. In subsequent years she had turned the company into one of the most successful businesses of its time.

Trying to find a solution to the irritating problem of persistent cloudiness caused by yeast deposits, she and Antoine de Müller took an old kitchen table and drilled holes in the top at oblique angles, in which they placed champagne bottles upside down. At regular intervals they turned the bottles, agitating them slightly before replacing them, still neck down, in the hole until all the sediment had completely settled in the neck of the bottle. The bottle was then opened, the deposits ejected by a swift wrist movement, and then the bottle placed upright and corked.

They managed to keep the process secret until 1821, but afterwards it became standard practice in the cellars of Champagne. The problem that remained in 1844 was that a lot of champagne was still wasted in ejecting the sediment; the introduction of the *à la glace*, or disgorging, procedure in 1884 solved this. In this process a small amount of liquid in the neck of the bottle was frozen and then the plug containing the deposits was removed. Losses were reduced to about an ounce, which before the final corking was balanced out with a mixture of old wines and spices typical of the wine-house.

The Industrial Revolution didn't bypass the sacred cellars of the champagne-houses. All these individual operations were, in time, undertaken by machinery. Whether disgorged by hand or machine, champagne is subject to a high degree of physical influence. It is in this sense a mechanical wine.

"Du vin Brut? Vous buvez de ce poison-là?"

CHAMPAGNE WAS ALSO affected by the vagaries of culinary fashions and trends. Astonishingly it was the English market and its special demands on French producers that were of crucial importance in the emergence of the champagne we now enjoy. The English were probably the first to add a *tirage* to the wine and give it a bit of fizz. Later they were also the first to demand dry wine. But that took a long time. From the Middle Ages until the first half of the seventeenth century, they liked their Champagne wines to be slightly acidy and light, to which they added spices and sweetening agents to suit the tastes of the time, thereby almost accidentally discovering sparkling wine. Excess acids plus carbon dioxide upset the stomach, so they had to be balanced out with additional sugar. As a result the champagne of the eighteenth and nineteenth centuries was not dry but incredibly sweet.

A few figures illustrate this. *Brut*, the most popular category today, contains 1.3 ounces of sugar per gallon of wine, and *demi-sec* has a maximum of 6.7 ounces. In 1820 this was the drier end of the scale, and even then only for wines intended for the English market. In Germany the norm was 20 ounces per gallon, the French needed almost 27 ounces, and the particularly important Russian market demanded an incredible 33 to 40 ounces of sugar per gallon in their wine.

The Russian imperial family were among the most important customers of champagne. Whereas his predecessor allowed various champagne-houses to advertise with his patronage, Alexander II was vain enough to demand his own private cuvée. To honor him, Roederer created the famous Cristal, then and now the most expensive champagne. It was sold in a clear lead-crystal bottle and at that time was produced exclusively for the imperial household, and with a sugar content of 33 ounces per gallon it could hardly be termed dry. After Russia was connected to the European railway networks, Alexander had the champagne imported by the trainload. Even if the Romanovs were notoriously slow at settling accounts, it was still a booming business for Roederer—until the October Revolution. The dethroned tsar, Nicholas II, who was also fond of his champagne, had accumulated considerable debts up to his involuntary downfall. After his death the immense amount of champagne produced for the imperial household was too heavy and sweet to sell anywhere outside Russia. The Bolsheviks, as expected, refused to honor the debts. Only years later did Roederer manage to sell the excess production to South America.

In 1903 a British food writer and journalist reported:

As to the champagnes found abroad, unless they are specially made for the English market, they must not be judged from an English standpoint, being as a rule far too sweet for our taste. An instance of this occurred to me at Rheims, when staying with one of the champagne magnates for some shooting owned by a syndicate of some of the large champagne shippers. We met for *déjeuner* at their Chalet de Chasse or club-house, each gentleman bringing his own wine. The result was that one saw from ten to a dozen different famous brands of champagne on the table. My host asked me which sort I would prefer. "Du vin Brut, if you have any," I replied. "Ah! Vous buvez de ce poison-là?" exclaimed he, smiling.[13]

This anecdote fails to make the reprinted edition of 1921, from which we could assume that the French had altered their drinking habits in the meantime.

In 1848 an English wine merchant named Burne had asked the champagne-house Perrier-Jouët for a few crates of dry champagne and had encountered fierce resistance. The French simply didn't want to supply such an order, and when it was eventually delivered the English didn't want to drink it. Mr. Burne, however, stuck to his guns, and time proved him right. By 1885 at the latest, dry champagne was *en vogue* in England and had almost completely supplanted the sweeter version—a drinking fashion that was soon to grip the rest of Europe. English wine drinkers in particular have always had a high regard for mature champagnes. But only really dry wines can be stored for so long. The ageing process softens the acids and creates another fuller and rounder taste that can't be produced with additional sugars. The aromas of such perfectly developed champagnes are reminiscent of roses, vanilla, hazelnuts, or cookies and are often described using the charming adjective "beguiling." The culture of dry champagne thus enabled the emergence of an unusually harmonious wine that becomes round and full only with time.

Le Marketing: Spreading the Word

DURING THE NINETEENTH century the sales figures for champagne climbed from a couple hundred thousand bottles to 25 million. The railway networks crisscrossed Europe and the aristocracy appreciably lost power, but champagne conquered the disparate but larger market of the middle class. The global spread of this luxury article was unthinkable without the input of ingenious advertising, much of which is taken for granted today.

A swarm of representatives of the great names of champagne followed the troops of Napoleon on the campaigns from 1804 to 1814—eloquent, hard-drinking men who felt at home on the parquet floors of the rich or in the military encampments of the army, discrete and undemanding but with a cutthroat instinct for business opportunities. The wine author·Patrick Forbes noted, "No sooner was the battle won than the retinue arrived for the victory celebrations and a short while later the sales organizations were being set up in the conquered territory."[14] One of the most successful characters of this new species was Louis Bohne. He represented the interests of Veuve Clicquot and specialized in avoiding English naval blockades and all other forms of war-related import bans, in particular to Russia. He smuggled bottles of champagne in barrels of coffee beans, chartered a Dutch ship for transport, and accelerated the sales of his illegal wares by spreading the rumor in Königsberg that although his champagne was all as good as sold, something could be done in isolated cases. "Oh! Honoured Friend, what a spectacle," he wrote to Madame Clicquot, "and how I wish you were here to enjoy it. You have two-thirds of the best society of Königsberg at your feet over your nectar."[15] Hardly surprising, as the nectar was the legendary 1811 vintage, the Cuvée de la Comète, considered an exceptional wine influenced by the miraculous passage of the Great Comet of 1811.

Champagne and the New World

CHARLES-HENRI HEIDSIECK ALSO saw in the endless expanses of Russia a gigantic market for his house. He traveled two thousand miles on the back of his white stallion, followed by an entourage of packhorses, to draw attention to his product. His arrival in Moscow was a spectacular event and his ride, in terms of business, a colossal success.

His son, Charles-Camille, visited America, which until his arrival in 1852, with a few exceptions, was terra incognita for the champagne business. Heidsieck Jr. was enthusiastic about the New World, which welcomed him with open arms. The handsome, six-foot-two-inch Frenchman became a social attraction. At the very latest, when he returned for his second visit with an arsenal of the best hunting weapons, the rapture of the Americans and their willingness to order his sparkling wines knew no bounds. Newspapers constantly informed their avid readers about which balls he was attending or where he was about to set off on a buffalo-hunting expedition. His ascendency was abruptly halted by the onset of the Civil War. His New York agent refused him payment for thousands of bottles of champagne that had been delivered to the southern states. As justification he cited recently passed laws, intended to isolate the South economically, absolving all business liabilities. That was the end of Heidsieck's trading company. He decided to head south to try to reclaim the money owed to him, where he was promptly arrested for spying and imprisoned on a swampy fever-infested island in the middle of the Mississippi delta. The prison flooded regularly at high tide, and the prisoners had to ward off alligators with wooden planks. French diplomats pleaded with Abraham Lincoln for the release of "Champagne Charlie," and eventually after a number of months this was granted, and more dead than alive he left the southern US.

After six months of recuperation he was fit enough to return to France. His business was bankrupt, and his wife had spent the family fortune paying off outstanding debts. One evening a stranger knocked at the door. An old missionary who was visiting his family in France presented the astonished Heidsieck with a pile of deeds for land in Colorado and a letter. The letter was from the brother of his former agent in New York who was so ashamed about the immense debts that Heidsieck had been burdened with that he felt obliged to compensate for the swindle. The deeds were priceless. The land included about one-third of what is now Denver. Heidsieck sold the land and repaid his remaining debts, and within a few months his champagne-house was back in business.

Of High-Flying and Loose Women

"Burgundy makes you think of silly things, Bordeaux makes you talk of them and Champagne makes you do them."
JEAN-ANTHELME BRILLAT-SAVARIN[16]

IN 1888 THE French National Assembly permitted billboards in public places for the first time. The first lithograph poster was commissioned by the now gone wine-house France-Champagne and was designed by Pierre Bonnard. It depicted a libertine beauty in a loose dress holding a glass of champagne bubbling over the rim[17]—too frivolous for the Americans, who on the occasion of the World's Fair of 1889 in Paris made an official protest against the image of lascivious womanhood, to no avail.

196   The man who was fastest to jump on the advertising bandwagon was Eugène Mercier. He caused a sensation before an international group of spectators beneath the newly erected Eiffel Tower when he transported the world's biggest wine barrel

up the Champ de Mars on a wagon pulled by twenty-four white oxen. He founded his own champagne-house at twenty, and suddenly you could find his name not only on billboards but also on fountain pens, ice buckets, corkscrews, fans, lipsticks, and, finally, at the World's Fair of 1900, a huge anchored hot-air balloon. Twelve people could sip champagne in its gondola while enjoying a unique view of Paris. On November 14, 1900, a sudden gust of wind put an end to the spectacle. The balloon tore away from its anchorage and was driven towards Champagne together with its occupants, who to begin with were not particularly disturbed and continued to drink merrily. Only towards evening when they tried in vain to cast the on-board anchor did the passengers begin to shout for help from their lofty platform, which unfortunately was interpreted by those on the ground as the drunken high jinks of revelers and promptly ignored. The adventure ended after sixteen hours in a small Belgian wood. The police, rushing to the scene, presented Mercier with a fine for illegally importing alcohol. As a result of this episode his name became known throughout the world. "It's the cheapest publicity I ever got," commented the entrepreneur.[18]

Otto von Bismarck, chancellor of the German Empire and not particularly highly regarded in France, did make some friends in Champagne when he disappointed Kaiser Wilhelm II, with whom he had little sympathy, by demanding champagne at a state banquet instead of German sparkling wine. "My patriotism stops short of my stomach," he informed the kaiser.[19] In 1890 after two years of joint governance, Bismarck was removed from office. While the kaiser's grandfather virtually drank his way through Champagne and was nicknamed by his subjects "King Clicquot," Wilhelm II preferred only German brands. When his yacht, *Meteor*, was ready to be launched in 1904 in New York, it was German *sekt* that was supposed to be smashed on the bows. Shortly before the ceremony, however,

Georg Kessler, a particularly mischievous Moët & Chandon agent, managed, with a considerable amount of dexterity, to swap the *sekt* with a bottle of his own champagne. The kaiser, on hearing the news, was so furious that he ordered his ambassador back to Germany. The name Moët & Chandon, however, was in all the newspapers the next day.[20]

In France the Belle Époque had long since begun. The great fleshpots on the Place Pigalle made Paris indisputably the City of Love. To treat a lady to a glass of champagne was then, as today, a distinctly ambiguous offer, and it can't be denied that champagne is inextricably linked to loose women. They value it not only because it is pleasant to drink and moreish, but also because of the obvious esteem it affords in the eyes of an admirer. The rapid incipient effect of the alcohol also helps both sides to quickly become acquainted.

The future King of England, Edward VII, on visiting Paris in his carefree days, caroused with the girls of Le Chabanais, the most lavish bordello of its time, in a bath filled to the brim with champagne. For their erotic games they used a Victorian copper bath in the form of a sphinx, and after bathing they proceeded to drink the contents. In 1905 another establishment, the Moulin Rouge, employed the staggering total of 796 dancers, who were responsible for the sales of 14,795 bottles of champagne. In addition to these, 32,109 bottles were sold outside of the partitioned booths. Drinking vessels fashionable at the time were the *coupes de champagne*, shallow, wide-brimmed glasses that apparently sat in the hand like a woman's breast. This trend did not help the champagne as the bouquet and fizz dissipate more quickly than in the narrower flute glasses. Struggling artists like Henri de Toulouse-Lautrec and Gustav Klimt were inspired by Bonnard's poster and were commissioned by the great champagne-houses to create their own free-flowing images on posters and bottle labels.

The Prince of Wales

WE MOVE ON to the year 1935. In the fashionable bathing resort of Le Touquet-Paris-Plage on the French side of the English Channel, a couple in love sat in the bar of a grand hotel and toasted each other with long-stemmed silver chalices. Elegantly dressed and with a seemingly unlimited budget, and usually surrounded by the jet set, they were among the favorite guests of the barkeeper Jack van Land, and so he named his cocktail creation the PRINCE OF WALES after the first person to sample it.

Edward VIII, Prince of Wales, son of George V and heir to the English throne, remained untouched by the puritanical zeitgeist in his home country. He spent his days on cruises or on safaris, which were interrupted only by prolonged visits to Paris. He was a modern offspring of the English dynasty and dedicated to the good life; he held extravagant parties, loved horse racing, was the first English prince to fly, and, of course, had a weakness for beautiful women.

Since 1934 he had had a passionate affair with the American Wallis Simpson, which had been extensively followed by the international tabloids. Wallis was depicted as a dominant, socially ambitious woman and the crown prince as her lapdog. But in England the press had been muzzled. When in January 1936 George V suddenly died, Edward's carefree life was over, as was the restraint of the English press. There was public speculation about the future of the relationship between Edward and Wallis. It was out of the question for a monarch to marry a commoner who was surrounded by scandal and had been divorced twice. Edward had to choose between Wallis and the crown, and he brought the constitutional monarchy of England to the brink of crisis. He decided against duty and for love, abdicated after almost a year on the throne, and was downgraded to the Duke of Windsor.

199

Champagne, Turbulence in Terroir

NOW LET US return to Paris at the end of the nineteenth century. While loose women were bathing in champagne, the bad times were beginning for the winegrowers. Four-fifths of them owned only a little more than an acre of land each, which may have been spread over a number of slopes. The situation, despite the long distances between plots, was not as bad as it sounds, because if there was a sudden frost or a hailstorm it was unlikely that they would lose all of the crops that their families had tended for generations. They were, however, dependant on selling their wares to the champagne-houses, and the railways that had boosted the rise of Champagne were now to be the curse of the winegrowers. The great wine-houses of the north had begun organizing the transport of cheap grapes from the Loire and southern France. For the first time, in the fall of 1890, there were so many containers full of "foreign" grapes at the station at Épernay that the passengers had trouble getting to the trains. A number of the larger champagne-houses had formed a cartel. Overnight, prices fell by 50 percent. The following winter was cold and hard and wolf packs returned to prowl through the vineyards. Winegrowers and their families were starving. The commissioning agents who bought grapes for the champagne-houses mercilessly beat down the prices. Only 51 percent of the pressed grapes had to come from Champagne, and there was some doubt as to whether the remaining 49 percent had to have anything at all to do with grapes; some producers used apple or pear juice, others were seen buying bulk amounts of rhubarb. The trust between winegrowers and producers had been shaken. A further problem for winegrowers came in the form of the phylloxera louse. For a long time they had hoped that their location in the north and the high chalk content of their soils would spare them the plague.

200

The Ministry for Agriculture and a number of the large wine-houses had launched initiatives to treat vines, but they were rejected by the enraged winegrowers. They even suspected that the inspectors were behind the spread of phylloxera lice in the vineyards and drove them off with clubs.

The difficult situation also made the winegrowers turn on each other. The winegrowing region of Champagne had long consisted of the large department of Marne, some of the department of Aisne, and the smaller department of Aube. Now Marne insisted on being the sole producer allowed to use the name "champagne," and in 1908 they finally managed to convince Paris of their case. The department of Aube was in uproar. Under their leader, the five-foot-tall Gaston Cheq, a crowd of forty thousand farmers armed with hoes gathered at the seat of the regional government in Troyes for an impressive and generally peaceful demonstration. Their arguments were heard, and in 1910 the senate recommended the reinclusion of Aube in the Champagne region. The news reached the telegraph offices of the department of Marne at 5 p.m., and by 9 p.m. the winegrowers and their families had stormed out onto the streets with axes, hatchets, and sharpened mattocks. They attacked the cellars of the large champagne-houses and plundered the estates of the owners and razed them to the ground. Towards morning a huge mob of ten thousand set off towards Épernay. They halted trains, upturned trucks, and attacked wine-houses. Confronted in Épernay by the army, the mob headed off towards Aÿ. Further wine-houses fell and cellars were destroyed; smashed barrels lay on the asphalt next to account books soaked in spilled wine, its vapors filling the streets. The cavalry tried to stop the pillagers, who reacted by chopping down telegraph poles and using the cables to hinder the progress of the riders along the roads. Stones and bottles were thrown, and the rioters took refuge in the wine merchants' tunnels, which riddled Aÿ like the holes in a rabbit warren. In neighboring vineyards the straw that was to protect vines from frost was set alight. Forty buildings, including six wine-houses, were completely destroyed and set ablaze. In the streets, rivers of the finest wines caused the drains to overflow while the rioters drank the champagne that the wine-houses were not supposed to sell. After twenty-four hours the riot was over. The anger of the winegrowers about price-fixing and corrupt commissioning agents, their despair after a series of bad harvests, and the threat from pests had been given an outlet. All of France was shocked.

The Champagne region was placed under military administration. However, there were still no legally binding definitions of what constituted the wine and the winegrowing area. In 1914, just as voting was beginning on a draft version submitted to the Chamber of Deputies, news arrived of the assassination of Franz Ferdinand in Sarajevo. The appellation of Champagne was only clearly defined in 1919, and the addition of foreign grapes, apples, or rhubarb was forbidden.

A Wine in the Trenches: The First World War

"In the little moment that remains to us between the crisis and the catastrophe, we may as well drink a glass of champagne."
PAUL CLAUDEL[21]

ON SEPTEMBER 18, 1914, Reims shook from the shelling of German artillery. The city had been spared the first few months of the war, but the cathedral, which for centuries had been the setting of coronations of emperors and kings, had now become the main objective of the bombardment. One of the first hits decapitated the smiling angel, one of the most famous sculptures on the facade of this richly decorated building. Thousands of squawking birds, ravens, crows, and pigeons living in the roof of the cathedral swarmed and circled above the catastrophe. Blocks of masonry cascaded down on the wounded who had sought refuge in the emergency hospital set up in the cathedral. Massive stone blocks buried doctors, nurses, and assistants, as well as priests rushing to save relics and diamond-studded coronation jewelry from the inferno. Incendiary bombs set alight the straw on which the wounded were lying, the fire quickly spreading to wooden pillars and roof timbers. With an almighty crash the great bells plummeted to the ground. The lead roof melted, transforming the outer statues and gargoyles into weird stalactites before the entire roof construction eventually collapsed. A sea of molten lead gushed into the ruins of the nave and transept. Four hundred buildings in the vicinity of the cathedral fell victim to the now-spreading conflagration. It was the first of the 1,050 days of bombardment that Reims was to suffer in the course of the next three and a half years. The inhabitants fled from the inferno into the *crayères* (chalk tunnels) that form a sometimes multilayered 150-mile network below the city and large parts of the region. Originally they were subterranean chalk quarries worked by Roman slaves; when the monks rediscovered them, they extended the tunnels as ideal storage space for wine. Now they were refuge to twenty thousand people escaping the nonstop pounding. What they didn't realize was that, for many of them, underground life would last for up to two years, a surreal shadow realm existing below the burning city. Hospitals, police stations, schools, gyms, and all sorts of trades—cobblers, clockmakers, butchers, bakers, and, of course, candlestick makers—were all relocated belowground. Six cows kept near the schools provided children with fresh milk. There were even cafés and opera, cinema, and theatre performances. A role in one of these subterranean performances became a patriotic honor for French actors. The Veuve Clicquot house held a champagne dinner in one of its tunnels for a couple hundred severely disabled war veterans. "Those who still had legs danced and champagne helped even those who were terribly disfigured to rekindle their spirits," commented one of those present.[22] Families who had managed to escape belowground tried to create a semblance of privacy among the riddling racks and shelves laden with wine. "We lived and slept among the bottles," one of them recollected.[23] Not everyone inhabiting the tunnels had as much respect for the contents. At the Pommery depot alone, 300,000 bottles quietly disappeared while soldiers were billeted there.

In local vineyards, as if in defiance of war, grapes of excellent quality were ripening in the fall of 1914. But a harvest in the middle of a war seemed impossible. The only available workforce for the heavy work consisted of the elderly, women, and children; the majority of men—and horses—were required at the front. Barrels, sugar, and money were in short supply. All telephones and telegraphs had either been destroyed or impounded by the military. Maurice Pol-Roger, the mayor of Épernay, however, was firmly committed to harvesting the crop. As it seemed futile to transport the grapes to the champagne-houses, he decided to bring the barrels, the grape presses, and all the other equipment from one vineyard to the next with a mobile task force, press the grapes on-site, and deposit the wine during the first fermentation at nearby farmhouses. During lulls in combat the wine would then be transported to the wine cellars, a complicated project that required the logistics of a minor campaign. Pol-Roger set up a system of runners and bike riders to keep communication channels open between all participants, and they succeeded in gathering 50 percent of the harvest. The later-famous 1914 vintage, as he expected, turned out to be an excellent wine. The first harvest of the war had its casualties. Time and again workers and transporters were attacked from the air. Soldiers helping out with the harvest, many women, and at least twenty children died for this vintage.

After unexpected advances deep into France, the Germans were forced back and the front ground to a halt in Champagne of all places. While previous wars were characterized by great battles with winners and losers, the First World War brought with it an ill-fated innovation—trench warfare. There were no winners, only losers enduring hunger, mud, disease, and death. The trenches stretched for five hundred miles from the Swiss border to the North Sea, and in them were millions of soldiers from both sides. In Champagne the trenches cut through the vineyards, which in winter turned into a grey, sticky, muddy version of hell. Some trenches collapsed, burying soldiers in the morass. In more than three years the lines did not alter much, and the trenches turned into rank cesspits teeming in lice, rats, and all sorts of other pests.

In violation of the Hague Convention the German military command ordered the use of toxic gases from 1915, and the war reached new, appalling dimensions. Vines were just as much affected as the soldiers, the drifting clouds of mustard gas and other killing agents defoliating the plants and contaminating the soil for years to come.

Almost all the great champagne-houses suffered considerable damage. Pommery and Lanson were razed to the ground. Moët & Chandon was almost completely destroyed, along with Napoleon's private hotel. Roederer and Ruinart were also hit hard. They were devastated by not only the destruction of their buildings and vineyards but also the collapse of sales markets for their bottles, which were still safely stored in their cellars. They discovered and courted a new form of clientele—the fighting troops and the French domestic market. Up until that time, French drinking habits were closely linked to their own particular regional winegrowing areas, but then the drinking of champagne became a patriotic gesture of an unbroken spirit. The cuvées were given names like Gloire française and Champagne anti-boche, as well as names honoring the Allies such as Champagne America and even the slightly long-winded Alliance Creaming Tommy's Special Dry Reserve. The Germans, too, ordered contingents of the famous sparkling wine through neutral intermediaries in Holland and Switzerland. Somehow the champagne-houses managed to survive. Four other vintages took place under the hail of bullets.

On July 14, 1918, the Germans launched a final assault in an attempt to reach Paris via Reims and failed. In November they signed a ceasefire agreement and seven months later the peace treaty.

All over France the corks popped. In Paris, at the Place de l'Opéra, fifty thousand sang "La Marseillaise," and at the Champs-Élysées a crowd gathered in the flush of victory. But this euphoria was tempered by the grim realization that 1.5 million French soldiers had died and 3 million were wounded, of which 1 million would remain permanently disabled. Champagne had lost half its population, some departments even two-thirds. The wine villages lay in ruins and forests had disappeared. Forty percent of the winegrowing areas ceased to exist; forty thousand acres had been so contaminated by toxic gases and bodies that they were declared red zones and cultivation was prohibited. Another bitter realization awaited the troubled winegrowers. An even older enemy than the Germans had performed well in the intervening years; the phylloxera louse had infested almost all vineyards. Only after reaching this low point could the great champagne-houses assert themselves and implement a replanting program with resistant American vines.

Les Années folles, the "Crazy Years," of the Roaring Twenties began. But the champagne-houses allowed themselves only a brief respite. The Russian market had disappeared because of the revolution, and the Americans had introduced Prohibition. A wave of pleasure-seeking emigrants flooded into a Paris swimming in champagne, and in their wake they brought jazz.

Pick Me Up

THE PICK ME UP, also known as Harry's Pick Me Up, was created in the 1920s by the celebrated barkeeper Harry MacElhone. Born in 1890 as the son of a Scottish jute-mill owner, he surfaced on the French Riviera in 1910, where he made a name for himself in the exclusive resort hotels. It was here that he was recruited by Tod Sloan, an American jockey, and his partner, Clancy, who were planning to open an American bar in Paris. Clancy had previously run a bar in downtown Manhattan. He had the bar, the mahogany paneling, and all the furniture shipped to Paris, and on November 26, 1911, they opened the New York Bar. MacElhone worked there for a couple of weeks before landing behind the bar of the Oak Room at the Plaza Hotel in New York. Later he transferred to Ciro's in London, at that time the rendezvous of the smart set and the trendiest dance club in Europe. In 1923 he returned to Paris and took over Sloan's and Clancy's bar, renaming it Harry's New York Bar. The well-established bar was a favorite meeting place for racehorse owners and the racing fraternity in general. After being taken over by MacElhone it became the favored meeting place for overseas Americans—artists, writers, musicians, and journalists who had fled to Europe to avoid Prohibition. In

1922, 36,000 Americans were living in exile, the strong dollar enabling them to live a Bohemian lifestyle.

For many years the Paris edition of the *Herald Tribune* carried regular ads with the phonetic version of the bar's address, "Sank Roo Doe Noo" (5, Rue Daunou), to assist freshly arriving Americans to reach his establishment.

The list of famous patrons is long, including F. Scott Fitzgerald, Noël Coward, Sinclair Lewis, Jack Dempsey, and George Gershwin, who composed parts of *An American in Paris* there. One of the bar's most loyal guests was Ernest Hemingway, who had lived in Paris since 1921 and was a close friend of MacElhone. They both had children of the same age who used to play together while their fathers went to the boxing club to train. In the 1920s Harry's Bar was the birthplace of many immortal cocktails, such as the BLOODY MARY, SIDECAR, WHITE LADY, and FRENCH 75. The very first hotdog in France was served there. The bar survived the Great Depression, the German occupation, and the economic recovery of the 1950s intact. After almost a hundred years you can still recapture some of the cosmopolitan atmosphere of Paris of the Roaring Twenties in a setting that has remained almost unaltered at Sank Roo Doe Noo.

IBF

AT FIRST GLANCE the recipe for this drink may appear somewhat unusual. In fact the IBF is a worthwhile, although slightly old-fashioned, mixture of cognac, triple sec, and a dash of fernet menta, topped up with champagne.

Its name and history again lead us back to Harry's New York Bar. In 1924 a group of hard-drinking American journalists met there. They planned an extensive drinking tour in the surrounding neighborhood including the Ritz Bar, the Pigalle, and a number of other stops, and so as not to lose sight of each other they came up with a rather quirky means of identification. A pin depicting a dead fly on a sugar cube was attached to the lapel of each participant. The group was initially called the Paris Barflies, which Harry and his friend, the journalist O. O. McIntyre, renamed the Brotherhood of International Bar Flies, subsequently abbreviated to IBF.

The strict conditions for joining and the secret rituals, with a newsletter every six months providing insider tips on the best bars—also called "watering holes" or "fly-traps"—made the club into an exclusive male domain. Ernest Hemingway, Burt Lancaster, George Carpenter, and even Teddy Roosevelt were all IBF members at some stage. In 1944 women were also granted membership, and female members included Marlene Dietrich and Coco Chanel.

Since the opening of Harry's Bar branches in Montreux, Munich, and Berlin, the number of bars generally and the complexity of the drinking community have grown, making it necessary to return to secret ceremonies to discover whether or not the person sitting next to you is indeed a member of the IBF.

Here is what you do: Smile at your neighbor and approach him or her, and go through the motions of swirling a brandy glass in your left hand. Then brush an imaginary fly off his or her shoulder with your right hand; if your suspect is an IBF member he or she will return the gesture. After a firm handshake both parties raise their right leg about eight inches off the ground and make a buzzing sound like a big, fat bluebottle.

A Cure for What Ails You

JUST AS PEOPLE were coming to terms with the consequences of the First World War, the Great Depression loomed. In the Champagne region, one excellent harvest followed the next.

The cellars were full to capacity, and 150 million bottles awaited delivery. The problem was a distinct lack of solvent purchasers. Again commercial agents traveled to America, where there were signs that Prohibition was coming to an end. With missionary zeal they extolled the healthy properties of their champagne. If they were to be believed, this sparkling wine was an all-round remedy, good against depression, appendicitis, and typhoid. Marshal Pétain, the commander-in-chief of the French Army, had emphasized the importance of champagne for morale and the courage of his troops during the First World War in the preface of a book on champagne with the exuberant title *Mon Docteur le Vin*.[24] And as the knight in shining armor, the champagne-houses rediscovered the man who at the beginning of the 1930s had been lost in the mists of time: Dom Pérignon. Eighteen years earlier, in 1915, they had tried to celebrate the two hundredth anniversary of his death with moderate success, and now in 1933, in the freshly renovated Hautvillers Abbey, a three-day festival was organized and dedicated to the 250th anniversary of Dom Pérignon's "invention" of bubbly champagne.[25] Champagne flowed in streams, and it didn't seem to bother anybody that genuine credit to the modest and industrious monk was washed away in a flood of marketing ideas. His name was flaunted on advertising billboards, road signs, and even the advertising bands of a particular brand of cigar. Moët & Chandon acquired the rights to the name and even today markets the prestige cuvée, Dom Pérignon.

Reserved for the German Armed Forces

SPREADING FASCISM IN Europe spoiled much of the celebration, and when in 1940 the Germans again occupied France it was only the Nazis who had reasons to drink champagne. After stealing 2 million bottles on their way to Paris, the Germans appointed Otto Klaebisch as *weinführer* in Champagne. Attempts by the French in the early days of occupation to hoodwink the Germans with cheap sparkling wine were no longer possible with Klaebisch. He had grown up in a wine-trading family and was brother-in-law to the German foreign minister, Joachim von Ribbentrop, who in turn had previously been a wine salesman for Kessler, a sparkling wine producer based in Rhineland. So the French champagne-houses were dealing with a *weinführer* who was an acknowledged expert and who treated Hitler's enemies unflinchingly and ruthlessly. The champagne-houses were forcibly placed under German administration. Sales were allowed only after consultation with the occupying forces. Most of the produce was stamped with an additional label, "Réservé à la Wehrmacht." Klaebisch decided the price that the wine merchants had to pay, and defiance was met with threats of abduction and forced labor. Count Robert-Jean de Vogüé, chairman of the local wine producers' collective and head of Moët & Chandon, together with his brother Bertrand de Vogüé, general director at Veuve Clicquot, were to suffer this destiny. Despite all the persecutions, Champagne became a center of French resistance, and again the *crayères* played a crucial role in wartime events. The underground tunnels were used as an arsenal by the resistance and for clandestine meetings. Allied pilots who had been shot down sought refuge there, with messengers conveying intelligence throughout the apparently endless network.

The Allied landing at Normandy was the beginning of the end of the war. The Champagne region had survived with fewer losses than in the previous war, and like all victories it had to be celebrated.

211

Champagne, Inc.: Sparkling Wine as a Global Player

TODAY THERE ARE still fifteen thousand winegrowers working on the almost 84,000 acres of land in the Champagne region. The numbers swell to 100,000 during the annual *vendange* (harvest), with the support of a host of grape pickers, back-basket carriers, loaders, and pressers. In 2011 over 323 million bottles with a value of US$6.2 billion left the cellars. Great Britain is still the main customer of this exclusive product. While the demands of the Anglo-Saxon market forced the trend for drier champagnes in the nineteenth century, producers are now reacting to an increased interest in rosé champagnes. Conventional rosé wines stem from red grapes whose maceration is interrupted when it has reached the desired color, and this is mainly governed by the grape skins. There are risks involved, as interrupting the process at the wrong time can badly affect profit margins. Rosé champagne producers, however, are permitted to mix prepressed regional red wines. One of the strictest wine regulations in the world offers greater freedom to producers of rosé champagne than to normal wine producers.

Even the area allowed for cultivation, strictly and clearly defined since 1927, will alter in the future. Since 2003 there have been moves for an expansion. At the same time, the existing 280,000 plots—after almost ninety years of cultivation as monocultures and the associated erosion and, in some cases, liberal use of pesticides—are being checked to see whether they even retain the mineral qualities demanded of a basis wine from Champagne.

The density of the grapevines in Champagne is considerably greater than in every other winegrowing area in the world. Paradoxically this has more of an effect on the quality than the quantity. The intense struggle for water and nutrients near the climatic boundary for growing vines forces the roots of densely planted vines to go deep into the light, chalky soil. The result is fewer, but high-grade, grapes full of minerals from the underlying rock strata. The price for one pound of these grapes lies between US$3.60 and US$3.70, albeit at the wholesale markets where the champagne-houses buy their stocks.

Monopolies and globalization have not spared champagne. For a long time now most of the great champagne-houses have operated under the aegis of luxury companies. In the meantime Dom Pérignon, Moët & Chandon, Veuve Clicquot, Ruinart, Mercier, and Krug belong to LVMH (Moët Hennesey Louis Vuitton), which in addition to selling exclusive spirits also has interests in the global market for fashion, handbags, and cosmetics.

On top of its traditional strengths in brut, demi-sec, rosé, and vintage champagnes, the company's marketing strategies are increasingly turning towards prestige cuvées. Here is what Stephan Holst from Maison des Champagnes, which over the last twenty years has offered one of the widest ranges of champagnes in Germany, has to say about the situation:

> You have to be absolutely clear that champagne, per se, is an exclusive, inimitable product that can be produced nowhere else in the world. I have experienced a number of German wine producers who have failed in attempting to copy champagne. You don't have to like it but you have to acknowledge its uniqueness. I have noticed a slow eroding of the middle classes. Customers who previously ordered a case of champagne for birthdays or anniversaries have switched to crémant or other sparkling wines. Parallel to this there has been an increase worldwide in the number of people with so much money that they don't know what to do with it and, figuratively, could even brush their teeth with Dom Pérignon. It is for this group that the prestige cuvées are being produced.

213

You can buy an outstanding Grand Cru champagne in a liquor store for about 26 euros [US$33]. After six further years of storage and without any real shift in quality of the contents it can be sold as a prestige cuvée for 145 euros [US$185] and this difference makes the people at Moët, among others, very happy.[26]

The fact that the profits of champagne producers are increasingly disproportionate to production seems to prove him right.

But serious investors still have to bring not only money with them, but also patience and expertise. Making a quick buck with a luxury product like champagne is not an option. Its sales figures react like a seismograph to every financial crash and every depression, globally. Those who invest in champagne must be able to think in decades or they will go under—the numerous major investors who have failed are testimony to this. In 2005 the traditional champagne-house Taittinger was acquired by the American Starwood Capital Group, which mostly dealt with hotels and resorts. A short time later, new economy stocks fell on global exchanges. After only two years the exasperated Americans threw in the towel. Pierre-Emmanuel Taittinger managed to unite the quarreling factions of heirs and, with the assistance of Crédit Agricole, brought the champagne-house back into family ownership.

An increasing number of winegrowers, most of them young, are no longer content to sell their grapes or basis wines to the larger champagne-houses, choosing instead to produce their own individual champagnes with some of their harvests. Freed from the demands of making immense quantities of wine with a standardized taste year after year, they produce champagnes that vary substantially in taste according to particular vintages or storage conditions. Even genuine champagnes following the strictures of the wine regulations are increasingly being produced, and real discoveries can be made for moderate prices.

Whether as the crowning moment of a completed business deal or a comfort in times of depression, the excuses for the pleasures of champagne are manifold. The search for a pretext shouldn't be taken too seriously and is probably best formulated by Lily Bollinger:

> I drink champagne when I am happy and when I am sad. Sometimes I drink it when alone. In company I consider it compulsory. I sip a little if I'm hungry. Otherwise I don't touch it—unless I'm thirsty of course.[27]

COCKTAIL RECIPES

EGGNOG (p.3)

2 oz brandy or other dark spirit

1 egg yolk

1/3 to 3/4 oz simple syrup

1 1/2 to 3 oz milk

Pinch of freshly ground nutmeg as garnish

Pour the brandy, egg yolk, simple syrup, and milk into a shaker with ice cubes and shake vigorously for 30 seconds. Strain into a large ice-filled glass and garnish with freshly ground nutmeg.

RÜDESHEIM COFFEE (p.3)

1 1/3 oz Asbach Uralt

Cup of sweet filter coffee

Sweetened whipped cream

Chocolate chips as garnish

Heat the Asbach Uralt, then mix it into the coffee. Add a generous dollop of sweetened whipped cream on top and garnish with chocolate chips.

SIDECAR (p.5)

1 1/2 oz cognac

1/2 oz orange triple sec

1/2 oz fresh lemon juice

Pour all ingredients into a shaker with ice cubes and shake well for 30 seconds. Strain into a pre-cooled cocktail or coupette glass.

BRANDY ALEXANDER (p.5)

1 1/3 oz brandy

3/4 oz white crème de cacao

1/3 oz cream

Freshly ground nutmeg as garnish

Pour the brandy, crème de cacao, and cream into a shaker with ice cubes and shake well for 30 seconds. Strain into a precooled cocktail or coupette glass and garnish with freshly ground nutmeg.

CHAMPAGNE COCKTAIL (p.5)

2 to 3 drops angostura

1 sugar cube

2 to 3 oz champagne

Orange and/or lemon zest

Put 2 to 3 drops of angostura onto a sugar cube and place it in a champagne flute, then fill the flute with champagne. Squeeze orange and/or lemon zest above the drink so that the essential oils coat the surface.

PISCO SOUR (p.18)

2 oz pisco

¾ oz triple sec

1 ⅓ oz fresh lime juice

1 egg white

Dash of gomme syrup

Slice of lime and angostura
as garnish

Pour the pisco, triple sec, lime juice, egg white, and gomme syrup into a shaker with ice cubes and shake well for 40 seconds. Strain the mixture into a tumbler with ice cubes or crushed ice, and garnish with a slice of lime and a couple of drops of angostura.

LUMUMBA (p.32)

1 ½ oz brandy

1 bar spoon (or 1 tsp) of cocoa

⅓ oz dark crème de cacao

5 oz milk

Pour all ingredients into a shaker with ice cubes and shake well for 20 seconds. Strain into a tumbler or a highball glass with ice cubes.

BLOODY MARY (p.208)

1 ½ oz vodka

⅓ oz lemon juice

Dashes of Worcestershire sauce, Tabasco, and freshly ground black pepper

5 oz tomato juice

Celery stick as garnish

Place the vodka, lemon juice, Worcestershire, Tabasco, pepper, and tomato juice into a large tumbler or highball glass, with or without ice cubes, and stir. Garnish with a celery stick.

MOSCOW MULE (p.38)

2 to 2 ½ oz ginger-infused vodka

3 to 5 oz ginger beer

Dash of lemon juice

Finely sliced cucumber as garnish

Pour the vodka and ginger beer into a tumbler, or traditionally into a copper beaker, and stir. The modern version includes a dash of lemon juice and a couple of fine slices of cucumber.

MANHATTAN (p.78)

2 oz rye whiskey

¾ oz vermouth

2 to 3 drops angostura

Cocktail cherry with stem as garnish

Pour the rye whiskey, vermouth, and angostura into an ice-filled mixing glass and stir. Strain the mixture into a precooled cocktail or coupette glass, and garnish with a cocktail cherry.

OLD-FASHIONED (p.77)

1 to 2 dashes of gomme or simple syrup

3 to 5 drops angostura or other bitters

2 ½ to 3 oz good bourbon or other mature spirit

Orange and/or lemon zest (optional)

Cocktail cherry with stem as garnish

Pour the gomme or simple syrup, angostura, and ½ oz of the spirit into a glass and stir well. Add ice and the remaining 2 to 2 ½ oz of spirits, and stir this mixture well for at least 40 seconds. The drink can be additionally flavored with the essential oils of orange and/or lemon peel by zesting the fruit above the glass. Garnish with a cocktail cherry.

BRANDY CRUSTA (p.78)

Orange wedge

Caster sugar

3 oz brandy

Dash of angostura, maraschino, Cointreau, and/or chocolate bitters

1/3 to 3/4 oz lemon juice (optional)

Orange peel as garnish

Moisten the rim of a wineglass with a wedge of orange and dip the rim in caster sugar to form the *crusta*. Then fill the glass with ice cubes and the brandy and flavor as desired with dashes of angostura, maraschino, Cointreau, and/or chocolate bitters, and stir the mixture in the glass. If it seems too sweet or too strong, add lemon juice. Garnish with an orange peel.

JAPANESE COCKTAIL (p.78)

2 oz cognac

1/4 oz orgeat

3 dashes angostura

Pour all ingredients into an ice-filled mixing glass and stir. Strain the mixture into a pre-cooled cocktail or coupette glass.

EAST INDIA COCKTAIL (p.78)

2 oz cognac

1/4 oz maraschino

1/4 oz curaçao

1 dash pineapple syrup

2 dashes angostura

Pour all ingredients into an ice-filled mixing glass and stir. Strain the mixture into a pre-cooled cocktail or coupette glass.

SAZERAC (p.78)

1 to 2 dashes gomme or
simple syrup

3 to 5 dashes Peychaud's bitters

1 bar spoon (or 1 tsp) absinthe

2 ½ to 3 oz rye whiskey

Lemon zest (optional)

Cocktail cherry with stem
as garnish

Pour the gomme or simple syrup, Peychaud's bitters, absinthe, and ½ oz of the rye whiskey into a mixing glass and stir well. Add ice and the remaining 2 to 2 ½ oz of rye, and stir for at least 40 seconds. Strain into a precooled coupette glass. The drink can be additionally flavored with the essential oils of lemon zest squeezed above the glass. Garnish with a cocktail cherry.

GREENPOINT (p.79)

2 oz rye whiskey

1 oz Punt e Mes

3 drops angostura

⅛ oz green or yellow chartreuse

Pour all ingredients into an ice-filled mixing glass and stir. Strain into a precooled cocktail or coupette glass.

BENSONHURST (p.79)

2 oz rye whiskey

1 oz Noilly Prat

¼ oz maraschino

1 bar spoon (or 1 tsp) cynar

Pour all ingredients into an ice-filled mixing glass and stir. Strain into a precooled cocktail or coupette glass.

RED HOOK (p.79)

2 oz rye whiskey

½ oz Punt e Mes

½ oz maraschino

Cocktail cherry with stem as garnish

Pour the rye whiskey, Punt e Mes, and maraschino into an ice-filled mixing glass and stir. Strain into a precooled cocktail or coupette glass, and garnish with a cocktail cherry.

GROG (p.95)

1 ⅓ to 2 oz rum

Hot water

Sugar (optional)

Spices (nutmeg, cinnamon, and/or cardamom) or lemon juice

Measure the rum into a heat-resistant mug and fill with hot water. Flavor with sugar, spices, and/or lemon juice as desired.

JULEP (p.79)

⅓ oz gomme or simple syrup

4 sprigs mint

3 oz spirit of choice

Lightly muddle the mint with the gomme or simple syrup and the chosen spirit and leave for a few minutes to marry the flavors. Strain the mixture into a silver julep cup or a highball glass filled with crushed ice.

SHARK'S TOOTH (p.110)

1 ½ oz dark rum

⅓ oz lime juice

⅓ oz lemon juice

⅓ oz grenadine

Club soda

Pour all ingredients into an ice-filled tumbler or highball glass and stir. Top up with soda.

ZOMBIE (p.110)

2 oz dark rum

¾ oz white rum

¾ oz cherry Heering

¾ oz curaçao

¾ oz grenadine

2 oz blood-orange juice

¾ oz overproof rum

Orange wedge as garnish

Pour all ingredients except the overproof rum and orange wedge into a shaker, shake well, and strain into a large highball glass filled with ice cubes or crushed ice. Float the overproof rum onto the mixture using an upturned spoon, then garnish with an orange wedge.

DR. FUNK (p.110)

2 oz dark rum

⅓ oz lemon juice

⅓ oz lime juice

⅓ oz grenadine

¼ oz absinthe

2 oz club soda

Pour all ingredients into a shaker, shake well, and strain into a tumbler or highball glass filled with ice cubes. Top up with soda.

SCORPION (p.112)

2 oz dark Jamaican rum

1/3 to 3/4 oz passion-fruit syrup

3/4 oz lemon juice

2 oz orange juice

Orange peel as garnish

Pour all liquid ingredients into a shaker, shake well, and strain into a large highball glass filled with ice cubes or crushed ice. Garnish with an orange peel.

SAMOAN FOG CUTTER (p.112)

2 oz dark rum

3/4 oz white rum

1/2 oz gin

1/2 oz brandy

2 oz lemon juice

1 oz orange juice

1/3 oz cream sherry

Orange wedge as garnish

Pour all ingredients except the sherry and orange wedge into a shaker, shake well, and strain into a large highball glass filled with ice cubes or crushed ice. Float the sherry onto the mixture using an upturned spoon, then garnish with an orange wedge.

MISSIONARY'S DOWNFALL (p.112)

2 oz white rum

1/2 oz peach brandy

3/4 oz lemon juice

1/3 oz simple syrup

2 oz pineapple juice

Sprig of mint as garnish

Pour all liquid ingredients into a shaker, shake well, and strain into a large highball glass filled with ice cubes or crushed ice. Garnish with a sprig of mint.

MAI TAI (p.112)

2 oz dark Jamaican rum

3/4 oz overproof rum

3/4 oz dry orange curaçao

1 oz orgeat

1 oz Rose's lime cordial

2 1/2 oz lemon juice

Sprig of mint as garnish

Pour all liquid ingredients into a shaker, shake well, and strain into a large highball glass filled with ice cubes or crushed ice. Garnish with a sprig of mint.

CUBA LIBRE (p.116)

4 slices of lime

1 1/2 oz white Cuban rum

5 oz cola

Squeeze the lime slices, then pour all ingredients into a highball glass and stir.

DAIQUIRI (p.116)

1 1/2 oz white Cuban rum

3/4 to 1 oz lime juice

1/2 oz simple syrup

Pour all ingredients into a shaker with ice cubes and shake well for 30 seconds. Strain the mixture into a precooled cocktail or coupette glass.

PAPA DOBLE (p.117)

1 ½ oz white Cuban rum
½ oz maraschino
¾ oz lime juice
¾ oz grapefruit juice, or ¼ of a peeled grapefruit for the frozen version

Pour all ingredients into a shaker with ice cubes and shake well for 30 seconds. Strain the mixture into a precooled cocktail or coupette glass. For the frozen version, pour all ingredients (substituting grapefruit segments for the grapefruit juice) into a blender together with a scoop of crushed ice and purée.

LA FLORIDITA DAIQUIRI (p.117)

1 ½ oz white Cuban rum
⅓ oz maraschino
⅓ oz lime juice
⅓ oz grapefruit juice

Pour all ingredients into a shaker with ice cubes and shake well for 30 seconds. Strain the mixture into a precooled cocktail or coupette glass. For the frozen version, pour all ingredients into a blender together with a scoop of crushed ice and purée.

FROZEN DAIQUIRI (p.117)

Pour daiquiri ingredients into a blender with a scoop of crushed ice and purée.

DRY MARTINI (p.129)

⅓ to 1 oz Noilly Prat

2 oz gin

2 dashes bitters

Olive or lemon zest as garnish

Pour the Noilly Prat, gin, and bitters into an ice-filled mixing glass and stir. Strain into a precooled cocktail or coupette glass, and garnish with an olive or lemon zest.

GIN AND FRENCH (p.131)

1 ½ oz gin

1 ½ oz Noilly Prat

Pour the ingredients into an ice-filled mixing glass and stir. Strain into a precooled cocktail or coupette glass.

GIN AND IT (p.131)

1 ½ oz gin

1 ½ oz carpano

Pour the ingredients into an ice-filled mixing glass and stir. Strain into a precooled cocktail or coupette glass.

GIN AND TONIC (p.147)

1 ½ oz gin

5 oz tonic

Wedge or slice of lemon as garnish

Pour the gin and tonic into a highball glass filled with ice cubes and stir. Garnish with a wedge or slice of lemon on the rim of the glass.

PINK GIN (p.143)

⅓ oz angostura

2 ½ oz gin

Pour the ingredients into an ice-filled mixing glass and stir. Strain into a precooled cocktail or coupette glass.

BLUE BLAZER (p.146)

2 oz overproof whisky

⅓ oz simple syrup

3 to 5 oz boiling water

Pour the whisky and simple syrup into one heat-proof mug with a handle and the boiling water into another. Carefully ignite the whisky and pour it into the hot water. Then pour the flaming whisky-water mixture into the empty mug and repeat the procedure, pouring the liquid back and forth with ever-increasing arcs. If there are problems with the flames, reduce the amount of water.

GIMLET (p.151)

2 oz gin

½ oz Rose's lime cordial

Wedge of lime

Lime zest

Pour the gin and lime cordial into an ice-filled mixing glass and stir. Squeeze the lime wedge into the mixture and stir. Strain into a precooled cocktail or coupette glass and sprinkle with lime zest.

VESPER (LYND) (p.152)

1 1/2 oz gin

1/2 oz vodka

1/3 oz Kina Lillet

Lemon zest

Pour the liquid ingredients into an ice-filled mixing glass and stir. Strain into a precooled cocktail or coupette glass and sprinkle with lemon zest.

KAMIKAZE (p.153)

2 oz vodka

1/2 oz triple sec

1/2 oz Rose's lime cordial

Large wedge of lime

Place all ingredients into an ice-filled mixing glass and stir. Strain into a precooled cocktail or coupette glass or a tumbler with ice cubes.

COSMOPOLITAN (p.153)

2 oz vodka

1/4 oz Cointreau

Large wedge of lime

1 oz cranberry juice

Place all ingredients into an ice-filled mixing glass and stir. Strain into a precooled cocktail or coupette glass.

PRINCE OF WALES (p.199)

1 oz cognac

1/2 oz bénédictine

3 dashes angostura

2 1/2 oz champagne

Pour all ingredients except the champagne into a mixing glass and stir. Strain into a champagne flute and then carefully top up with champagne. This cocktail can also be served in an ice-filled bejeweled silver chalice!

PICK ME UP (p.207)

1 oz cognac

3 dashes grenadine

3 dashes angostura

1/3 oz lemon juice

2 1/2 oz champagne

Pour all ingredients except the champagne into a ice-filled shaker and shake well for 10 seconds. Strain into a champagne flute and carefully top up with champagne.

WHITE LADY (p.208)

1 1/3 oz gin

3/4 oz triple sec

3/4 oz lemon juice

Half an egg white

Pour all ingredients into an ice-filled shaker and shake well for 30 seconds. Strain into a pre-cooled cocktail or coupette glass.

FRENCH 75 (p.208)

1 oz gin

3/4 oz lemon juice

1 bar spoon (or 1 tsp) confectioner's sugar

3 oz champagne

Pour all ingredients except the champagne into an ice-filled shaker and shake well for 10 seconds. Strain into a champagne flute and carefully top up with champagne. This drink can also be served in a tumbler with ice cubes.

IBF (p.208)

1 oz brandy

1 bar spoon (or 1 tsp) fernet menta

1 bar spoon (or 1 tsp) triple sec

2 ½ oz champagne

Pour all ingredients except the champagne in an ice-filled mixing glass and stir. Strain into a champagne flute and carefully top up with champagne.

NOTES

PREFACE

[1]   "Frank Sinatra," http://en.wikiquote.org/wiki/Frank_Sinatra.

FIRST SEMESTER: BRANDY

[1]   Hugh Johnson, *Vintage: The Story of Wine* (New York: Simon and Schuster, 1989), 180.

[2]   Nicholas Faith, *Cognac* (London: Octopus Publishing Group, 2004), 103.

[3]   Ibid., 104.

[4]   Bureau National Interprofessionnel du Cognac, http://www.cognac.fr/cognac/_en/4_pro/index.aspx?page=marches_campagne.

[5]   Lord Byron, *Don Juan* (1837; Project Gutenberg, 2007), http://www.gutenberg.org/files/21700/21700-h/21700-h.htm.

SECOND SEMESTER: VODKA

[1]   "Noël Coward Quotes," http://www.brainyquote.com/quotes/quotes/n/noelcoward128225.html.

[2]   Hervé Chayette and Alain Weill, *Cocktails* (Paris: Éditions Baleine, 2013).

[3]   "Without Feathers Quotes," http://www.goodreads.com/work/quotes/1843009-without-feathers?page=1.

4 John 4:13–14 (American Standard Version).

5 Sonja Margolina, *Wodka: Trinken und Macht in Russland* (Berlin: WJS Verlag, 2004).

6 Pavel Parfenovich Zablotskii-Desiatovskii, quoted in David Christian, *Living Water: Vodka and Russian Society on the Eve of Emancipation* (New York: Oxford University Press, 1990, reprinted 2001), 76–77.

7 Giles Fletcher, *Of the Russe Common Wealth* (1591), quoted in Mark Lawrence Schrad, *Vodka Politics: Alcohol, Autocracy, and the Secret History of the Russian State* (New York: Oxford University Press, 2014), 81.

8 Christian, *Living Water*, 180.

9 Quoted in Margolina, *Wodka*, 66.

10 "*Das Proletariat ist eine aufsteigende Klasse. Es braucht nicht den Rausch zur Betäubung oder als Stimulus... Es braucht Klarheit, Klarheit und nochmals Klarheit. Deshalb, ich wiederhole es, keine Schwächung, Vergeudung, Verw‚stung von Kräften.*" Quoted as a German translation from the original Russian in Clara Zetkin, "Erinnerungen an Lenin (Januar 1925)," in *Ausgewählte Reden und Schriften* (Berlin: Institut für Marxismus-Leninismus beim ZK der SED, 1960).

THIRD SEMESTER: WHISKY

1 "Logan Pearsall Smith Quote," http://izquotes.com/quote/351530.

2 "The Place to Be: 100 Years of New York's Hottest Scenes," *New York Magazine*, http://nymag.com/news/articles/03/12/100yearsof-hotscenes/5.htm.

3 "W.C. Fields Quotes," http://www.brainyquote.com/quotes/quotes/w/wcfields102057.html.

4 Museum of the American Cocktail, "World Cocktail Day: May 13, 2007," (blog), February 21, 2007, http://www.museumoftheamericancocktail.org.

⁵ Harry Johnson, *Bartenders' Manual*, rev. ed. (Newark, NJ: Charles E. Graham & Co., 1934), 162.

⁶ "8 Proverbs with Whiskey," http://www.special-dictionary.com/proverbs/keywords/whiskey/.

⁷ "Jerry Vale Quote," http://izquotes.com/quote/189260.

⁸ "Fifty Best Drinking Quotes," http://www.thefiftybest.com/useful_info/best_drinking_quotes/.

⁹ John Powers, John Jameson, and William Jameson, *Truths about Whisky* (London: Sutton, Sharpe & Co., 1879).

¹⁰ "Igor Stravinsky Quotes," http://thinkexist.com/quotation/my_god-so_much_i_like_to_drink_scotch_that/209681.html.

¹¹ "Logic," http://en.wikiquote.org/wiki/Logic.

FOURTH SEMESTER: RUM

¹ Robert Louis Stevenson, *Treasure Island* (Ware, UK: Wordsworth, 1993).

² Quoted in Tom Colls, "What Did They Do with the Drunken Sailor?" *BBC Today*, July 30, 2010, http://news.bbc.co.uk/today/hi/today/newsid_8859000/8859506.stm.

³ Colls, "What Did They Do with the Drunken Sailor?"

⁴ Quoted in Colls, "What Did They Do with the Drunken Sailor?"

⁵ Quoted in Edward L. Lowell, *The Hessians and the Other German Auxiliaries of Great Britain in the Revolutionary War* (New York: Harper & Brothers, 1884), 57.

⁶ Ned Ward, *A Trip to Jamaica* (1698), quoted in Myra Jehlen and Michael Warner, eds., *English Literatures of America: 1500–1800* (London: Routledge), 300.

⁷ "Flaschengeist der frühen Globalisierung." Martina Wimmer, "Das Rauschgold der Antillen," *mare* 75 (2009), http://www.mare.de/index.php?article_id=1770&setCookie=1.

⁸ Ibid.

⁹ Quoted in David Watts, *The West Indies: Patterns of Development,*

Culture and Environmental Change since 1492 (Cambridge: Cambridge University Press, 1987), 128.

10 Richard Ligon, *A True and Exact History of the Island of Barbados* (1673; repr., Indianapolis: Hackett Publishing, 2011), 80. Citation refers to the 2011 edition.

11 Ibid., 82.

12 Benjamin Franklin, *The Autobiography of Benjamin Franklin*, 57, http://www.ushistory.org/franklin/autobiography/page57.htm.

13 John Adams, *The Works of John Adams* vol. X (Boston: Little, Brown, 1856), 345, https://archive.org/stream/worksofjohnadams10adam/worksofjohnadams10adam_djvu.txt.

14 Heinrich Heine, *Germany: A Winter's Tale*, quoted at *The LiederNet Archive*, http://www.recmusic.org/lieder/get_text.html?TextId=68944.

15 John J. Pershing, *My Life before the World War, 1860–1917: A Memoir* (Lexington: University of Kentucky Press, 2013).

16 Quoted in Anistatia Miller and Jared Brown with Dave Broom and Nick Strangeway, *Cuba: The Legend of Rum* (London: Havana Club Collection, Mixellany Books, 2009), 140, http://en.calameo.com/read/000301956fe3adbb10592.

17 Ernest Hemingway, *Islands in the Stream* (New York: Charles Scribner's Sons, 1970), 215.

18 Ibid., 296.

19 Antonio Meilan, *De los mas famosos cocteles cubanos* (Place: Visual Publishing, 1997), 28.

20 "Einige Barkeeper, ein paar Werftratten, mehrere heruntergekommene Pelotaspieler und ehemalige Stierkämpfer, zwei baskische Priester und verschiedene im Exil lebende Grafen und Herzöge." Quoted in Axel von Frohn, "Agenten: Dank des Vaterlandes," *Der Spiegel*, July 26, 1999, http://www.spiegel.de/spiegel/print/d-14010981.html.

21 Hernando Calvo Ospina, *Bacardi: The Hidden War*, trans. Stephen Wilkinson (London: Pluto Press, 2002).

FIFTH SEMESTER: GIN

1   William Grimes, *Straight Up or On the Rocks: The Story of the American Cocktail* (New York: Simon and Schuster, 1993).

2   Frank P. Newman, *American Bar, Boissons Anglaises et Américaines* (Paris: Société française d'imprimerie et de librairie, 1904).

3   Luis Buñuel, *My Last Breath* (New York: Vintage, 1984), 42.

4   Ibid., 44.

5   "Robert Benchley Facts," http://biography.yourdictionary.com/robert-benchley.

6   Dorothy Parker, *The Collected Dorothy Parker* (London: Penguin, 2007).

7   "Fifty Best Drinking Quotes," http://www.thefiftybest.com/useful_info/best_drinking_quotes/.

8   "Famous Martini Quotes," http://www.martiniwarehouse.com/famous-martini-quotes_ep_79.html.

9   George Burns, quoted in Joseph Scott and Donald Bain, *The World's Best Bartenders' Guide* (New York: Berkley Publishing Group, 1998), 92.

10 Ernest Hemingway, *Across the River and into the Trees* (New York: Charles Scribner's Sons, 1950).

11 Quoted in Leo Segedin, *Martinis: Theory and Practice*, http://www.leopoldsegedin.com/essay_detail_martinis.cfm.

12 Richard Barnett, *The Book of Gin* (New York: Grove Press, 2011).

13 Quoted in James Mew and John Ashton, *Drinks of the World* (London: Leadenhall Press, 1892), 132.

14 B. R. Mitchell and P. Deane, Abstract of British Historical Statistics *(Cambridge:* Cambridge University Press, 1962), cited in Ernest L. Abel, "The Gin Epidemic: Much Ado about What?" *Alcohol and Alcoholism* 49, no. 1 (2014), http://alcalc.oxfordjournals.org/content/36/5/401#ref-26.

15 *The Balance and Columbian Repository* 5, no. 19 (1806), 146, quoted at http://en.wikipedia.org/wiki/Cocktail#cite_note-4.

[16] Alexander von Humboldt and Aimé Bonpland, *Personal Narrative of Travels to the Equinoctial Regions of America*, trans. Thomasina Ross (London: George Bell & Sons, 1907), http://ebooks.adelaide.edu.au/h/humboldt/alexander/travels/complete.html.

[17] Charles Dickens, *Sketches by Boz* (1903; Project Gutenberg, 2009), chap. XXII, http://www.gutenberg.org/files/882/882-h/882-h.htm.

[18] Jerry Thomas, *How to Mix Drinks* (New York: Dick and Fitzgerald, 1862).

[19] Theodora Sutcliffe, diffordsguide.com (April 2012), 12.

[20] Jim Wright, "A Whiskey Journal," http://www.awhiskeyjournal.com/martini-worship-is-it-wrong/.

[21] Quoted in Richard Langworth, ed., *Churchill by Himself: The Definitive Collection of Quotations* (London: Ebury Press, 2008), 353.

[22] Rémy Desquesnes, *Normandie 1944* (Rennes: Éditions Ouest-France, 1996).

[23] Raymond Chandler, *The High Window* (London: Penguin, 2011).

[24] Grimes, *Straight Up or On the Rocks*.

[25] Ibid., xvi.

SIXTH SEMESTER: TEQUILA

[1] Malcolm Lowry, *Under the Volcano* (New York: New American Library, 1971), 292.

[2] Consejo Regulador del Tequila, http://www.crt.org.mx/index.php?lang=en.

[3] *El Arbol de Las Maravillas: The Maguey*, http://www.usc.edu/dept/ideaLAB/people/labore/maguey.

SEVENTH SEMESTER: CHAMPAGNE

[1] Cardinal de Bernis, *Complete Works of Monsieur le C. de B*** of the Académie Françoise* (1771), quoted in *History of Champagne*, Union of Champagne Houses, http://www.maisons-champagne.com/en/bonal_gb/pages/03/01-02.

[2] Ibid.

3   Quoted in Don Kladstrup and Petie Kladstrup, *Champagne: How the World's Most Glamorous Wine Triumphed over War and Hard Times* (New York: HarperCollins, 2005), 43. Many of the stories in this section are drawn from this book, particularly chapter 2, and have not been individually cited.

4   Harriet Welty Rochefort, *Joie de Vivre: Secrets of Wining, Dining, and Romancing Like the French* (New York: St. Martin's Press, 2012), 32.

5   History of Champagne, Union of Champagne Houses, http://www.maisons-champagne.com/en/bonal_gb/pages/04/04-05.

6   Quoted in "Odette Pol-Roger," *The Telegraph*, December 30, 2000, http://www.telegraph.co.uk/news/obituaries/1379766/Odette-Pol-Roger.html.

7   Guglielmo Ferrero, *The Reconstruction of Europe: Talleyrand and the Congress of Vienna, 1814–1815*, trans. Theodore R. Jaeckel (New York: G.P. Putnam's Sons, 1941), 248, https://archive.org/details/reconstructionofo11003mbp.

8   *Moët & Chandon Champagne*, 14, http://dc347.4shared.com/doc/Nx5Qos9A/preview.html.

9   Wilhelm Busch, "Die fromme Helene," in *Und die Moral von der Geschicht* (Berlin: Bertelsmann, 1959).

10 *The Holy Rule of St Benedict*, chap. 48, *Of the Daily Work*, trans. Rev. Boniface Verheyen, www.holyrule.com/part10.htm.

11 Caimin O'Brien and Jean Farrelly, "Shinrone, Forest Glass Furnaces in County Offaly," https://www.offalyhistory.com/reading-resources/archaeology/forest-glass-furnaces-in-county-offaly.

12 "Robert Mansell," *Wikipedia*, last modified July 24, 2014, http://en.wikipedia.org/wiki/Robert_Mansell.

13 Lieut.-Col. Newnham-Davis, *The Gourmet's Guide to Europe* (London: Grant Richards, 1903), 48.

14 Patrick Forbes, *Champagne: The Wine, the Land and the People* (London: David and Charles, 1967).

[15] Quoted in Leo A. Loubère, *The Red and White: The History of Wine in France and Italy in the Nineteenth Century* (New York: State University of New York Press, 1978), 248–49.

[16] "Wine," http://en.wikiquote.org/wiki/Wine.

[17] Kladstrup and Kladstrup, *Champagne*, 120.

[18] Ibid., 120–22.

[19] Quoted in Kladstrup and Kladstrup, *Champagne*, 122.

[20] Kladstrup and Kladstrup, *Champagne*, 123.

[21] "Paul Claudel," http://en.wikiquote.org/wiki/Paul_Claudel.

[22] Quoted in Maurice de Waleffe, *Quand Paris était un Paradis: Mémoires 1900–1939* (Paris: Denoël, 1947).

[23] Kladstrup and Kladstrup, *Champagne*, 181.

[24] Gaston Derys, *Mon docteur le vin* (Paris: Draeger frères, 1936).

[25] Harry Haddon, "Bubby History Lesson: Part One," 2 *Oceans Vibe News*, July 21, 2011, http://www.2oceansvibe.com/2011/07/21/bubbly-history-lesson-part-one/#ixzz3ByMvqzBN.

[26] Personal communication, June 11, 2013.

[27] Quoted in Kladstrup and Kladstrup, *Champagne*, 5.

SELECTED BIBLIOGRAPHY

Amis, Kingsley. *Everyday Drinking: The Distilled Kingsley Amis.*
New York: Bloomsbury, 2008.

Barnett, Richard. *The Book of Gin.* New York: Grove Press, 2011.

Berry, Jeff. *Beachbum Berry Remixed.* San Jose: SLG, 2010.

Buñuel, Luis. *My Last Breath.* New York: Vintage, 1984.

Chandler, Raymond. *The High Window.* London: Penguin, 2011.

Chayette, Hervé, and Alain Weill. *Cocktails.* Paris: Èditions Baleine,
2013.

Christian, David. *Living Water: Vodka and Russian Society on the
Eve of Emancipation.* New York: Oxford University Press, 1990,
reprinted 2001.

Craddock, Harry. *The Savoy Cocktail Book.* London: Constable,
1930.

Faith, Nicholas. *Cognac.* London: Octopus Publishing Group, 2004.

Ferrero, Guglielmo. *The Reconstruction of Europe: Talleyrand and
the Congress of Vienna, 1814–1815.* Translated by Theodore R.
Jaeckel. New York: G. P. Putnam's Sons, 1941.

Forbes, Patrick. *Champagne: The Wine, the Land and the People.*
London: David and Charles, 1967.

Grimes, William. *Straight Up or On the Rocks: The Story of the
American Cocktail.* New York: Simon and Schuster, 1993.

Haigh, Ted. *Vintage Spirits & Forgotten Cocktails*. Gloucester, MA: Quarry Books, 2004.

Hemingway, Ernest. *Islands in the Stream*. New York: Charles Scribner's Sons, 1970.

Herlihy, Patricia. *The Alcoholic Empire: Vodka and Politics in Late Imperial Russia*. New York: Oxford University Press, 2002.

Jerofejew, Wenedikt. *Die Reise nach Petuschki*. Munich: Piper, 1978.

Johnson, Harry. *Bartenders' Manual*, rev. ed. Newark, NJ: Charles E. Graham & Co., 1934.

Johnson, Hugh. *Vintage: The Story of Wine*. New York: Simon and Schuster, 1989.

Kirsten, Sven. *The Book of Tiki*. Cologne: Taschen, 2000.

Kladstrup, Don, and Petie Kladstrup. *Champagne: How the World's Most Glamorous Wine Triumphed Over War and Hard Times*. New York: HarperCollins, 2005.

Ligon, Richard. *A True and Exact History of the Island of Barbados*. Indianapolis: Hackett Publishing, 2011. First published 1657.

Loubère, Leo A. *The Red and White: The History of Wine in France and Italy in the Nineteenth Century*. New York: State University of New York Press, 1978.

Lowell, Edward L. *The Hessians and the Other German Auxiliaries of Great Britain in the Revolutionary War*. New York: Harper & Brothers, 1884.

Lowry, Malcolm. *Under the Volcano*. New York: New American Library, 1971.

MacElhone, Harry. *Barflies and Cocktails*. Paris: Lecram Press, 1927.

Margolina, Sonja. *Wodka: Trinken und Macht in Russland*. Berlin: WJS Verlag, 2004.

Meier, Frank. *The Artistry of Mixing Drinks*. Paris: Fryam Press, 1936.

Mew, James, and John Ashton. *Drinks of the World*. London: Leadenhall Press, 1892.

Miller, Anistatia, and Jared Brown. *Spirituous Journey: A History of Drink.* Book 2, *From Publicans to Master Mixologists.* London: Mixellany Books, 2009.

Miller, Anistatia, and Jared Brown, with Dave Broom and Nick Strangeway. *Cuba: The Legend of Rum.* London: Mixellany Books, 2009, http://en.calameo.com/read/000301956fe3adbb10592.

Moruzzi, Peter. *Havana before Castro: When Cuba Was a Tropical Playground.* Layton, UT: Gibbs Smith, 2008.

Newman, Frank P. *American Bar, Boissons Anglaises et Américaines.* Paris: Société française d'imprimerie et de librairie, 1904.

Ospina, Hernando Calvo. *Bacardi: The Hidden War.* Translated by Stephen Wilkinson. London: Pluto Press, 2002.

Pfaller, Robert. *Wofür es sich zu leben lohnt: Elemente materialistischer Philosophie.* Frankfurt: S. Fischer Verlag, 2011.

Powers, John, John Jameson, and William Jameson, *Truths about Whisky.* London: Sutton, Sharpe & Co., 1879.

Richter, Peter. *Über das Trinken.* Munich: Goldmann/Random House, 2011.

Schmidt, William. *The Flowing Bowl: When and What to Drink.* New York: Mud Puddle Books, 2010. First published 1891 by Jenkins & McCowan.

Schrad, Mark Lawrence. *Vodka Politics: Alcohol, Autocracy, and the Secret History of the Russian State.* New York: Oxford University Press, 2014.

Sorokin, Vladimir. "Flaschendrehen auf dem Gogol-Boulevard Moskaus erogene Zonen: eine Gebrauchsanleitung." *Frankfurter Allgemeine Zeitung,* January 11, 2011.

Sundermeier, Jörg Hrsg. *Das Buch vom Trinken.* Berlin: Verbrecher Verlag, 2004.

Tarling, W. J. *Café Royal Cocktail Book.* London: Pall Mall Ltd., 1937.

Thomas, Jerry. *How to Mix Drinks.* New York: Dick and Fitzgerald, 1862.

von Humboldt, Alexander, and Aimé Bonpland. *Personal Narrative of Travels to the Equinoctial Regions of America.* Translated by Thomasina Ross. London: George Bell & Sons, 1907, http://ebooks. adelaide.edu.au/h/humboldt/alexander/travels/complete.html.

Watts, David. *The West Indies: Patterns of Development, Culture and Environmental Change since 1492.* Cambridge: Cambridge University Press, 1987.

Wondrich, David. *Esquire Drinks.* New York: Hearst Books, 2002.

Wondrich, David. *Imbibe!* New York: Perigee, 2007.